Leading Lean
Software Development

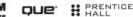

Leading Lean Software Development

Results Are Not the Point

Mary and Tom Poppendieck

✦✦ Addison-Wesley

Upper Saddle River, NJ • Boston • Indianapolis • San Francisco
New York • Toronto • Montreal • London • Munich • Paris • Madrid
Capetown • Sydney • Tokyo • Singapore • Mexico City

The publisher offers excellent discounts on this book when ordered in quantity for bulk purchases or special sales, which may include electronic versions and/or custom covers and content particular to your business, training goals, marketing focus, and branding interests. For more information, please contact:

U.S. Corporate and Government Sales
(800) 382-3419
corpsales@pearsontechgroup.com

For sales outside the United States please contact:

International Sales
international@pearson.com

Visit us on the Web: informit.com/aw

Library of Congress Cataloging-in-Publication Data

Poppendieck, Mary.
  Leading lean software development : results are not the point / Mary and Tom Poppendieck.
      p. cm.
  Includes bibliographical references and index.
  ISBN 0-321-62070-4 (pbk. : alk. paper)
1. Management information systems. 2. Computer software—Development. 3. Organizational effectiveness. I. Poppendieck, Tom. II. Title.
  HD30.213.P65 2010
  658.4'038011—dc22   2009035319

ISBN-13: 978-0-321-62070-5
ISBN-10:   0-321-62070-4
Text printed in the United States on recycled paper at RR Donnelly in Crawfordsville, Indiana.
First printing, October 2009.

Contents

Foreword

I was a relative newbie to both agile and lean when I first met Mary and Tom Poppendieck at an Agile Conference in Salt Lake City in 2003, so of course I started our conversation with the question that had been bothering me: "How do you reconcile the lean view that tests are waste with the need for tests in software development?" Mary's immediate response: "Unit tests are what let you stop the line."

I've learned a lot about both agile and lean since then, and the more I learn, the more I appreciate the profound understanding that led to that simple answer so clearly tying multiple agile practices to fundamental lean principles.

So, when Mary asked me to review her new book, I jumped at the chance, and I wasn't disappointed. The approach of framing various views into lean leadership provided fresh perspectives on many of the issues that we must all address if we are to be effective in developing software in the twenty-first century. I could rave on about the book, but that would just keep you from reading it, so I decided to limit myself to sharing my three favorite parts of the book (in chronological order)—not an easy task when the whole book is packed with valuable information.

Since I'm a geek at heart, my first favorite part of the book was Chapter 2, Technical Excellence, with its fresh look at agile practices as a continuation and extension of the fundamentals expressed in the early days of computer science by giants such as Dijkstra, Parnas, and Mills. Seeing agile practices as an evolution of the best of the past, rather than as a revolution that rejects the past, is an important step in enabling adoption of the best that agile has to offer.

Since I'm an idealist, my second favorite part of the book was in Chapter 4, Relentless Improvement, with the discussion of the need for a shared vision of what success will look like for your organization. When you couple this with the material in the same chapter about the importance of managers as mentors in developing problem solvers, you start to see the potential for an organization where everyone works every day to remove the impediments to future success.

Finally, since I'm a realist, my third favorite part of the book was Chapter 5, Great People. "Success comes from people. Results are not the point. Developing people so that they can achieve successful results is the point." Statistically speaking, no large company has all above-average employees, suppliers, and customers. However, by following the principles and advice in this book, any company, large or small, has the potential of getting above-average results from its average employees, suppliers, and customers. That's really what business success is all about.

If I read the book again, would I pick the same three favorite parts? I don't know, but I'll find out. As soon as the book is published, I'll be starting book clubs across our company to share these ideas and see where they lead us. I encourage all of you to do the same.

Dottie Acton
Senior Fellow
Lockheed Martin

Introduction: Framing

Weathering the Perfect Storm[1]

Sweden's Handelsbanken has placed a large sum of money in an account at the Riksbank in a bid to help the central bank safeguard the financial system.

> —*Stockholm, June 17, 2009 (Reuters)*

Svenska Handelsbanken is one of the top 25 banks in Europe. It was not just the only bank that survived the Swedish banking crisis in the 1990s without asking for government support—it has also done very well in the 2008/2009 crisis. Handelsbanken did not have to raise capital or ask for government support and its shares have been the best performing European bank stock by a wide margin. Despite its large size Handelsbanken has, in many ways, acted as a shock absorber, not a shock amplifier, to the financial system.[2]

In 1970, Svenska Handelsbanken was 100 years old and deeply troubled. It was trying mightily to become the largest bank in Sweden, and costs had gotten out of control. To make a bad situation worse, a small provincial bank in northern Sweden was eating into its market share. When the Handelsbanken management team abruptly resigned, its board decided to recruit the head of the upstart competitor as Handelsbanken's new managing director. Dr. Jan Wallander was a professional economist turned banker who had his own ideas about how to run a bank.

The first thing Wallander did was to make it clear that growth is not the point; profitability is what matters. He insisted that everyone in the bank stop trying to bring in as much revenue as possible and start focusing on generating

---

1. Information in this section is from Wallander, "Budgeting—An Unnecessary Evil," 1999.
2. Jacket text for Kroner. *Svenska Handelsbanken: A Blueprint for Better Banking,* 2009.

profitable revenue instead. To accomplish this goal, he had information systems publish a few key metrics for each branch immediately after the end of each month, numbers such as the cost-to-income ratio (the inverse of profitability) and income per employee (productivity). Then he gave branch managers the freedom to manage their affairs locally. They could decide which products to sell, how much money to spend, how many employees to hire, and so on. Wallander felt that central control got in the way of the people closest to customers, slowed down their reaction time, and stifled their creativity. So decision-making authority devolved to branch managers; staff groups were dramatically reduced in number and size, and those that remained had to sell their services to the branches.

Each month branch managers could see how they stood relative to their peers on the key measures. Wallander believed that this kind of competition among branches provided a continuing challenge that drove each branch to constantly improve the things that really mattered. To keep this competition friendly, there were no bonuses based on the relative internal standings. Instead, Wallander established one of the earliest profit-sharing programs in Sweden, with payouts to a pension fund based on the overall profitability of the company relative to its external competitors.

The bank's goal was to be more profitable than comparable banks. From 1972 onward, Handelsbanken has been more profitable than the mean of all of its competitors, and generally it has been the most profitable bank in Sweden, although occasionally it was in second or third place. Shortly after Wallander took over, two Swedish banks merged to form a bank much larger than Handelsbanken; it took 23 years for Handelsbanken to grow back into the largest bank in Sweden—this time without explicitly trying.

The results of Wallander's approach were both immediate and long-lasting. Svenska Handelsbanken is among the most cost-efficient banks *in the world*. Moody ranks its financial strength among the top ten European banks, something that comes in handy during the periodic financial crises that plague the banking industry. It has continued to grow, expanding to other Nordic countries as well as the UK. Frequently ranked as a top place to work, Handelsbanken has the most satisfied customers, the lowest employee turnover, and the highest investor return of any Swedish bank.

Jan Wallander understood that the most effective, responsive organization is one where small unit leaders make local decisions. He devised an organizational structure, governance approach, and culture that reliably engaged the creativity and dedication of knowledge workers at hundreds of local branches. Four decades later, his vision is credited with helping Handelsbanken weather one of the worst financial storms in a century.

The Leadership Frame of Great Companies

What does Handelsbanken have in common with Nucor Steel, SAS Institute, W. L. Gore, Southwest Airlines, Semco, and Toyota? Each of these companies has developed a *culture of high involvement*, each thrives in *an industry of high change*, and each has sustained *best-in-industry performance* over time. And each company credits its unique culture for its success. Interestingly, the cultures of these companies are not all that unique; in fact, they are remarkably similar. Consider these descriptions of company culture, direct from each company's Web site:

Nucor Steel[3]

Our Culture:
Safety First
Eliminating Hierarchy
Granting Trust and Freedom
Giving All Workers a Stake in the Company
Turning Everyone into a Decision Maker
Inspiring a Work Ethic

SAS Institute[4]

If you treat employees as if they make a difference to the company, they will make a difference to the company. That has been the employee-focused philosophy behind SAS' corporate culture since our founding in 1976. At the heart of this unique business model is a simple idea: satisfied employees create satisfied customers.

"We've worked hard to create a corporate culture that is based on trust between our employees and the company," explains SAS President and CEO Jim Goodnight, "a culture that rewards innovation, encourages employees to try new things and yet doesn't penalize them for taking chances, and a culture that cares about employees' personal and professional growth."

W. L. Gore & Associates[5]

How we work at Gore sets us apart. Since Bill Gore founded the company in 1958, Gore has been a team-based, flat lattice organization that fosters personal initiative. There are no traditional organizational charts, no chains of command, nor predetermined channels of communication.

Instead, we communicate directly with each other and are accountable to fellow members of our multi-disciplined teams. We encourage hands-on innovation, involving those closest to a project in decision making. Teams organize around opportunities and leaders emerge.

---

3. www.nucor.com/story/chapter3/.
4. www.sas.com/jobs/corporate/index.html.
5. www.gore.com/en_xx/aboutus/culture/index.html.

Southwest Airlines[6]

The mission of Southwest Airlines is dedication to the highest quality of Customer Service delivered with a sense of warmth, friendliness, individual pride, and Company Spirit.

We are committed to provide our Employees a stable work environment with equal opportunity for learning and personal growth. Creativity and innovation are encouraged for improving the effectiveness of Southwest Airlines. Above all, Employees will be provided the same concern, respect, and caring attitude within the organization that they are expected to share externally with every Southwest Customer.

Southwest Airlines is famous for its remarkable management philosophy: employees first, customers second, shareholders a distant third. When we look at other truly successful companies, we notice that they have a similar philosophy. In these companies, front-line people are highly valued, are expected to make local decisions, and are effectively engaged in delivering superior customer outcomes. As a result, the companies gain two significant advantages: (1) Workers routinely dedicate their intelligence and creativity to help the company be successful, and (2) the company is adaptive; it can detect and quickly respond to changing market conditions and opportunities.

The purpose of this book is to explore how we might adapt the way these great companies frame the role of leadership to organizations involved in developing software-intensive systems.

Frames

Deep frames pervade TPS that fundamentally alter how the system is understood and therefore how to proceed with implementation. If managers and program leaders fail to understand the frameworks underlying TPS, they miss the point and therefore fail to achieve the expected results.[7]

When coauthor Tom isn't thinking about software development, he pursues his passion, which is photography. He captures stunning scenic views and creates dynamic photo journals of conferences. When you look at his photographs, you see the world through his eyes; he has carefully framed each photograph to guide your attention to the subject and purpose of the image, whether it is an

---

6. www.southwest.com/about_swa/mission.html.
7. We thank Michael Ballé, Godefroy Beauvallet, Art Smalley, and Durward Sobek for their paper "The Thinking Production System," 2006, which inspired the theme of this book. This quote is from that paper. TPS is an abbreviation for the Toyota Production System, and also the Thinking People System.

engaged conversation, a sweeping view of a spectacular sunrise, or a tightly framed view of an incongruous detail. The first thing Tom does when he creates a photograph is to decide on the perspective and framing that will lead to an effective composition. Sometimes he creates a frame with his hands to help him concentrate both on how the elements inside the photograph flow together and on which things to leave out of the frame because they would detract from the subject. Only after Tom has framed a picture does he consider the details of focus, depth of field, exposure, improving the lighting, and so on. In the end, each of Tom's photographs tells a story about the subject from his chosen perspective.

According to cognitive scientists, we all interpret our surroundings through frames—mental constructs that shape our perspective of the world. Frames are sets of beliefs about what elements to pay attention to and how these elements interact with each other. Frames place significant limits on our perspective; we can see only what our frames tell us is meaningful, and we usually ignore what lies outside the boundaries. Most of us are unaware of the way our background and experience shape the way we frame our decisions and actions; only a few of us consciously adjust our frames as if we were photographers. In fact, we seldom even think about the direction in which we are pointing our cameras.

Everyone shapes his or her view of the world through framing, and people with different backgrounds are likely to see their surroundings through vastly different frames. By themselves, frames are not inherently good or bad; they just are. However, evidence has shown that certain frames are more likely than others to lead to long-term business success. For example, as we will see later, Southwest Airlines frames its business in a strikingly different manner from most other airlines. And over its almost 40-year life span, Southwest has been more successful than airlines employing different frames, including airlines that have copied many of Southwest's practices. Similarly, Toyota frames its business differently from the Big Three automakers in Detroit, and although most automakers have adopted lean practices, their thinking frames have not really changed. Like Southwest, Toyota is a major player in the automotive business, and not coincidentally, Toyota, Southwest Airlines, and Svenska Handelsbanken all see the world through similar frames.

Whatever frame you use limits the questions you think to ask, the decision alternatives you consider, and the consequences you anticipate from those decisions. Sometimes you may be surprised and perhaps disappointed when things don't work out as expected. It is possible that the execution of the decision was at fault, or that events conspired to change the results. But it is more likely that your frame of reference, your thinking system, is the culprit. If you are not seeing the results you expect from your current direction, consider moving to a different place, re-aim your camera, and look at the problem through a different frame.

Framing the System Development Process

This book is divided into six chapters. Each chapter contains four frames, so over the course of the book we will look through 24 different frames to get a good picture of how a lean development process should work. Taken as a whole, the 24 frames present a coherent leadership framework for system development. We conclude each chapter with a portrait of the leader who is responsible for creating focus through its four frames. (See Figure I-1.)

Chapter 1, Systems Thinking, starts, appropriately enough, by focusing on customers. It examines the nature of customer demand, distinguishing between value demand and failure demand. It investigates how our work systems can predictably and effectively anticipate and deal with demand, and how our policies often interfere and create waste. The chapter concludes with a portrait of a leader who creates a vision of how to delight customers.

Chapter 2, Technical Excellence, covers the basics of excellent software development—low-dependency architecture, a test-driven development process, an evolutionary development approach, and the importance of deep expertise among developers. The highlighted leader in this chapter is the competency leader.

Chapter 3, Reliable Delivery, starts by finding the biggest constraint in the system and learning how to manage the risk posed by that constraint. It discusses workflow and schedule, and the essential contribution of feedback. The highlighted leader is the product champion—the same leader we met in Chapter 1, but this time in the role of leading implementation.

Chapter 4, Relentless Improvement, discusses the essential characteristic of any lean organization: constant, ongoing, never-be-satisfied improvement. It shows how improvement works, suggests some tools, and features the manager as mentor of improvement.

Chapter 5, Great People, starts with the assumption that great results come from great people, so the essential question is how to create great people. It starts with the basic tenet that people treat others the way they are treated, then walks through the four Ps: Purpose, Passion, Persistence, and Pride. The chapter highlights the front-line leader, who has the most influence on the way people think about their work.

Chapter 6, Aligned Leaders, discusses and gives examples of developing alignment on the leadership team. It has several lists of ideas for your leadership team to ponder as you turn theory into practice.

Figure I-1 *The big picture*

Acknowledgments

In February of 2001, a small group of people who were passionate about software development met at the Snowbird ski resort near Salt Lake City, Utah. At this famous meeting, the Agile Manifesto was born. A November 2001 meeting in Chicago led to the incorporation of Agile Alliance "to provide an unbiased forum within which the community can freely work to discuss, promote, and improve agile development processes."[1] Both before and after these momentous events, many people worked tirelessly to change the frame through which software development is perceived and the way in which software developers work. As unlikely as it seemed at the time, agile development approaches have become mainstream methods, and the more urgent problem these days is learning how to reap the benefits of agile development beyond the low-hanging fruit.

We owe a great debt of gratitude to those who had the vision and courage to lead the way, and to the many who have subsequently become instrumental in growing agile methods into an effective framework for software and system development. Our work truly stands on the shoulders of giants.

While we were writing this book, the agile and lean community characteristically came to our aid with insightful reviews, comments, and corrections. The people who helped us out are too numerous to mention, and there is always the fear that by naming a few, we will leave out others who should also be mentioned. However, we will take that chance as we express special gratitude to those whose words or efforts are specifically cited in this book.

Heartfelt thanks go to Dottie Acton for writing the foreword for this book; we sincerely appreciate her support. We owe a deep debt of gratitude to Ted Rivera, Paul Gibson, and Sue McKinney for helping us understand Agile@IBM and prepare the case study in Chapter 6. We also thank Helen and Charlie for telling their stories. Thanks to Maria Wesslegård, Johan Nordin, and Daniel Eriksson, who showed us what life was like in the real world and convinced us that a book on lean leadership should be written. We wrote the book with Maria in mind and tried to make it useful to people in her leadership role.

---

1. From the Agile Alliance Bylaws.

Thanks to Henrik Kniberg and Mattias Skarin for their insightful value stream map and the long discussions we had about practical approaches to improvement; and to Mr. Nobuaki Katayama, Chisako Katayama, and Kenji Hiranabe for helping us understand the role of a chief engineer at Toyota. Thanks to Bob Martin for gathering thoughts of industry leaders on clean code, and to Bjarne Stroustrup, Grady Booch, Dave Thomas, Michael Feathers, and Ward Cunningham for their insights on this topic. Thanks to Barry Boehm for letting us publish his historical graphs and for his encouragement. And thanks also to Kent Beck, our series editor, for his support.

Thanks to Jason Yip, Arun Batchu, Lisa Crispin, Janet Gregory, Masayuki Yamaguchi, and John Shook for key insights. And a special thanks to those who graciously allowed us to use their words in sidebars: Ola Ellnestam, Samuel Crescêncio, Carsten Jakobsen, Tomo Lennox, Olve Maudal, and Tom Stephen.

We had many reviewers who contributed excellent comments that helped to shape this book, and, of course, picking out a few to thank always leaves us at risk of forgetting someone. But we'll take the risk and extend special appreciation to the contributions of Rick Mugridge, Ryan Martens, Hubert Smits, Dustin Poppendieck, Bob Corrick, and Bas Vodde.

Finally, thanks to the Addison-Wesley team members, especially Greg Doench, for all of their help and support in publishing this book.

Chapter 1

Systems Thinking

Snapshot

Southwest Airlines is a company that has defied the odds against success in the rough world of the airline industry and become a model for others to follow—a model that has been enormously difficult to copy. Why? Because would-be imitators copy the parts of the system that fit their mental models, but they don't copy the way these parts work together as a system. They fail to appreciate the fundamentally different way of thinking behind the Southwest Airlines system: *systems thinking*.

For decades, John Seddon has used systems thinking to dramatically improve service organizations. "To take a systems view is to think about the organization from the outside-in, to understand customer demand and to design a system that meets it," Seddon says. "To enable control in this high variety environment, it is necessary to integrate decision-making with work (so the workers control the work) and use measures derived from the work. . . . If workers are controlling the work, they need managers to be working on the things beyond the control of the workers which affect the system conditions: the way work works. The result is an adaptive, customer-centric system."[1]

Seddon's approach to systems thinking begins by asking an organization to answer five questions:[2] (1) **Purpose:** What is the purpose of this organization? (2) **Demand:** What is the nature of customer demand? (3) **Capability:** What is the system predictably achieving? (4) **Flow:** How does the work work? (5) **System conditions:** What are the causes of waste in the system? We discuss these five questions in this chapter. Then we introduce the leader whose job it is to bring systems thinking to the creation of a product idea, the *product champion*. We will meet the product champion again in Chapter 3, leading the product development effort.

1. Seddon, *Systems Thinking in the Public Sector*, 2008, p. 70.
2. Seddon, *Freedom from Command and Control: Rethinking Management for Lean Service*, 2005, pp. 101–10.

A Different Way to Run an Airline

Are empty airplane seats waste? If you were an airline executive, what would your answer be?

Every month the Airline Transport Association publishes the load factors (revenue passenger miles divided by available seat miles—a utilization measure) for U.S. airlines. Business reporters are quick to praise airlines that increased load factors over the previous year. Financial analysts maintain that once an airline load factor exceeds its break-even point, more and more revenue will hit the bottom line. So it's pretty clear that empty seats are waste—unless you are an airline passenger. Or Southwest Airlines.

Completely full airplanes aren't very comfortable. It's hard to find space for carry-on luggage, and people carry on a lot more these days, since most U.S. airlines are charging to check bags. But the real problem comes during the holidays when bad weather wreaks havoc with airline schedules, and there is no spare capacity. Far too many airline passengers have spent Thanksgiving in Denver or Christmas in Chicago instead of getting all the way home for the holidays.

It costs airlines a lot to untangle the mess of a winter storm at a hub, especially with load factors approaching 100%. To soften the financial blow, U.S. airlines long ago stopped providing lodging for passengers who were stranded because of a weather-caused delay, but they still have to find a way to get those passengers to their destination. Inconvenienced passengers are not happy, but most airlines don't seem to worry about the cost of annoyed customers. After all, the bad weather wasn't their fault.

Over the years, Southwest Airlines has reported load factors that were approximately 10% lower than those of other airlines of similar size. This might lead you to suspect that Southwest has been struggling financially—but you would be wrong. Donald Converse summed up the amazing track record of Southwest Airlines in *Fast Company* magazine in June 2008:[3]

> Founded in 1971, Southwest Airlines began to establish a consistent pattern of deviating from convention. In 1978 the airline industry was deregulated and 120 plus airlines have gone bankrupt since. Why, in this difficult environment, has SWA continued to grow and thrive? Notably, SWA is the only airline to continuously show a profit every year since 1973. How has SWA managed to increase its traffic by as much as 139%? Here are some facts that might help to understand how SWA has achieved this incredible record:
>
> • The company consistently leads the industry in low fares and dominates the short haul market with an average of 60% market share.

---

3. Converse, "Thank You Herb!," 2008.

- The company serves over 2400 customers per employee annually—making SWA employees by far the most productive workforce in the airline industry.
- Employee turnover averages 6.4%—again one of the best records in the industry.
- SWA is consistently ranked in the top 100 of the best U.S. companies to work for.
- They have never been forced to lay off employees regardless of external market factors such as recession or high fuel prices.
- They have the best record for baggage handling in the industry.
- They have the best on-time performance record.
- Fewest customer complaints.
- Youngest fleet of airplanes, and the best safety record!

Southwest's stated purpose is to make flying possible for those who would not otherwise be able to afford it. Thus Southwest sees its main competitor as the car, not other airlines.[4] Southwest started out in Texas serving three cities—Houston, Dallas, and San Antonio—that form a triangle, about a four-hour drive, or an hour flight, apart. About a year after it was founded, Southwest had four planes on these routes, but it was running out of money, so it sold one of the planes. However, executives decided that canceling a quarter of its flights would be a disaster—this would not lead to higher load factors; it would lead to many fewer customers.

This was the start of Southwest's famous ability to rapidly turn around aircraft at the gate. The ground operations manager decided that planes could be emptied of passengers and filled up for the next flight in ten minutes, allowing three planes to fly the schedule designed for four.[5] What Southwest realized is that load factors don't take into account the time that airplanes spend on the ground. By operating with fewer planes, Southwest saved significantly on capital investment and labor costs. Maintaining the same number of flights provided plenty of options for passengers and empty seats for growing traffic and absorbing variation—at a small marginal cost. James Parker, former Southwest CEO, notes:[6]

---

4. In Europe, Southwest would compete with trains, but in the United States there are few equivalent train systems.
5. Southwest planes used to leave the gate before everyone was seated, encouraging people to find a seat. This is no longer allowed, and turnaround times are a bit longer these days.
6. Parker, *Do the Right Thing: How Dedicated Employees Create Loyal Customers and Large Profits*, 2008, p. 57. Italics in the original.

With Southwest's predominantly short and medium haul route structure, an increase in turnaround times of 20 minutes per flight would reduce the available flying time for each aircraft by about two hours every day. Spreading this effect over the entire fleet of more than 450 airplanes would mean the loss of about 900 hours of flying every day. Remember, an aircraft doesn't make any money sitting on the ground. So Southwest would have to buy at least 80 more airplanes. With a list price of around $40 million per 737, this comes to a tidy sum of well over $3 billion. *This is money Southwest doesn't have to spend because of its efficient turnaround.*

Southwest realizes that increasing its revenue potential is more profitable than trying to make as much money as possible on every flight, and customers get more of what they want at the same time. Southwest's airplanes may be less full than those of its competitors, but the planes spend a lot more time in the air, which more than compensates for the lower load factors. By one account, the typical Southwest 737 is used 11.5 hours a day, compared with an average of 8.6 hours for other carriers.[7] Rapid aircraft turnaround leading to high capital equipment utilization bears a resemblance to the use of short setup times in manufacturing, pioneered by Toyota. Both companies discovered new, counterintuitive ways to make more productive use of both capital equipment and people while maintaining increased flexibility in the face of variation in demand. In both cases, their approach trumped the apparent economies of scale enjoyed by their competitors.

Since Southwest can turn a plane around much faster than other airlines, the people involved can be assigned to a new plane more quickly, and thus they are more productive. Short turnarounds have been difficult for other airlines to copy; Southwest's times average 15 to 20 minutes faster than those of their best competitors.[8] One of the reasons short turnarounds are so difficult to emulate is that many different departments must be coordinated in a short span of time: pilots, flight attendants, caterers, cabin cleaners, gate agents, operations agents, ramp agents, ticket agents, baggage agents, freight agents, fuelers, mechanics. Southwest nurtures a strong culture of cooperation across these departments; people from different areas routinely help each other out. At many other airlines, work rules and measurement systems discourage such cooperation.[9]

---

7. Freiberg and Freiberg, *Nuts: Southwest Airlines' Crazy Recipe for Business and Personal Success*, 1998, p. 51.
8. Parker, *Do the Right Thing: How Dedicated Employees Create Loyal Customers and Large Profits*, 2008, p. 57.
9. See Grittell, *The Southwest Way*, 2003, Chapter 3.

Any Pilot Can Fly Any Plane, Any Plane Can Fly Any Route

We were flying from Los Angeles to Denver on Southwest. We were pleasantly surprised by the waiting area: a double row of comfortable seats with small tables and power outlets in between, right at the gate, and free! It was just what we road warriors look for in an airline club room, especially when the flight is delayed. And our flight was late, due to fog in San Francisco. When it arrived, we experienced the famous rapid turnaround with a well-managed boarding queue. But alas, we were not going to depart on that plane; the pilot announced that it had a mechanical problem.

We were asked to go to another airplane and please take the same seat; we didn't have boarding passes, after all. The plane was about 70% full—typical for Southwest—so most of the center seats were empty and no one was too worried about seating. A quick exit from the plane and a short walk brought us to a gate where the plane we were now going to take was just pulling up. It was empty in short order, and two agents stood at the gate checking each of us off on a paper list as we boarded. Soon we were all in the same seats with the same crew and the same luggage in the hold. Less than a half hour after the mechanical problem was discovered, we were leaving in a different plane.

Not long after that trip we found ourselves in Atlanta, flying home to Minneapolis on a late-evening flight, this time on a different airline. Again, fog took its toll. As the evening wore on, our flight was delayed, first to 11:00 P.M. Then 11:30 P.M. Then a quarter past midnight. I checked the arrival time of the plane coming in to our departing gate to be sure we would have a plane. An arrival was scheduled at 11:05 P.M.—over an hour before our flight was scheduled to depart. Surely this could not be our plane. How could a simple turnaround take 80 minutes? We were soon to find out.

We went to the gate and found our future cabin crew already there; they'd been waiting for the plane for a couple of hours, just like us. In this traditional system, there was no concept that a flight and its crew could simply be assigned the next available plane; everyone had to wait for the appropriate aircraft to arrive. We could see why Southwest achieves higher productivity through its emphasis on simplicity: Any flight and any crew can use any available plane.

When the plane we were to take finally arrived, it seemed to take forever for people to get off. Of course it was completely full, but even worse, it was overflowing with carry-on luggage. The airline had a $15 luggage fee, which encouraged passengers to carry on everything they could. As we boarded, the same thing happened—the plane was completely full and almost everyone was overburdened with luggage. It took forever to get all the luggage stowed or checked. The impact of luggage fees on turnaround times seems to be lost on most airlines. One wonders if the fees cover the decreased aircraft utilization.

Mary and Tom Poppendieck

Jim Parker, Southwest's former CEO, claims that Southwest Airlines isn't really in the airline business at all. The company is in the customer service business; it just happens to fly airplanes.[10] He believes that the secret to success in the customer service business is to take good care of your employees, because then they will take good care of your customers, and satisfied customers lead to a successful business. So Southwest focuses on three things: Create a great place to work, provide customers with what they really want, and make sure that the airline always makes a profit so it can stay in business for the long term.

Frame 1: Customer Focus

If you think of your organization as a system,[11] then a clear, customer-focused purpose that can be used to drive holistic decisions is the starting point for systems thinking. Start by asking yourself, "Who are my customers, and what do they really want from my organization?" This is not as easy as it sounds, because it may not be clear who your customers really are. So let's start by defining whom we mean by customers.

Who Are Your Customers?

A customer is anyone who *pays for, uses, supports,* or *derives value from* the systems you create. Thus you probably have a lot of different customers. But wait; there's more. If you are working on a subsystem of a larger system, you have customers of your subsystem and customers of the overall system. So arriving at clarity about who your customers are can be challenging.

We recommend that you simplify the issue of identifying your customers by considering the whole system you are involved in creating, not just the software. If you are creating a subsystem of a larger system, think of those creating the other parts of the system as partners and focus on understanding the customers of the overall system. For example, if you are developing the software for a medical device programmer, the primary customers are those whose lives are improved by the medical device, followed closely by the medical personnel who select, deliver, and program the medical device. If you are developing soft-

---

10. Parker, *Do the Right Thing: How Dedicated Employees Create Loyal Customers and Large Profits,* 2008, p. 65.
11. We use the word *system* in two ways: First, there is your organization's work system, and second, there are the systems you deliver to customers. The meaning should be clear from context. Systems thinking should be applied to both types of systems.

ware to automate a business process, the purpose of the software is to support the most effective business process possible, and the most appropriate measurements of success would be the business results generated by the improved business process.

Customers Who Pay for the System

Often the first customers who come to mind are the sponsors who pay for your systems. Ask yourself, "Why do these customers spend good money for my systems? What purpose are they trying to achieve? What are their key constraints?" Sponsors usually have a clear purpose: They know the overall results they expect from an investment. Cost is frequently constrained by a limit beyond which the investment would not make sense, and sometimes there is a deadline beyond which the system would not be useful.

Sponsors usually don't care about the details of the system, as long as their purpose is served. Thus it is very important to be clear about what this purpose is and to focus on it separately from the details of implementation. The objective is to be sure that the sponsor's purpose is achieved.

Customers Who Use the System

Customers who use your system may not be the same as those who pay for the system, and sometimes these users have a different purpose. They have a job to do, and they want the system to help them do their job more effectively, more comfortably, and more intuitively. As Carl Kessler and John Sweitzer say in *Outside-in Software Development*, "If your product makes end-users feel smart, effective, and in control of their work, you have a winning product."[12]

Customers Who Support the System

When you release a system, you may breathe a sigh of relief now that your work is done; but the work is just beginning for those who support the system. Do you know how *consumable* your systems are—that is, how rapidly and easily your customers can begin realizing value from your system? What does it take to install a system or a release? How difficult is it to use? How much training is required?

You should also understand how *robust* your systems are. How often do they fail in normal use? How long does it take to recover? How easy is it to find and eliminate the cause? What does a failure cost your customers?

---

12. Kessler and Sweitzer, *Outside-in Software Development: A Practical Approach to Building Successful Stakeholder-Based Products*, 2008, p. 25.

Customers Who Derive Value from the System

One of the most effective ways to create a competitive advantage is to help your customers be successful. So ask yourself whether you know how long it takes your customers to start deriving value from your systems. Is there anything you can do to help them?

Many companies expand their business by understanding their customers' value chain and helping their *customers' customers* be successful. For example, if a company helps its customers develop a truly effective call center, or sell software tools that increase the effectiveness of financial analysts, *their* customers will be delighted.

Product Owners Aren't Customers

I was giving a talk at a company with maybe 70 people in the room. "How many here are developers?" my host asked. About 50 people raised their hands. "And how many of you developers understand the purpose of the code you work on?" Only two hands stayed up!

We found a similar sentiment in the developers who attended our class over the next two days; few of them knew why they were working on their assigned stories. I challenged them to take responsibility for understanding and achieving the purpose of their work; they should spend time with the production workers in the manufacturing plant and find out how well the system was working for them. As it turned out, many had already done that, but the issues the production workers thought were important never made it to the developers' "to do" list.

"We are a central IT department," the department manager told me. "When we implemented Scrum, we decided that the IT people in the business units should be the product owners. But the problem is they are actually project managers, so they usually tell the development teams exactly what to do without telling them why. They are measured on how many new features get into the system, so they don't put priority on maintenance work, even though our system annoys the production workers and often slows down factory production."

Product managers and product owners are not customers. Their job should be to connect the development teams with customers, but that clearly wasn't happening here. Instead, the product owners represented a handover between the development teams and their real customers, keeping developers from engaging in the purpose of their work.

Later in our class we did a problem-solving exercise, and two groups independently decided to work on the problem of not being allowed to do the maintenance work they knew should be done. Both groups came up with the same solution to the problem: They decided they would reserve 20% of the velocity of each iteration to work on tasks of their own choosing, which would give them time to fix the system so they could be proud of it.

Mary Poppendieck

What Is Your Purpose?

A simple statement of purpose *from a customer's perspective* can do wonders to clarify what is important and what is not. For example, everyone at Southwest knows that the company's purpose is to make flying affordable and enjoyable for everyone. This means that costs have to be low and hassles minimized. This purpose guides both strategic initiatives and day-to-day decisions at all levels of the company.

Once you have identified your customers, it is time to come to a clear understanding of your organization's purpose from your customers' perspective. Create a brief, crisp statement of what is important for your organization to succeed. This is what your work system must deliver. Note: Your purpose is probably *not* to develop software. It is a rare customer who wants software; customers want their problems solved. If customers could solve their problems without software, they would be delighted.

As an example, let's look at how we would describe the purpose of the development group in the sidebar "Product Owners Aren't Customers." In this case, the primary customers were the users, the production operators; another important customer was the sponsor; and a third set of customers were the operations people who supported the system. The purpose of the development group was to provide a production information system that made production operators' jobs easier while improving quality and productivity in the manufacturing plant.

Let's look at another example. Werner Vogels, CTO of Amazon.com, defines the purpose of his IT organization thus: Provide a highly available, highly scalable technology platform for Amazon.com and its business partners.[13] By "available," Vogels means that shoppers can always browse a site and put things in their shopping basket, even if other parts of the system aren't working. By "scalable," Vogels means that there should be positive, not negative, economies of scale, and scaling should be available on demand. Over the past several years, pursuing this purpose has turned Amazon.com into an impressive technology provider as well as a retailer, while Amazon's IT department has become a true profit center.

---

13. Vogels, "A Conversation with Werner Vogels," 2006; see also the videos Vogels, "Availability & Consistency," 2007, and Vogels, Keynote, 2008.

What Is the Nature of Customer Demand?

The next step in establishing a systems view of your organization is to understand the patterns of customer demand for the products and services you provide. Customer demand comes in two forms. First there is demand for products and services that provide value. Second, when a product or service doesn't meet the customers' expectations, there is demand for failure remediation—that is, demand to fix something that appears to be broken, inadequate, or difficult to use, configure, or modify.

Failure Demand

Failure demand is the demand on the resources of an organization caused by its own failures. Support calls, for example, are almost always failure demand. They may be caused by some aspect of the system that is unclear to a user, or they may be caused by an outright failure of the system to perform.

Change requests may also be failure demand; for example, a change request may come from a failure on your part to understand your customers or a premature decision on your part about what customers actually want. Even if you deliver exactly what your customers asked for, once they see it they may realize that it doesn't solve their problem; from *your customer's* perspective change requests in this case are failure demand.

An insidious form of failure demand is the demand on your resources created by technical debt: things such as defects you have chosen to ignore, messy coding practices, duplication, lack of effective test automation, a tightly coupled architecture, multiple code branches—anything that makes it difficult to respond to a request for a change. All these things increase the demand on your capacity when customers ask for changes, even if the changes themselves are value demand.

Demand from support organizations that have to deal with your systems is usually failure demand. When your product is difficult to integrate with other systems, database migrations between versions are a nightmare, or intermittent lockups bring down the data center, you have serious failure demand. Even if your software performs exactly the way it was designed to operate, if it gives operations and support organizations problems, both you and they are wasting valuable time.

What Is Failure Demand?

We were explaining failure demand to a management team. I asked, "Is the support manager here?" Yes, he was.

"So how much of the demand on your organization do you think is failure demand?"

"About 95%," he was quick to reply.

Later that day I was giving a talk to a larger group and a question came from the audience: "You say that we should be able to rapidly update our code. But how can we do that when so many of our customers have customized versions of our software?"

Suddenly the magnitude of the support problem dawned on me. "It sounds to me like you have a huge branching problem," I replied. And they did. The branching and support policies had created ever-growing failure demand on the organization.

Mary Poppendieck

The purpose of looking for failure demand is to *identify as much failure demand as possible*, because failure demand is waste that you can do something about. In the beginning you should expect to find a *lot* of failure demand. Welcome it; do *not* penalize anyone for it. Failure demand is created by the way your work is done; exposing it gives you the opportunity for significant improvement. Your primary objective is to find and eliminate failure demand so that you have more time to accommodate additional value demand.

Once you have identified failure demand, calculate what percentage of the demand on your organization is failure demand. It is likely to be a big number; we have seen estimates between 30% and 70%. Think about it: If one-third of your demand is failure demand, you would increase the capacity of your organization by 50% if you could eliminate that failure demand. Eliminating failure demand provides a huge opportunity for increased productivity. In Chapter 4, Relentless Improvement, you will find ideas for ways to uncover the causes and reduce the amount of failure demand.

Of course, failure demand is not going to go away overnight, and while it exists, your secondary objective is to remediate each problem as rapidly as possible. John Seddon says, "As a rule of thumb, end-to-end time from the customer's point of view is almost always an essential measure in any 'break-fix' system."[14] A break-fix system starts with a customer in distress (something is broken) and ends when the problem is resolved (fixed). For all failure demand that you choose to fix, the essential customer-focused measurement is the request-to-resolution time. Clearly, your first priority should be to eliminate the

---

14. Seddon, *Freedom from Command and Control: Rethinking Management for Lean Service*, 2005, p. 106.

failure demand, but as long as it's there, minimize your customers' pain by fixing their problem as rapidly as possible.

Value Demand

The primary demand on your organization should be value demand. This demand can be in the form of requests for work that will add value from a customer's perspective, or it can be in the form of unmet needs that customers don't know they have, but that you discover and satisfy through your products and services. Value demand, when satisfied, usually generates revenue for your organization.

Almost every software development organization we know of has more demand for its services than it can accommodate, so a good question to ask is "What portion of incoming value demand does my organization have the capacity to satisfy?" If value demand exceeds your capacity to deliver, there are two steps to take: (1) Focus on eliminating failure demand so you have more time to work on value demand, and (2) evaluate how you filter value demand to decide which work you will accept and which you will turn down.

Once you have a good idea about the volume of value demand your organization is experiencing, how you qualify it, and what percentage you can accept, the next step is to establish a customer-focused view of the value you deliver. What do your customers really value? Once you understand what customers value, you can establish customer-centric measures to focus everyone on improving customer outcomes, rather than meeting internal targets. If you provide visibility into what it means to deliver customer value, development teams can act independently and creatively to give customers more of what they really want.

Examples of good customer-centric measurements might be the following:

1. Time-to-market for product development (for the whole product)

2. End-to-end response time for customer requests (request-to-resolution time)

3. Success of a product in the marketplace (profitability, market share)

4. Business benefits attributable to a new system (measureable business improvement)

5. Customer time-to-value after delivery (consumability)

6. Impact of escaped (post-release) defects (customer downtime, financial impact)

Frame 2: System Capability

Once you understand your customers and what it means to deliver value to those customers, the next step is to gain a clear understanding of your capability to deliver that value. What capabilities do you need to be successful in the marketplace, both now and in the future? It is important to have the capability to deliver what customers want today, but it is also necessary to look into the future and make sure that today's efforts are moving your organization toward tomorrow's success. Realistic long-term planning and risk assessment, along with understanding the current and future competitive environment, are essential ingredients of sustainable success. If people and teams are going to use their creative energy to decide what is important to do today, they need to understand both the immediate customer needs and the challenges of the future.

What Is Your System Predictably Achieving?

The starting point for improving your capability to satisfy customers is to understand how your current work methods actually work, what they are currently capable of delivering. You need to understand how your capability compares with the needs of your customers and the capability of your competitors, both now and in the future.

Understanding Capability

If you want to know how well your organization is performing, don't just look at a few data points; look at a sequence of data over time. All systems exhibit variation, and looking at an occasional data point does not tell you much about how much variation there is in your system. In fact, random data points give a distorted view of your current capability.

A good way to visualize capability is to create a time series chart. Let's say that you want to look at your capability to quickly respond to a particular type of demand, for example, small urgent requests from customers. When a request arrives, give it a date stamp; when the request is closed out, subtract the arrival date from the current date to get the end-to-end response time, then plot these times. A time series plot of response times for small urgent requests might look something like Figure 1-1.

Your immediate reaction to a chart like this might be to look for the cause of the long delays for several of the requests. You don't have to look very far—your *work methods* are the cause. This is a chart showing what your work system is currently capable of delivering. You are not going to change things by

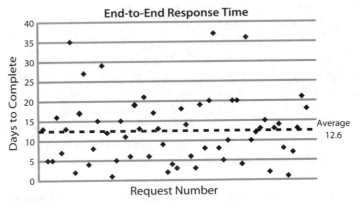

Figure 1-1   *Time series chart of end-to-end response time for small urgent requests*

looking for scapegoats or setting more aggressive targets. Your current way of working produces the results in the chart; if you don't like the results, you have to change the way the work is done.

W. Edwards Deming worked to spread an understanding of variation to industry leaders, but we think that his message is often distorted. We frequently see efforts aimed at removing variation from every process, without recognizing that such efforts usually make things worse. When you try to remove normal (common-cause) variation from a process, the process actually gets worse, not better. Deming pointed out that almost all variation (perhaps 95%) is common-cause variation—it is inherent in the system—and the only way to remove it is to change the way work is done. He concluded that most variation is a management problem. So if you are looking for scapegoats, start by looking in the mirror.

Positive or Negative Reinforcement?

A well-known approach to training is to give positive reinforcement when someone does something especially well, because this is supposed to lead to more of the same behavior.

We heard of a pilot training center that decided to test this theory. Careful records were kept of the results of positive and negative reinforcement of pilots in training. Much to the surprise of the researchers, they found that whenever a trainee pilot was given positive reinforcement, performance got worse, and whenever negative reinforcement was given, performance always improved! The training center concluded that giving negative feedback for poor performance was an effective training technique, and that positive feedback for good performance should be avoided.

Figure 1-2   *Performance of a pilot in training*

What's wrong with this research? Consider a time series of the performance of a pilot in Figure 1-2.

This time series shows expected variation in performance—variation due to random causes largely unrelated to pilot skill. Assume that the pilot is praised at the high points (circled). Of course, performance will appear to be lower the next time! If the pilot is reprimanded at the low points (boxed), performance would appear to improve.

The evidence shows very little about positive or negative reinforcement, but it clearly indicates that those gathering the data did not understand variation.

Tom Poppendieck

What Does Your System Need to Achieve?

The first step in changing the way work is done is to develop an understanding of what capabilities you need for both short- and long-term success. Do you have competitors who are better at delivering value to your customers than you are, or is there a threat that such competitors might emerge in the future? Could you attain a meaningful competitive advantage from significant improvements? Will your performance deteriorate over time if you proceed down your current path? Will your architecture support sustainable growth? Are you building up technical debt that will slow you down in the future?

Once you understand where you need to be in order to be successful, both now and in the future, you can create a long-term challenge that will make it clear to everyone what the organization needs to happen in order to be successful both now and over the long run. This will enable people and teams to balance short-term or narrowly focused decisions against long-term and system-wide imperatives.

Don't Set Targets

You should *not* set targets. Your current system is what it is; targets are not going to change its capability. You *measure* system capability; you do not prescribe it. As Deming once said, "If you have a stable system, then there is no use to specify a goal. You will get whatever the system will deliver. A goal beyond the capability of the system will not be reached. If you have not a stable system, then there is no point in setting a goal. There is no way to know what the system will produce: it has no capability."[15]

Think of it this way. Let's say you set a target that is beyond the capability of your system, a goal that your current work processes cannot achieve. Since the target is a strong motivator (no argument there), people have three choices: (1) redesign the work, (2) distort the system (for instance, by ignoring defects), or (3) cheat (game the system) to hit the target.[16] If people do not have the know-how to redesign the system, they are left with two options: distort or game the system.

Suppose the people do have the know-how to redesign the work. In our experience, redesigned work is likely to produce far better results than an arbitrary target—but where is the motivation to surpass the target? Similarly, if you set a target below the current system capability, you are likely to get less than the system is capable of delivering, because there is little motivation to surpass the target.

▼————————————————————————————————▼

Goals Gone Wild

Managers have no doubt heard that they should set challenging goals in order to motivate the best performance. But in the paper "Goals Gone Wild,"[17] researchers from four top business schools question this practice. They agree that goals are powerful motivators, so powerful that the goals often have severe side effects, ranging from dangerous products to unethical behavior to seriously underperforming systems to reduced learning.

There may be too many goals, causing people to choose the ones they like. Or they can be too specific, causing sub-optimizing behavior. Or they can be too challenging, causing people to meet them at all costs—inducing unnecessary risk taking, cheating, or gaming. The authors issue this warning: "Goals may cause systematic problems in organizations due to narrowed focus, unethical behavior, increased risk taking, decreased cooperation, and

---

15. Deming, *Out of the Crisis*, 2000, p. 76.
16. From Seddon, *Systems Thinking in the Public Sector*, 2008, p. 97.
17. Ordóñez et al., "Goals Gone Wild: The Systematic Side Effects of Over-Prescribing Goal Setting," 2009. Italics in the original. See also Bazerman, "When Goal Setting Goes Bad," 2009.

decreased intrinsic motivation." And they postulate, *"Aggressive goal setting within an organization will foster an organizational climate ripe for unethical behavior."*

There is no question that goals influence behavior; it's just that they are a blunt instrument. So be careful what you ask for; you will probably get it.

Mary Poppendieck

A target is a predetermined level of performance that people are expected to achieve; if there is significant variance from the target (or plan), explanations are usually required. Targets are generally associated with incentives; people are rewarded or punished based on their variance from the target.

Incentive systems based on performance targets make the assumption that if people would only try harder, they could achieve better results—hence targets communicate an implicit assumption that people are not currently contributing their best efforts. Wouldn't it be better to challenge people and teams to excel at delivering exceptional customer outcomes and communicate trust that they will do their best?

Use Relative Goals with Caution

Not all goals are based on predetermined targets; they can be based on relative measures. For example, goals can be based on performance relative to competitors, performance relative to peers, or performance compared to past performance. Relative performance goals do not attempt to set a fixed level of performance for the future; they look backward to see how actual performance compares against the performance of others. In most sports, winning or losing depends upon relative performance: A swimmer only has to swim faster than seven other swimmers in order to win; a baseball team has to score more runs than the other team.

Relative goals can be very motivating, and they have some advantages over targets or plans. Relative goals are not based on a prediction of the future, nor do they encourage people to distort or game the system; and finally, they don't act as a floor on performance. On the other hand, relative goals leave competitors with little motivation to help each other out—quite the contrary: Relative goals can motivate competitors to sabotage each other's performance. Thus ranking performance relative to peers can be damaging inside a company, especially if reward systems are based on this ranking. If, however, the competition is friendly and performance rewards are shared equally among all competitors, the destructive side effects of tracking performance against peers can be mitigated.

Challenge: Pull from the Future

Perhaps the best way to engage people in making the organization better is to create a long-term vision of where you want to be—where you need to be to survive—and challenge everyone to help move the organization from where it is now to where it needs to be. Challenge people and teams to improve the way work is done by redesigning their work methods. Challenge them to develop systems that provide clear business value. Challenge them to devise an architecture that will meet future growth projections. Challenge them to create new products that will be successful in the marketplace.

Let's say that you would like to decrease the "hardening" time at the end of a release cycle. A target might be "Cut the verification time in half!" Given enough emphasis on this target, the verification time will probably be cut in half, but often at the expense of more defects escaping to production.

A far better approach is to challenge teams to redesign the way development works so that defects are discovered and fixed as soon as possible after they are injected into the code. With this challenge, a team would quit focusing on how many features are delivered and start thinking about how to make sure that every delivered feature is defect-free. The team would introduce automated tests and continuous integration and adopt the practice of stopping to fix every defect as soon as it is detected. When done well, this approach has a track record of dramatically decreasing back-end testing time—by far more than half—at the same time as it increases quality and productivity. But these results are achieved only when a team works to improve the capability of its work methods to produce defect-free code. They are rarely achieved by a decree that system verification time must be cut in half.

Challenges are different from fixed performance targets:

1. Challenges are not necessarily SMART;[18] they are open-ended, customer-centric, and designed to elicit passion and pride.

2. Challenges communicate confidence that people and teams are intelligent, innovative, capable of thinking for themselves, and trusted to do their best to further the purpose of the organization.

3. Challenges flow from a long-term vision of what is necessary to be successful over time and contain enough information that people and teams can act independently and with confidence that their work will contribute to achieving the vision.

4. Thus challenges are a pull from the future rather than a forecast of the future.

---

18. SMART goals are specific, measurable, attainable, realistic, timely.

Frame 3: End-to-End Flow

Far too often, providing customer value is thought of as a series of separate input-process-output steps, rather than an integrated flow of work through an organization. But if no one takes an end-to-end view of a customer problem or a product as it moves through a work system, customer problems fall into the cracks between departments, hard-earned knowledge evaporates at handovers, and the things that customers will really value get lost along the way. Developing an understanding of the end-to-end flow of work through a work system is fundamental to systems thinking.

One way to evaluate the end-to-end workflow through your system is to draw a process flow map—also known as a value stream map—of the end-to-end flow of a product or a customer problem as it makes its way through your organization. There are two reasons for drawing these maps. They help you

1. Discover the reasons for failure demand, so it can be eliminated

2. Find waste in the workflow, so it can be removed

Eliminate Failure Demand

Failure demand is waste. So the best questions to ask are "Why is the process producing failure demand? What can be changed to prevent failure demand?" In general, your bias should be against creating a process map for failure demand, because every activity on that map would be waste. But there are times when a process map for failure demand can help you discover how to reduce and eventually eliminate the waste.

Failure Demand Process Map

We were at a Web portal company drawing a process map of the critical defect resolution process. The group wanted to start their map when a critical defect report reached the development team. But critical defect resolution is a break-fix problem, so the process should always be mapped starting when the customer discovers that something is broken (see Figure 1-3).

"I'm one of your customers," I said to get the mapping process started in the right place. "So let's say that I discover a critical defect. What do I do?"

"Call Level 1 customer support."

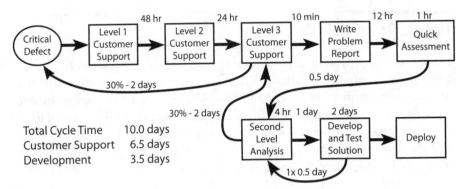

Figure 1-3   *Critical defect process map*

Total Cycle Time   10.0 days
Customer Support   6.5 days
Development   3.5 days

"Right. I know how that goes: They tell me I must be doing something wrong; nothing can be wrong with your system. So how long does it take me to convince them that it's your problem, not mine?"

"Maybe a couple of days" came the sheepish answer. Next my problem moves to Level 2 customer support; a day later my problem makes it to Level 3 customer support. Often there is not enough information at this point, so they need to get back to me about 30% of the time. This might take two days.

Just over a day later my problem reaches the development team, which looks at the problem report immediately. Thirty percent of the time they have to get back to Level 3 customer support, which takes another two days. But often (30% of the time) Level 3 customer support needs to get back to me to answer the development team's question. It takes two days to contact me and another day to get the answer back to the development team.

Once it's clear what the problem is, it takes four hours to develop a solution and one day to wait for testing, which takes another two days. An additional half day, on the average, is needed to fix problems discovered in testing. Finally the fix is deployed.

All told it takes an average of six and a half days for the customer support process and another three and a half days for development. So it takes an average of ten days to solve my problem.

"What if the first six and a half days disappeared?" I asked.

"You mean have customers call developers directly?" The development VP was appalled. It didn't seem like a productive path to take.

But then someone spoke up from the back of the room. "We did that," she said. "A few years ago when I was working in another company, we were going crazy, we needed to try something. So we got the CEO to let us bypass customer support. It worked well."

"Who answered the phones?" the development VP challenged.

"The developers did, in rotation," she responded.

"How much of their time did *that* take?" He was clearly skeptical.

"Well, we did a lot of experiments, and we quickly settled on two rules: (1) Immediately after a release, the responsible team staffed the phones. (2) Developers were required to create a knowledge base report accessible to customers for every call, before they could close it out.

"With those two rules, we were astonished at the results. We had 800 developers. Before we changed the process, 60% of development time was spent on critical defects. After we changed the process, 20% of development time was spent on critical defects."

By connecting developers directly with customers, this company effectively gained 320 experienced developers—for free.

Mary Poppendieck

Remember, all time spent handling failure demand is waste. So it is usually better to create a map of the process that *creates* failure, rather than mapping the process that *handles* failure. Your objective is not to handle failure demand more efficiently; it is to eliminate failure altogether. Before mapping the flow of failure demand, ask yourself, "What is causing the development process to produce failure demand in the first place? What can be changed in the process to prevent (or dramatically reduce) the failure demand?"

In particular, we recommend that you think hard before creating a process map for handling a change approval process. Customers don't usually see change approval systems as a value; they see the *changes they need* as a value, but asking for permission to make the change is annoying. If customers see your change request approval process as a nuisance, that process is handling failure demand. Instead of improving your change request approval process, consider why you should have one in the first place. A change request approval process for a system under development is usually a sign that the development process can't absorb new ideas or handle typical variation in your customers' situation. Perhaps you are making decisions too soon, or waiting too long to ask for feedback, or not leaving enough space in your plan to accommodate that feedback. Perhaps your customer engagement and collaboration practices are ineffective. Ask yourself, "How can we reorganize our process so it can discover changes more rapidly and accommodate changes more easily?"

Map Value Demand

A value stream map is a diagram of the end-to-end flow of value-creating work through your process; its purpose is to help you understand the workflow for value demand so you can improve your process. Usually a value stream map starts when a customer has a need and ends when the need is met; however, a time-to-market map may start when a product concept is approved and end when customers start realizing value from the product. Before you start a value stream map, use a time series chart, as we discussed in Frame 2: System Capability, to visualize the end-to-end flow time for an average item moving through your system. This is your current capability. The value stream map will show you how much of that time is spent actually adding value.[19]

Value Stream Map

Henrik Kniberg showed a value stream map of the development process at a video game development company.[20] The company was experiencing very long development times, which led to missed market windows and high overhead costs, not to mention the toll that lack of success took on the people developing the products.

Henrik described the value stream like this:

When someone—call him Sam—came up with an idea for a new game, he took a couple of hours to prepare a concept presentation. After about a month, the presentation was made to the idea review committee, and since this was a good idea, it went into the game backlog. This was not the only game in the queue, however; there were several others, so it took six months for graphics and sound designers to become available (see Figure 1-4).

Once the designers were free, Lisa assigned the new game to them, and two months later the design was done. Only a week was wasted during those two months, but when the game was designed, it was put in the design-ready queue, where it languished for six months. When the development team finally got to the game, it was working on two other games at the same time, so it took three months to complete development, even though the team spent only one month of that time actually working on Sam's game. When the team was done, the game sat in the product-ready queue for six months, waiting for final integration and deployment. Finally, over two years after Sam initially had his idea, the game was released. During those two years, only three and a half months—or 14% of the time—were spent actually adding value to the game.

---

19. More examples of value stream maps can be found in Poppendieck, *Implementing Lean Software Development: From Concept to Cash*, 2006, pp. 83–92.
20. Henrik Kniberg of Crisp, a Stockholm company, drew this value stream map at the Deep Lean Conference in Stockholm, September 2008. Mattias Skarin of Crisp helped us understand the case in more detail. Used with permission.

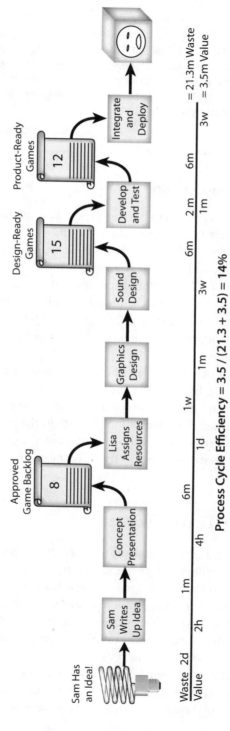

Process Cycle Efficiency = 3.5 / (21.3 + 3.5) = 14%

Figure 1-4   *Time-to-market value stream map*

23

Diagnosis:

There is obviously too much in-process inventory in this system, too many handovers, and a lot of multitasking. To address all of these issues at the same time, the company created cross-functional teams, each of which developed one game at a time, end-to-end, with no handovers. The first team demonstrated that it could repeatedly develop new games in less than four months (six times faster than before).

Mary and Tom Poppendieck

Find the Biggest Opportunity

The purpose of a value stream map is to help spot opportunities to improve your process capability. When you compare the value-added time to the total process time, you get a feel for how much better things could be. Ask yourself, "Why do we have so much non-value-adding time? Is it really necessary? What's causing it?"

Generally the biggest delays or loopbacks in a value stream map provide the biggest opportunity for improving the process capability. We recommend that you pick the most likely opportunity and tackle it. Forget the value stream map while you work on improving your process; you can draw a new one once you have changed the process.

Don't take the ratio of value-added time to total process cycle time (the process cycle efficiency) too literally. We find that after the process is improved, a new value stream map might show that the process cycle efficiency has *decreased*! Why? Because there was a lot of waste in the process that was not recognized when the first value stream map was drawn; once you get used to seeing and removing waste, you tend to find a lot more of it.

Frame 4: Policy-Driven Waste

Waste is anything that depletes resources of *time*, *effort*, *space*, or *money* without adding customer value. Most people do not frame their view of a system in terms of waste, so waste tends to fall outside their field of view. You can remove only the waste you see, so it is important to adjust the way you look at work so that the always-present waste becomes clearly visible.

You would be amazed at how much waste in a system is caused by the system itself, that is, by the way the work in the system is done. Too often waste is disguised under the cloak of habit or conventional wisdom—and more often than not, these sources of waste are embedded in the policies and standard procedures of the organization. Unless and until these policies change, the waste is not going to go away.

How Can Policies Cause Waste?

There are many ways that policies can cause waste. For example, leaders in many companies believe that developers should not talk to customers because this is a waste of valuable developer time. In Frame 3: End-to-End Flow, we discussed a critical defect process in which three levels of customer support insulated developers from customers (see Figure 1-3). By simply removing the three levels of customer support and having developers talk directly to customers, *40% of the total time of 800 developers was freed up.* This is not an isolated case. We will see in a case study in Chapter 6 that direct developer-customer interaction delivered more of the right content, increased sales, and dramatically reduced support calls.

Of course, simply providing direct customer-developer interaction does not necessarily eliminate the biggest cause of waste; other policies can overwhelm the advantages of good customer interaction.

"We Felt Like Pawns in a Game"

"I was part of a team where we had very strong pull incentives, from a customer point of view. We could add features and reprioritize every two weeks if we wanted to. We had in fact worked very hard to turn a waterfall company more flexible. And succeeded in a way. We listened to the customers, the ones really using the product. And we could build a release rather quickly.

"What we, the team, didn't realize was how hard the product was to install. This dawned on me when I went to a site using the product to do an upgrade. The end user asked me why he couldn't do the upgrade himself. He pointed out that he was a very seasoned end user. He had lots and lots of experience with computers and programming. I told him I didn't doubt his capabilities and explained how things were for me. I was told to travel tens of thousands of kilometers through Europe to do upgrades of systems that could have been designed to be more easily upgraded if one would have thought of it earlier. I kept on telling him about how I felt it should have been done and we felt more and more like pawns in a game. I guess he did more than I.

"What I realized at a later point was this: The upgrades and responsibilities for the data the application generated were regulated with contracts. The customer wasn't allowed to do upgrades; this was controlled by contracts.

"So, I guess, whatever your intentions are during the development of a product, they can easily be destroyed by early thoughts (or lack thereof) on how to handle your customers."

Ola Ellnestam, CEO, Owner, and Agile Coach at Agical AB, Sweden

Another example of policy-driven waste was depicted in the time-to-market value stream map in Frame 3: End-to-End Flow (see Figure 1-4). A quick glance showed that three long queues were the cause of most of the delay in getting products to market, yet the organization was blind to them. This was probably because the queues were not the responsibility of any department manager; their real purpose was to buffer departments from the variation of neighboring departments. Failure to see the impact of queues is often caused by focusing exclusively on department-level performance or by trying to achieve high utilization of scarce talent. These policies leave most companies oblivious to the tremendous drag local optimization has on time-to-market and end-to-end flow and hence on cost, revenue, and yes, even utilization.

The Five Biggest Causes of Policy-Driven Waste

In our experience, the most common causes of policy-driven waste in software development are

1. Complexity

2. Economies of scale

3. Separating decision making from work

4. Wishful thinking

5. Technical debt

Complexity

In "No Silver Bullet" Fred Brooks wrote, "Software entities are more complex for their size than perhaps any other human construct. . . . Many of the classic problems of developing software products derive from this essential complexity and its nonlinear increases with size."[21] We know this. And yet . . .

1. Our software systems contain far more features than are ever going to be used.[22] Those extra features increase the complexity of the code, driving up costs nonlinearly. If even half of our code is unnecessary—a conservative estimate—the cost of the system with that extra code is not just double; it's perhaps ten times more expensive than it needs to be. Our best opportunity to improve software development productivity is this: Stop putting features into our systems that aren't absolutely necessary.

---

21. Brooks, "No Silver Bullet: Essence and Accidents of Software Engineering," 1986.
22. More detail on this is provided in Poppendieck, *Implementing Lean Software Development: From Concept to Cash*, 2006, p. 24.

2. Many of our policies are predicated on the assumption that scope is non-negotiable. This leaves us no way to stop adding those unnecessary features. We need a process that lets us develop the first 20% of a system, get it in production, get feedback, and add features incrementally as time and money permit. We need policies that say: If something has to be compromised—cost, schedule, or scope—the default choice should *routinely* be scope.

3. Even our measurements give subtle messages that we should squeeze as much code into a system as possible. We measure productivity based on lines of code or function points, as if these things were good. They're not; they're bad. Function points might provide interesting *relative data*, but they should never be used as performance metrics.

4. We need to keep our code bases simple. This means we shouldn't add features until they are needed. Forget just in case; develop just in time. We need architectures that foster incremental development. We need policies that make refactoring—removing complexity introduced when changing the code—a normal and expected part of adding new features.

5. Our customers often want to use software to automate their complex processes. This is not a good idea. Business processes should be simplified first and automated later. How often do we help our customers simplify their processes before automating them?

The lean frame of reference focuses on simplicity. Lean thinkers know that complexity clogs up the flow of work and inevitably slows things down. The cost of complexity is hidden; it has a second-order effect on cost, so we just don't see it in our financial systems. This makes complexity all the more pernicious—it's hard to cost-justify spending money to keep things simple.

At the end of this chapter we introduce the concept of *ideation*, the process of coming up with a design so fitting to the problem that it seems inevitable. Solutions that "just fit" are necessarily simple; great designs always make us wonder how something so obvious could have escaped us for so long.

Cut Scope, Meet the Deadline

"We were doing very well," they said. "The code base was solid, our velocity was stable, we were proud of the way our system was coming along. But we weren't getting done fast enough for the management team. So one day our boss took the senior people aside and offered us a very large bonus if we could meet the deadline. We mean, it was *really* big."

I was surprised at their candor, since they were presenting at a public conference.

"We agreed to go for it. We worked day and night and weekends. We shoveled code out as fast as we could. We stopped testing; it didn't matter if it worked, it just had to be done. And we made it; we got the bonus.

"But the code is a mess. Nothing works right. The work-arounds are terrible. It's going to take us years to clean it up."

I wasn't surprised. I could tell they were not proud of what they had done.

"What do you think you should have done?" came a question from the audience.

They were quick to answer: "We should have said *no*. We should have been late."

I wasn't so sure. I had been at their company a year before, and I admired their boss. He was a good manager in an impossible position, I suspected. I was pretty sure that missing the deadline was *not* an option.

Later at break I asked to the two speakers, "Wouldn't it have been possible to cut scope and meet the deadline without abandoning your testing discipline?"

"Oh, yes, definitely!" came the immediate reply. "A lot of what we coded isn't being used yet anyway. But we couldn't. When you visited us a year ago, you told our management that they had to cut scope if they wanted to succeed. So a senior engineer went around to all the managers and got an agreement on moving a bunch of features to later releases. But once that was done, no one was willing to cut any more. We couldn't even talk about it."

I think that management was not close enough to the work to realize that delaying the implementation of major features was an easy and logical option. I expect they had no idea of the havoc they would create by setting impossible goals and leaving the team to figure out how to reach them. It was a very costly mistake.

In my experience, cutting scope and meeting the deadline is almost always the best approach.

Mary Poppendieck

Economies of Scale

Many of our instincts, policies, and procedures are rooted in the economies of scale, which drove huge improvements in productivity as industrial production replaced craft production in the first half of the twentieth century. But during the second half of that century, it became apparent that in any system with high variety, the economies of flow outperform the economies of scale, even in manufacturing. Software groups develop one-of-a-kind systems—the essence of variety. It should be obvious that we should base our policies and processes on the economies of flow. And yet . . .

1. It's difficult to abandon batch and queue mentality. We sort work into batches so we can assign each batch to the appropriate specialist, making maximum use of the specialist's time and skills. Full utilization of our most skilled workers is considered essential, and people are conditioned to focus on doing their part of the work without regard to its impact on the next step or the final customers. As a result, neither our workflow nor our workers are capable of absorbing variety.

2. It is so difficult to abandon batch and queue mentality that we fail to see queues that are staring us in the face. We can't figure out why it takes so long for things to move through our backlog-laden processes. We are blind to lists of customer requests that would take years to clear. We can't bring ourselves to shorten our queues because it would mean saying no to customers rather than letting their requests die a slow death.

3. Instead of designing a system that can absorb urgent requests, we pull workers off their current job to rush a yet-more-important job through our system. We ask people to work on three, five, ten, or more things at once. We are blind to the enormous amount of time wasted in context switching. It never occurs to us that if we did one thing at a time rather than three, everything would get done a lot faster and we would deliver value a lot sooner.

4. Sometimes we do let people work on one thing at a time, and then use computer systems to make sure that everyone is busy all of the time. We schedule projects and assign teams with an eye to full utilization. This scheme has little capability to absorb ever-present variation, so it is absorbed in the ramp-up time of newly formed teams. It would be much better to assign work to established teams than to reconstitute teams around projects.

5. We create annual budgets or long project plans that justify every person by committing to what they will deliver. Then we dump this big batch of work on our organization all at once. We must deliver everything that was promised, but as time goes on, reality intervenes. Customers want other things but aren't willing to pay more or give up what was promised. We know this system never works, but we don't see a way to escape the policy of making big batch promises.

Lean thinking uses economies of flow, rather than economies of scale, to frame the world we look at. Variety is an essential ingredient of software development, and so we need processes that absorb the variety gracefully. We will discuss such flow processes in Chapter 3. The problem is, when the world is framed with economies of scale, these approaches seem counterintuitive.

Separating Decision Making from Work

Any solution to a problem is necessarily simplified and abstracted when removed from its source, and it is for this reason that a design should not be separated from the concrete context in which it is implemented. We know that our deepest insights into our work are based on the tacit knowledge we get from being there: watching, experiencing, and getting our hands dirty. We know that great designs come from designers who are deeply engaged with solving the problem. We know that throwing things over the wall doesn't work. And yet . . .

1. There is widespread belief that it's not necessary for managers to understand work they manage. Yet without a technical background, managers are not in a position to provide guidance to technical workers. Some managers simply establish targets and leave it to workers to figure out how to meet them. Others put a team together and charter the members with figuring out how to do the right thing. From a lean perspective, the fundamental job of managers is to understand how the work they manage works, and then focus on how to make it better.[23] This is not to say that all leaders must know all the answers; the critical thing is that they *know what questions to ask*.

2. We have created organizational cultures where the only available career path is to leave the technical details behind. We do not honor or adequately reward the seasoned architect or brilliant user interaction designer. What future awaits a tech lead who can reinvent the testing process and put together a set of tools that runs every bit of code through every operating system and database every single night? When the only career path for these people is to leave their core expertise behind and become managers, we will never have top-notch technical leadership on the ground, where we need it.

3. In *Lean Product and Process Development*, Allen Ward writes that handoffs (handovers) are the biggest waste in product development. He says that a handoff occurs whenever we separate *responsibility* (what to do),

---

23. See Seddon, *Freedom from Command and Control: Rethinking Management for Lean Service*, 2005, Chapter 4.

knowledge (how to do it), *action* (doing the work), and *feedback* (learning from the results).[24] Our processes are full of these handovers, and we fail to see what's wrong with them. But in practice, many day-to-day decisions are based on tacit knowledge, which gets left behind in a handover. We must think that tacit knowledge transfers by magic, if we understand tacit knowledge in the first place.

4. Our language betrays us when we talk about "The Business." With these words we separate development decisions from the work they are auto-mating (see Figure 1-5).

Even agile software development methodologies make this mistake. They may recommend a "customer" or a "product owner" who is supposed to decide what all of our customers want and prioritize the order of develop-ment. But the most successful development occurs when developers talk directly to customers or are part of business teams. And those things called requirements? They are really candidate solutions; separating require-ments from implementation is just another form of handover.

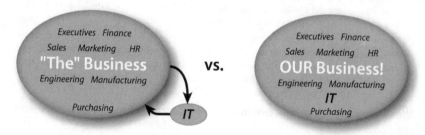

Figure 1-5   *From "the" business to "our" business*

5. Once our systems are deployed, there are policies and interpretations of laws (Sarbanes-Oxley, for example) that keep developers away from their code. So we walk away and leave the support team to deal with any prob-lems that occur. The support team members are the ones who get the phone calls in the middle of the night, yet we wonder why they don't like frequent deployments. They are the victims of our risky design practices, but we are not interested in hearing about the causes of system failures. Perhaps our world would be a better place if all developers had to walk in the shoes of the operations and support team for a month every year.

---

24. Ward, *Lean Product and Process Development*, 2007, p. 43. We use the word *hand-over* instead of *handoff* because it seems to translate better into other languages.

Ever since Adam Smith wrote about division of labor in a pin factory,[25] it has been commonly accepted wisdom that division of labor increases productivity—the more specialization the better. Fortunately, this "fact" was lost on Toyota's Taiichi Ohno, who devised a system where multiskilled workers and easy-to-reconfigure machines are more productive than specialists. There are two reasons for this: First, lean systems are designed to absorb variety, and second, they are designed to be relentlessly improved as the workers devise ever better ways to do the work. In the context of system development, Adam Smith was dead wrong.

Developer on Site

What CIO wouldn't love to read this kind of article?

Agile Development and SOA at Standard Life[26]

Thursday, 18th October 2007

Investors Chronicle is not famed for its hyperbole, but it certainly likes what it sees in Standard Life. . . . its rise has been "little short of meteoric", the magazine gushes. Half-year financials show how huge leaps in efficiency led to a 71% jump in operating profit and a 31% rise in new business.

A great deal of the credit for that gilded resurgence is being placed at the door of Standard Life's IT organization. . . . It has created one of the most advanced implementations of service-oriented architecture, put into practice lean processes and radically shaken up the structure of the development of its core applications, with IT staff "embedded" within the business units they deliver to.

We were pretty impressed, because we had been there two years earlier. We read on:

Keith Jones, CIO recalls: "The light bulb moment for me was when [Mary Poppendieck] said that something like 60% of all code that is delivered is never exercised. I thought that was astonishing, that there must be some terrible companies out there doing some really bad things. Then she said, 'By the way, we have done a sample of Standard Life's projects and it's something like 64% for you guys'."

The article goes on to say that the leadership group asked themselves why they had analysts and developers located in a different place from their customers. Why not have the people building the software located with the business team, listening to what customers are struggling with, talking with the people creating the business case? So Standard Life created one department, roughly half IS staff and half pensions people, all sitting together and working as a team.

---

25. Smith, *An Inquiry into the Nature and Causes of the Wealth of Nations*, 1776.
26. Swabey, "Agility Applied at Standard Life," 2007.

Putting developers on the business team is a successful pattern. We once taught a class at a bank that scanned mortgage closing papers to archive them digitally. It had a large lean effort for the paper scanning process; the problem was the lean teams could not get anyone to make changes to the workflow software that governed their work. The changes seemed so minor that they couldn't get enough priority. The leader of the lean effort complained, "In the past 18 months, I have submitted 1536 requests for changes to the software, and not *one* of them has been implemented."

I knew the workflow software they were using and I was pretty sure that it was relatively easy to configure. So I suggested that they put a couple of developers on the operations teams for a while and just let them help their teammates out. We later heard that this approach was very successful, and much of the software development work is now done by developers who are embedded in cross-functional business teams.

Mary Poppendieck

Wishful Thinking[27]

Frederick Winslow Taylor got one thing right. He insisted that work improvement should be based on the scientific method. Taiichi Ohno embraced this idea—but instead of having "experts" measure and improve the work of production workers, he trained production workers to measure and improve their own work. We know that making decisions based on data rather than opinion is the right approach. Being in software, we can create tools to gather any data we want any day of the week. And yet . . .

1. We chase the latest ideas in software development without bothering with the scientific method. We think it is a waste of time to understand the theory, create hypotheses, run experiments, gather data, and find out what really works in our environment. We fail to appreciate that "best practices" are somebody else's solutions to their problems, not necessarily the right solutions to our problems. We adopt new development approaches with an unhealthy dose of wishful thinking, rather than determining the most appropriate practices for our environment—and then we are surprised at the disappointing results.

2. We manage by looking at single data points instead of a series of data in context. We set targets without understanding our process capability relative

---

27. The idea of wishful thinking as waste, as well as many other ideas in this section, are from Allen Ward (*Lean Product and Process Development*, 2007).

to the target. We don't appreciate the fact that trying to remove normal (common-cause) variation will make the situation worse, not better.

3. We don't like uncertainty, so we try to make decisions and get them out of the way. Our natural inclination is to look at one alternative for solving a problem, because we think that's cheaper and faster than looking at several alternatives. For tough problems, this is usually wrong; making early decisions when we are the most ignorant is the least likely way to get good results and the most likely way to force us to start over again.

4. Despite our prowess in handling information, we have very few techniques for preserving knowledge. One approach has been to collect massive, detailed documents. But who reads them? Even search engines fail us. Another approach has been whiteboards, coupled with a camera if we really need to save the sketches. Still another approach is to video a whiteboard talk on the fundamental architecture of an application. There is no doubt a middle ground, but we're still searching for it. We might learn a lesson from the open-source movement, where all communication is written and the focus is on making the communication system extremely simple, appropriately concise, quickly searchable, and never bypassed by verbal communication.

5. We feel a great sense of accomplishment when our code passes its tests and we celebrate because it meets the specification—as if the specification could contain everything we needed to think about. What about that security hole or the memory leak or the ungraceful exit from the database that occasionally causes a lockup? How easy will the system be to install, interface to, populate with data? Thinking we're done when the regression tests pass is wishful thinking.

When you think of learning as uncovering the shortcomings of plans, somehow plan-driven development loses its charm. Instead, creating useful knowledge becomes the essence of developing a new product. But there's more to learn about than the product being developed; we also learn about our process for developing products. Constant learning is the essence of improving both the product itself and the product development process.

Technical Debt

We know that all successful software gets changed.[28] So if we think we're working on code that will be successful, we know we need to keep it easy to change.

---

28. See Brooks, "No Silver Bullet: Essence and Accidents of Software Engineering," 1986.

Anything that makes code difficult to change is technical debt.[29] We know that technical debt drives the total cost of software ownership relentlessly higher, and that eventually we will have to pay it off or the system will go bankrupt. And yet . . .

1. We tolerate obscure code, instead of making sure that all code reveals its intentions to the next person who comes along. Developers, especially apprentices, should be taught how to write "clean code":[30] code that is simple and direct, with straightforward logic. Senior technical people need to ensure that messy code, even if it passes the tests, is never admitted into the code base.

2. Far too often we don't take the time for refactoring: consolidating changes into existing code. Refactoring is essential for iterative development. Adding new features to existing code creates complexity, ambiguity, and duplication; refactoring pays down the debt.

3. We run regression tests on our systems before deployment. At first they are quick, but with each addition of code, regression tests take longer and longer and longer. As the regression deficit[31] grows, we increase the interval between releases. The only way to break this unending cycle of increasing release overhead is to decrease the regression deficit. If we had started with automated test harnesses back when the code base was small and added to and maintained them, we could make changes to our code almost as quickly today as when the code base was new.

4. We know that dependencies are one of the biggest generators of technical debt, and yet we are ambivalent about replacing obsolete systems with massive dependencies. We must develop, and migrate to, architectures that minimize dependencies. We have known for a long time how to do this: Focus on information hiding[32] and separation of concerns.[33]

---

29. The idea of debt as a metaphor was introduced by Ward Cunningham, "The WyCash Portfolio Management System," 1992.

30. See Martin, *Clean Code: A Handbook of Agile Software Craftsmanship*, 2009. Definitions are from pp. 7–11.

31. We first heard the term *regression deficit* from Owen Rogers.

32. *Information hiding* means putting features that change together into a single module. See Parnas, "On the Criteria to Be Used in Decomposing Systems into Modules," 1972.

33. *Separation of concerns* means keeping features that will change separately in different modules. See Dijkstra, "On the Role of Scientific Thought," 1982.

5. We branch code for many reasons: to isolate new development, to focus on an individual application, to create parallel feature sets. And we know that the longer two branches of code are apart, the harder they will be to merge. And yet we wait for days to build our code, and worse, we delay system testing until the end of development. We don't realize that this isn't necessary anymore; the big bang is obsolete.

We need to expose technical debt for what it is: a costly burden to be avoided lest it lead us into bankruptcy. Chapter 2 will look at software development through a technical frame and discuss solid techniques for avoiding technical debt.

Portrait: Product Champion, Take 1

We close out this chapter by taking a look at what is probably the most important part of the system development process—even though it happens before most people would think the development process has begun. Before you dive into developing a system, it is critical to define its purpose *in customer terms*, just as you defined the purpose of your organization in customer terms earlier in this chapter.

When Thomas Edison invented the light bulb in 1879, it was a rather useless novelty. So he invented an electric power distribution system, formed a company to distribute power, and built a steam power-generating plant—to make the light bulb broadly useful. Edison's genius lay in his ability to envision how people would want to use light bulbs and to imagine a fully developed marketplace. We saw this same genius in Steve Jobs, as the iPod and iPhone came to life as complete ecosystems. This is the essential challenge of development: imagining how people will want to use a product and envisioning a complete system and fully developed marketplace. We call this *ideation*.[34]

Just as Edison went on to found the companies that brought his light bulb to the masses, we expect that ideation leaders will remain at the helm as their concepts are implemented. After all, people develop a certain passion around their creative ideas and are eager to bring them to life. In honor of that passion and dedication, we call this leader a *product champion*.[35]

---

34. The term *ideation* is from Tim Brown, CEO of IDEO, as described in Brown, "Design Thinking," 2008.
35. The term *product champion* is borrowed from 3M, where Mary worked for 20 years. The term *chief engineer* is widely used for the same role and is interchangeable with *product champion*.

A product champion, much like an entrepreneur, has business responsibility for the success or failure of the product. This means that for a product with a profit-and-loss statement (P&L), they are responsible for the P&L of that product. This is why the product champion leads the ideation effort—if ideation is not done well, the product will not be successful.[36]

The Story of a Chief Engineer

Mr. Nobuaki Katayama, former chief engineer of the Lexus/SC, IS, & Altezza, took the time to discuss the job of a chief engineer with a group of us on a study tour of Japan in April 2009.[37] He noted that new car development is led by a chief engineer who is responsible for the business success of the car. This person should have a passion for the car; so if the car is to be a sports car, the chief engineer should *love* to drive fast.

Toyota develops new cars in three phases: creation, development, and production.

Creation: The creation stage of a new car is the backbone of the development process, and also the most difficult part. During this stage planning and concept development take place, including market research, predevelopment, styling, and cost and profit targets. The chief engineer negotiates with section heads (heads of body styling, engine, transmission, etc.) concerning what kind of performance and key features the car will have, what it will take to develop the car, and so on. Creation is not timeboxed; work continues until the concept is ready and typically takes about a year. As handshake agreements are reached, the product concept is refined and reviewed and, ultimately, approved by the board.

Development: This is the easier part of creating a new car, and Toyota is good at it. A schedule of 20 to 24 months is established by the chief engineer, who leads the work, with support from section managers. There are clear milestones that can be expected to be met, with, of course, more negotiations and ongoing design decisions.

---

36. See Levine, *A Tale of Two Systems: Lean and Agile Software Development for Business Leaders*, 2009, for an in-depth example of the role of a chief engineer in software development.

37. This meeting summary is used with permission. Some information in this sidebar is from a presentation by Kenji Hiranabe at Agile 2008, reporting on a presentation by Mr. Nobuaki Katayama to Developers Summit 2008, February 13, 2008, Gajoen, Tokyo (Hiranabe, "New Car Development at Toyota," 2008). Used with permission.

Keeping development on schedule requires honest communication and a philosophy of "bad news first" so that problems can be addressed as early as possible. Key decisions during development are made by choosing among well-developed options so that the best combination of quality, cost, and delivery can be achieved.

Production: The chief engineer remains responsible for the business success of the car as it goes into production and over its lifetime.

Mary and Tom Poppendieck

For the sake of simplicity, we use the term *product* champion, although we recognize that you may not use the word *product* to refer to your systems. You may be developing

1. Software as a product

2. Software embedded in a product

3. Software enabling a process

4. Software under contract

In the first two cases, the product champion should be the person with business responsibility for the final product. With larger systems, the champion may need assistance with subsystem leadership. Even then, division into subsystems should not be along technology lines, but along subsystem lines, for example, an engine for a car, a medical device programmer, the human interface for an electronic device, and so on.

In the third case—software that enables a process—it is particularly important that the product champion (actually, in this case, the process champion) be responsible for the design and success of the overall process, not just the software.

The fourth case—software developed under contract—is the most problematic for a product champion, especially if the contracting party divorces software development from the rest of system development. In the end, software developed under contract serves a broader purpose, and it would be best to have a product champion responsible for the broader purpose guiding the learning and feedback necessary for system development. We recognize that this is not always possible, but in any case, the product champion(s) must keep the whole system in mind.

A product champion leads two critical activities: a customer-facing role and a technology-facing role. Very often these roles reside in one person, but they can also be successfully shared by two people working in close harmony. In either case, the product champion initiates development by leading a team through the ideation phase.

Customer-Facing Ideation

IDEO is a design firm in California that has been extraordinarily successful at discovering unmet needs and matching them with technically feasible, commercially viable designs. These have led to a remarkable lineup of products that have been extremely successful in delighting customers. As design awards pile up year after year, IDEO has gone into the business of helping other companies copy its design process.[38]

IDEO's design approach is outlined by general manager Tom Kelley in *The Art of Innovation*:[39]

1. *Understand* the market, the client, the technology, and the perceived constraints on the problem. Later we often challenge those constraints, but it's important to understand current perceptions.

2. *Observe* real people in real life situations to find out what makes them tick; what confuses them, what they like, what they hate, where they have latent needs not addressed by current products and services.

3. *Visualize* new-to-the-world concepts and the customers who will use them. Some people think of this step as predicting the future, and it is probably the most brainstorming-intensive phase of the process.

4. *Evaluate* and refine the prototypes in a series of quick iterations. We try not to get too attached to the first few prototypes, because we know they'll change. No idea is so good that it can't be improved upon, and we plan on a *series* of improvements. . . . We watch for what works and what doesn't, what confuses people, what they seem to like, and we incrementally improve the product.

5. *Implement* the new concept for commercialization.

We can find no better summary of how to go about ideation. First frame the problem with its constraints. Then become an ethnographer and carefully observe people in that frame. This isn't about focus groups or market studies; go and watch the people who will use the product. Get inside their heads.

The next step is to visualize, model, and discuss what was observed. Add to the mix a forward-looking view of technology trends over the next few years. You want to skate to where the puck is going,[40] and our technology puck moves fast. Brainstorm, concoct scenarios, tell stories about customers, whip up some prototypes, keep ideas alive.

---

38. This section summarizes sections of Brown, "Design Thinking," 2008. See also Brown, "Strategy by Design," 2007.
39. From Kelley and Littman, *The Art of Innovation*, 2001, pp. 6–7.
40. Hockey star Wayne Gretzky gave the secret to his success: "I skate to where the puck will be, not to where it is."

Visualization leads to evaluation, a series of quick experiments that incrementally improve the product. "It doesn't matter how clever you are, your first idea about something is never right," says Tim Brown, CEO of IDEO. "So the great value of prototyping—and prototyping quickly and inexpensively—is that you learn about the idea and make it better."[41]

So *That's* How They Do It!

I have always loved cooking, and for years my kitchen was equipped with the same gadgets that I had grown up with as a child. Then a company called OXO invented a new kind of measuring cup. It's called an angled measuring cup, and it has an indentation so you can read the liquid level by looking *inside* the cup. I immediately loved it. No more bending over or holding the cup up high to read the liquid level on the outside of the cup. I could simply glance down inside the measuring cup and see the level. I bought several for my house and plenty for gifts.

Then I started seeing other OXO products: A peeler that felt a lot better in my hand. Utensils that were easy to store. Great cutting boards. Soon my kitchen was full of OXO gadgets. I wondered, "How can a company routinely come out with improvements on cooking tools that have been around for decades? How did they know that I would rather not bend over to measure liquids, that I prefer a bigger handle on a peeler? I didn't even know it myself!"

Then I read about how IDEO does ethnography; they call it archaeology. They go into houses of people like me and watch me using a measuring cup. They look for times when I'm a bit uncomfortable—bending over or holding a full cup high in the air. They notice when I pick up the peeler that I use an uncomfortable grip. And they invent a gadget that gets rid of these annoyances that I didn't even know were there.

So *that's* how they do it! Simple enough, really. You'd think that if we used the same approach, we might get similar results—fantastic systems that solve problems our customers didn't even know they had.

Mary Poppendieck

In due time, a product concept is ready for implementation. Ideation should not be a long, drawn-out affair, and the resulting concept should be at a high level to leave plenty of room for further learning.

---

41. Brown, "The Deans of Design," 2006.

Technology-Facing Ideation

Envisioning the product from a customer perspective is not enough in software development. Without an equally effective technology vision—let's call it an architecture—you aren't ready to proceed. The same design steps that worked to create a customer-centric view of the product can be used to develop the architectural vision:

1. *Understand:* Technology is forever changing. Start by understanding where it has been and, especially, where it is likely to go over the life of the product.

2. *Observe:* Take some time to observe the people struggling with the problem, from a technology point of view. The technical-facing concept and the customer-facing concept gain their integrity as a system when they are developed together and inform each other.

3. *Visualize:* Model, discuss, brainstorm, test ideas with spikes.[42] Inform these discussions with a keen awareness of where technology is heading and what will be possible over the life of the product.

4. *Evaluate:* Don't get caught up in the first idea that comes to mind. Experiment. Select three or four options and use set-based design during implementation to make the final choice. Above all, remember that a good software architecture is one that facilitates change in the code over the short term and evolution of the architecture over the long term.

5. *Implement:* At this point the architecture is a technical vision that will grow and evolve as development proceeds and learning takes place. It's time to start implementation.

The ideation phase will be done when it is done; it shouldn't have a deadline. It's not that ideation takes a lot of time; it usually doesn't. But without a breakaway concept, there can be no breakaway product. So don't short-change this important step. Develop a clear vision of how the product will meet market needs, how the architecture will support that vision, and how development will proceed. We call this a *product concept.* A product concept is not a detailed plan; it is a framework for proceeding with development.

What is the difference between a detailed plan and a framework for proceeding? Think of it this way: Plans are subject to change as learning occurs, whereas frameworks provide a space for learning to occur. So if you find that

---

42. A *spike* is a quick technical prototype to test out the viability of a technical approach.

you have to make substantial changes to the product concept after approval, it was too detailed and did not provide for learning.

How do you know when ideation is done? This differs from one context to another, so we don't have a canned answer. In companies with good ideation processes, the product champion knows when the concept is developed sufficiently to move on to implementation. If you aren't quite sure, you'll have to experiment and find out what works for you. We recommend that you start your experiments with a bias toward action. If you wonder whether you're ready to start implementation, the answer is probably yes.

Your Shot

1. Answer John Seddon's five questions about your organization:
   a. *Purpose:* What is the purpose of this organization?
   b. *Demand:* What is the nature of customer demand?
   c. *Capability:* What is the system predictably achieving?
   d. *Flow:* How does the work work?
   e. *System conditions:* What are the causes of waste in the system?

2. Choose two to five customer-centric measurements for your system. Some you might consider are
   a. Time-to-market for product development (for the whole product)
   b. End-to-end response time for customer requests (request-to-resolution time)
   c. Success of the product in the marketplace (profitability, market share)
   d. Business benefits attributable to a new system (measureable business improvement)
   e. Customer time-to-value after delivery (consumability)
   f. Impact of escaped (post-release) defects (customer downtime, financial impact)

3. Create time series charts for each of your customer-centric measures. (Some people call these charts the "voice of the process.") If the data doesn't exist, now would be a good time to start measuring.
   a. What do the charts say to you?
   b. Are your work processes stable?
   c. Can you distinguish between common-cause and special-cause variation?
   d. Is the way you do work delivering the results your customers expect?
   e. If not, what should be done?

4. Analyze how you handle requests from your customers:
   a. How much value demand do you receive in a month?

b. How much failure demand do you receive in a month?

c. What is the ratio of failure demand to value demand?

d. What kind of approval process do you use to filter customer demand?

e. What criteria are used?

f. What percentage of the requests are accepted?

g. How long does the approval process take?

h. How long on the average does it take for customers to find out about rejected requests?

i. Do you measure after the fact to see that the projected customer outcomes are achieved?

j. How long does an average approved request take to complete?

k. What do your customers think about your approval process?

5. Gather a team that includes the person responsible for an end-to-end process, if that person exists. Sketch a value stream map of an actual end-to-end flow of a customer demand through your organization's various processes, through the customer's processes, and back to the original customer.

a. What is the total cycle time?

b. How much of that time was spent adding value?

6. Have the team brainstorm the goals, policies, and beliefs that cause waste that might exist in your organization in each of the five categories:

a. Complexity

b. Economies of scale

c. Separating decision making from work

d. Wishful thinking

e. Technical debt

7. How does ideation take place in your company?

a. Does your organization have the role of product champion or chief engineer?

b. How do you move ideas from the fuzzy front end of product development into an approved product concept?

c. How does it work for you?

Chapter 2

Technical Excellence

Snapshot

We invite you to take a walk through the history of software engineering, starting the year it was named—1968. We're looking for concepts that turned out to be important, and ideas that ended up as passing fads. We learn that all of the critical technical practices that form the basis of agile software development had precursors in software engineering's first five years. We discover that project management practices that have been touted throughout the years as the answer to "the software crisis" have by and large had disappointing results. We conclude that we should focus our search for enduring system development practices primarily through a technical frame of reference.

We explore four essential technical concepts that have withstood the test of time, starting with the classic approach to dealing with software's essential complexity: low-dependency architecture. We move on to the holy grail of software development: finding a process in which errors are discovered earlier rather than later. This brings us to the ideas of Edsger Dijkstra and Harlan Mills, who first articulated the constructionist concepts that underlie test-driven development[1] and continuous integration.[2] We look at evolutionary development, which fueled the hidden revolutions of the Internet, personal computing, and open-source software. And we investigate expertise, arguably the most important ingredient of technical excellence. To wrap up the chapter, we explore the role of competency leaders.

---

1. Dijkstra, "Structured Programming," 1969.
2. Mills, "Top Down Programming in Large Systems," 1971.

Facts, Fads, and Fallacies

During the 1840s, more than 1.7 million immigrants arrived in the United States—almost three times as many as had come in the preceding decade. Many headed to farmland in the upper Midwest, traveling mostly on rutted roads to their homesteads. State governments had little money to build and maintain roads; there had been an economic crash in the 1830s. Then in 1844, word spread that someone in Toronto had invented a new technology, a better, cheaper way to build roads. Roads surfaced with wooden planks—widely available in the densely forested upper Midwest—cost a third as much as gravel roads. According to the hype, plank roads would provide a much smoother ride, so loads could be twice as heavy and travel time could be cut in half. Maintenance would be minimal; the planks would last for eight to ten years. Return on investment was projected to be 20% per year. And best of all, plank roads would be good for society. Neighbors could visit each other and families could make it to church even in bad weather.

For the next several years, there was a massive boom in plank road construction. Completion of a road was accompanied by great civic fanfare. Travel was fast and the plank roads quickly became popular. Success stories fueled intense interest across the Midwest. New companies formed, shares were sold to thousands of local investors, and in a few short years, 10,000 miles of plank roads were built. And for a few short years, everyone was pleased with the roads.

But it didn't take long for the planks to rot—perhaps three or four years. Rotted planks tripped horses and toppled carriages. But the tolls had yet to generate enough revenue to pay for repairs, so deteriorating plank roads were neglected and became more and more dangerous. People started evading tolls on degenerated roads, and income plummeted. By 1853 plank road construction had stopped and companies began abandoning their roads in droves. State governments took over the legacy road system and switched to dirt and gravel for repairs.

"Plank Road Fever is a good example of an information cascade,"[3] James Surowiecki wrote in *The Wisdom of Crowds*. "The first plank roads were a huge success. People looking for a solution to the road problem found one ready-made at hand. As more people built plank roads, their legitimacy became more entrenched and the desire to consider alternate solutions shrank. It was

---

3. Surowiecki, *The Wisdom of Crowds*, 2004, Chapter 3. The quote is from p. 52. An information cascade occurs when someone who is considered an expert makes a decision and others copy the decision rather than doing their own analysis. As more people copy the decision, its credibility increases.

years before the fundamental weakness of plank roads—they didn't last long enough—became obvious."

Over the years we have seen our share of plank roads in software development. There's the good idea, the hype, the initial successes, the bandwagon, and, after a few years, the rotting planks. Given this history, we expect there may be some contemporary plank roads; so how do we recognize them? To answer this question, we decided to study software history and look for patterns in the way key issues were framed, so that we could see which frames turned into fads. We didn't have far to go; our bookshelves are overflowing with software books dating back into the 1960s. To get started, we pulled out eight books with *structured* in the title. We don't hear much about structured programming anymore. Could it be that "structure" was an early software plank road?

Structured Programming

Arguably, structured programming had its beginnings at the 1968 NATO Conference on Software Engineering in Garmisch, Germany, where some of the greatest minds in software development came together to discuss "the software crisis." Why was it so difficult to create reliable large software systems? Edsger W. Dijkstra, a professor from Technological University in Eindhoven, the Netherlands, presented a paper titled "Complexity Controlled by Hierarchical Ordering of Function and Variability.[4]" In this paper he proposed that complex systems should be constructed as a sequence of levels of abstraction, or a hierarchy of layers, where each layer acts as a virtual machine for the layer above.

At about the same time as the conference, Dijkstra published "A Constructive Approach to the Problem of Program Correctness,"[5] perhaps his most misunderstood contribution to software development. In 1975, Peter Freeman summarized this concept:[6]

> The second procedural suggestion of Dijkstra is more subtle and seems to have been missed by many of those attempting to follow his suggestions. . . . Dijkstra suggests the following procedure for constructing correct programs: analyze how a proof can be given that a class of computations obeys certain requirements—that is, explicitly state the conditions which must hold if we are to prove that an

---

4. Dijkstra, "Complexity Controlled by Hierarchical Ordering of Function and Variability," 1968, available at http://homepages.cs.ncl.ac.uk/brian.randell/NATO/index.html.
5. Dijkstra, "A Constructive Approach to the Problem of Program Correctness," 1968.
6. See Freeman, *Software Systems Principles: A Survey,* 1975, pp. 489–90.

algorithm performs correctly; then write a program that makes the conditions come true.

Thus structured programming is a way of thinking that leads to constructive programming; it is not an exact process that can be precisely specified . . . to develop a more explicit definition of structured programming may be detrimental; we have no desire to impede the process of discovering structures and techniques to help us program constructively.

Today *hierarchical layers* very similar to those described by Dijkstra lie at the core of many of our systems, from Internet protocols to multitiered architectures. But Freeman was correct; hierarchical layers are not the only way to program constructively. Dijkstra's constructionist approach was a precursor of today's *test-driven development*, in which one starts by describing or writing examples of what the code must do in order to perform correctly (also known as tests), then writes the code that causes each example to behave as expected.

Dijkstra summed up his philosophy this way: "Those who want really reliable software will discover that they must find means of avoiding the majority of bugs to start with, and as a result the programming process will become cheaper. If you want more effective programmers, you will discover that they should not waste their time debugging—they should not introduce bugs to start with."[7] This is the holy grail of software development, and so the goal of structured development was enthusiastically embraced. But techniques for constructing error-free code were often flawed, as we shall see later.

Top Down Programming

Harlan Mills, a fellow at IBM, read Dijkstra's work with keen interest and deep understanding.[8] He experimented with ways to build programs "from the point of view of provability" as Dijkstra suggested. Mills discovered that in order to always know that a program is correct, the statements have to be developed in a particular order; a statement should not depend on future statements for its correctness. This means that programmers should take a recursive approach: Start with a statement that works, add a new statement and make sure that they both work, then add another and be sure all three work, and so on. He generalized this idea: If it held for statements, it should also hold for programs. So, for example, code to open files should be written before code to access the files. In particular, the job control code for a system should be written first and then programs added incrementally, exactly the opposite of practice at the time. Mills tested this idea on a major project for the *New York Times*; he started

---

7. Dijkstra, "The Humble Programmer," 1972.
8. See Mills, *Software Productivity*, 1988, p. 3.

with a working skeleton of a system and added modules one at a time, checking after each addition that the overall system still worked. The results were widely reported—the project had impressive quality and productivity, with almost no defects discovered during integration, acceptance testing, and the first year of operation.[9]

Mills realized that trying to resolve discrepancies discovered during integration was an unsolvable problem, so he recommended that *Top Down Programming*-modules should be integrated into a system as they are written, rather than at the end. His approach might be called "stepwise integration," a precursor of today's *continuous integration*. Mills noted that those who used this technique experienced a dramatic improvement in the integration process. "There was simply no integration crunch at the end of software development."[10]

But to most people at the time, "top down programming" was a catchphrase that lent itself to many interpretations, few related to the stepwise integration that Mills had in mind. He wrote, "I am happy that people are using the term. I will be even happier when they begin using the idea." Mills said he could tell whether or not people were using his idea: "My principal criterion for judging whether top down programming was actually used is [the] absence of any difficulty at integration. The proof of the pudding is in the eating!"[11]

What Happened to Structured Programming?

From 1970 until 1980, everything had to be *structured*. It was as if structured programming and its derivatives were *the* answer to every problem that existed in software development. In 1982 Gerald Weinberg complained that *structured programming* could be used interchangeably with *our latest computer* in statements like this:[12]

> If you are having problems in data processing, you can solve them by installing *our latest computer*. *Our latest computer* is more cost effective and easier to use. Your people will love *our latest computer*, although you won't need so many people once *our latest computer* has been installed. Conversion? No problem! With *our latest computer*, you'll start to realize savings in a few weeks, at most.

And as we have seen, there was a very good reason why structured programming was popular: It was framed by core technical concepts that have withstood the test of time, concepts such as hierarchical layers and stepwise

---

9. Baker, "System Quality Through Structured Programming," 1972, pp. 339–43.
10. Mills, *Software Productivity*, 1988, p. 5.
11. Ibid., p. 4.
12. Weinberg, *Rethinking Systems Analysis and Design*, 1982, p. 21. Italics in the original.

integration. Constructive programming followed a more torturous path. Various methods for constructing proofs of correctness were devised, including Hoare logic and Bertrand Meyer's Design by Contract. But these proved to be too difficult to be widely adopted. It wasn't until xUnit frameworks became available in the late 1990s that a practical approach to constructive programming evolved.

The theories of Dijkstra and Mills—build code *from the point of view of provability* and avoid big-bang integration—were difficult to apply in practice, especially with the computers and tools that were available at the time. Without a good implementation of these core technical fundamentals, structured programming lost some of its potential, and it never quite lived up to the hype that made it so popular in the first place.

Object-Oriented Programming

While Dijkstra and Mills framed the software problem as establishing confidence that code is correct, David Parnas created a new frame to address the emerging and potentially bigger problem: software maintenance. As we see in Figure 2-1, maintenance costs were half of all computer costs by 1970 and growing rapidly.

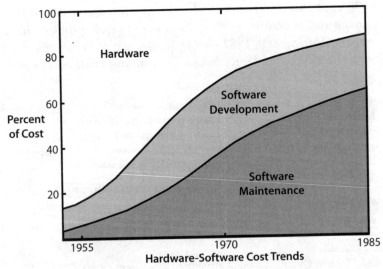

Figure 2-1   *The growing impact of maintenance (From Boehm, "Software Engineering," 1976, pp. 1226–41. Used with permission.)*

Both Dijkstra and Parnas understood that the basic problems with software were its complexity and the inability of a human mind to understand in detail the complexities of a large system. But while Dijkstra counted on a hierarchy of abstractions to organize the complexity into understandable layers, Parnas realized that this was not the only solution to the complexity problem. He agreed with Dijkstra's "divide and conquer" mantra, but he proposed a new criterion for decomposing systems into modules that would render the software easier to maintain. He called this principle *information hiding*.[13]

Parnas noted that the most common criterion used for system decomposition was the flow of the program, but this approach resulted in modules with complex interfaces. Worse, typical changes in things such as input format or storage location would require a change in every module. He proposed that instead, the criteria for decomposition should be such that each module has knowledge of (and responsibility for) a single design decision that it hides from all other modules. In addition, interfaces should be chosen to reveal as little as possible about the inner workings of the module. Later writers rephrased these criteria: Modules should have high cohesiveness within themselves and loose coupling between each other.

In the 1960s, Ole-Johan Dahl and Kristen Nygaard developed the programming language Simula at the Norwegian Computer Center in Oslo. Simula, the first object-oriented language, was specifically designed for doing simulations. It introduced many now-familiar concepts such as objects, classes, subclasses, inheritance, and dynamic object creation. In 1972, Dahl, Dijkstra, and Hoare published a book called *Structured Programming*.[14] At the time, structured programming was considered to include the concepts of object orientation, but over time the term *structured* became limited to hierarchical structures, and object-orientated programming was left out of most writing on structured development.

Smalltalk, created at Xerox PARC and modeled on Simula, was a popular general-purpose object-oriented programming language in the 1980s. Despite its enthusiastic following, Smalltalk was not widely supported and was supplanted, first by C++ and then by Java in the late 1990s.

In 1994, more than 20 years after his first article on information hiding, Parnas wrote, "The first step in controlling software aging is applying the old slogan, 'design for change.' Since the early 70's we have known how to design software for change. The principle to be applied is known by various names,

---

13. Parnas, "On the Criteria to Be Used in Decomposing Systems into Modules," 1972.
14. Dahl, Dijkstra, and Hoare, *Structured Programming: A.P.I.C. Studies in Data Processing No. 8*, 1972.

e.g. 'information hiding,' 'abstraction,' 'separation of concerns,' 'data hiding,' or most recently, *'object orientation.'*[15]

Over those two decades, IT departments had discovered that the cost of maintenance and integration increasingly dominated all other costs. When they discovered that hierarchical structure did not necessarily produce maintainable code, they turned to object-oriented development. Because the basis for modularization and factoring is the likelihood of future change, in theory at least, object-oriented software is designed from the start in a way that should be easy to maintain.

But many developers found object-oriented thinking difficult, and it took time to learn to produce well-factored object-oriented code. Moreover, good patterns for programming with objects had to be developed, disseminated, and used effectively. Thus while *in theory* object-oriented development produces code that is easy to change, in practice, object-oriented systems can be as difficult to change as any other, especially when information hiding is not deeply understood and effectively used.

High-Level Languages

It's interesting to contemplate that in 1970, most systems were written in assembly language, aided by macros for common control structures. It's not that high-level languages didn't exist. In the mid-1950s, Grace Hooper developed FLOW-MATIC, a precursor of COBOL, and John Backus led the development of FORTRAN. However, at that time computers were highly constrained in memory, storage, and processing power, so assembly language was considered necessary to optimize hardware usage. In fact, on Barry Boehm's first day as a programmer in 1955, his supervisor said to him: "Now listen. We're paying this computer six hundred dollars an hour, and we're paying you two dollars an hour, and I want you to act accordingly."[16] With that kind of economics, assembly language made a lot of sense.

But as computers grew bigger, faster, and cheaper, the cost of software first equaled and then began to rapidly outstrip the cost of the hardware (see Figure 2-1). The objective shifted from optimizing hardware to optimizing people, and high-level languages came into widespread use. Most people expected that this would lead to productivity and quality improvements in software even as they enabled people with less technical experience to program computers. And at first, that's more or less what happened.

---

15. Parnas, "Software Aging," 1994. Italics added.
16. Boehm, "An Early Application Generator and Other Recollections," 1997.

Dijkstra summarized the impact of high-level languages thus: "COBOL was designed with the avowed intention that it should make programming by professional programmers superfluous by allowing the 'user' . . . to write down what he wanted in 'plain English' that everyone could read and understand. We all know that that splendid dream did not come true. . . . COBOL, instead of doing away with professional programmers, became the major programming vehicle for ever growing numbers of them."[17] He explained that high-level languages removed drudgery from programming, which made the job more complex and required higher-caliber people who "still produced, as willingly as before, large chunks of un-understandable code, the only difference being that now they did it on a more grandiose scale, and high-level bugs had replaced low-level ones."

Later, even higher-level languages such as SQL, MAPPER, and PowerBuilder came into fashion, and you only have to replace *COBOL* in Dijkstra's statement with these names to figure out how they fared. Like plank roads, most high-level languages produced immediate, impressive improvements at a low cost. But it didn't take long for the shine to wear off. While it was relatively easy to create initial applications, there was often little appreciation of how to design maintainable applications. In a short time—much shorter than anticipated—the initial software started to age, and maintenance was much more expensive than anticipated. Unlike plank roads, high-level languages provided lasting benefits, but the longest-term benefits came only when solid technical approaches to managing complexity were used at the same time.

The Life Cycle Concept

At the beginning of the 1970s, programming and software development were thought of as one and the same thing. But by the end of the decade, programming had become just one step in a larger process called the *software life cycle*. This happened at the same time that the cost of computing was undergoing a seismic shift, as we saw in the graph in Figure 2-1. With the relative cost of software to hardware growing rapidly and the cost of software maintenance dominating that growth, the search was on for a way to control these costs.

In the mid-1970s, Michael Fagan of IBM published "Design and Code Inspections to Reduce Errors in Program Development."[18] He reported that over half of the time spent on a program was wasted in non-value-adding layers of testing and claimed that rework in the first half of development is 10 to 100 times less expensive than rework done in the second half. Like Dijkstra and

---

17. Dijkstra, "Two Views of Programming," 1975.
18. See Fagan, "Design and Code Inspections to Reduce Errors in Program Development," 1976. Fagan published several earlier versions of the same paper. This is the final version.

Mills, Fagan felt that the solution was to find and fix errors as early as possible. However, Fagan's approach was different. He framed development as three processes: design, coding, and testing, each process with an input and an output. At the end of each process, he added a formal inspection step to be sure that the output met predefined exit criteria. Fagan's work helped to establish the frame of thinking that casts software development as a series of sequential input-process-output steps, with formal validation at the end of each step.

Barry Boehm extended Fagan's approach by emphasizing four more processes. In his 1976 "Software Engineering" article[19] he drew a classic waterfall picture, as seen in Figure 2-2.[20] Boehm called this series of processes the "software life cycle." He cited Fagan's work and his own studies to show that the biggest opportunity for cost reduction was finding errors as soon as possible, by inserting a formal inspection at the end of each process.

Separation of Design from Implementation

The problem with the life cycle concept is not the idea that it is good to find defects early; it certainly is! The problem is twofold. First, large batches of work tend to queue up during each process step, and so defects are not detected at the point of insertion; they have to wait to be uncovered in a batch validation step. Dijkstra's idea was to code the program in such a way that at every step of program construction, one had confidence in the program's correctness. Dijkstra's approach to thinking about eliminating defects in software development was *exactly the opposite* of the life cycle process: State a condition that must hold if you are to prove that code performs correctly, and then write code that makes the condition come true.

The second problem with the life cycle concept is the separation of design from implementation. Dijkstra said, "Honestly, I cannot see how these activities [design and programming] allow a rigid separation if we are going to do a decent job. ... I am convinced that the quality of the product can never be established afterwards. Whether the correctness of a piece of software can be guaranteed or not depends greatly on the structure of the thing made. This means that the ability to convince users, or yourself, that the product is good, is closely intertwined with the design process itself."[21]

---

19. Boehm, "Software Engineering," 1976.
20. The first "waterfall" diagram was published by Winston Royce (Royce, "Managing the Development of Large Software Systems," 1970) and discussed in Poppendieck, *Lean Software Development: An Agile Toolkit*, 2003, p. 24. The paper by Boehm in 1976 (ibid.) reemphasized the life cycle concept and had a significant impact on its subsequent popularity.
21. Naur and Randell, *Software Engineering: Report on a Conference Sponsored by the NATO Science Committee*, 1968.

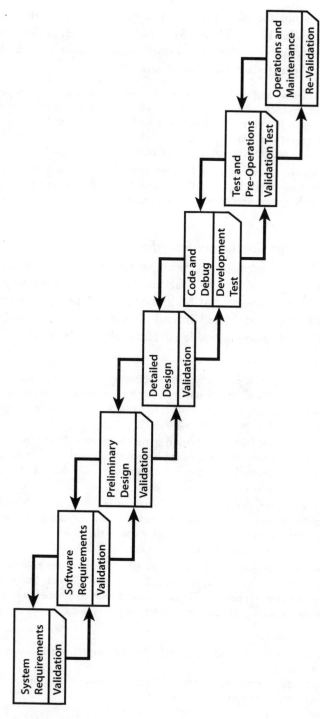

Figure 2-2 Boehm's original version of the software life cycle (From Boehm, "Software Engineering," 1976. Used with permission.)

Dijkstra was not the only one who felt you cannot separate design from implementation. In 1982 William Swartout and Robert Balzer, who once thought sequential development was a good idea, wrote in "On the Inevitable Intertwining of Specification and Implementation":[22]

> For several years we and others have been carefully pointing out how important it is to separate specification from implementation. In this view, one first completely specifies a system in a formal language at a high level of abstraction in an implementation-free manner. Then, as a separate phase, the implementation issues are considered and a program realizing the specification is produced. . . .
>
> All current software methodologies have adopted a common model that separates specification from implementation. Unfortunately, this model is overly naive, and does not match reality. Specification and implementation are, in fact, intimately intertwined.

Life Cycle Concept Considered Harmful

It didn't take long for a serious outcry against the life cycle concept to be heard. It came from no less than Dan McCracken, author of computer language textbooks and former president of ACM, and Michael Jackson, inventor of a system development method framed around objects. In 1982 they published the note "Life Cycle Concept Considered Harmful" in *ACM SIGSOFT*. They said:[23]

> 1. Any form of life cycle is a project management structure imposed on system development. To contend that a life cycle scheme, even with variations, can be applied to all system development is either to fly in the face of reality or to assume a life cycle so rudimentary as to be vacuous.
>
> The elaborate life cycle [similar to Boehm's] may have seemed to be the only possible approach in the past when managing huge projects with inadequate development tools. (That it seemed to be the only choice, obviously did not prevent many such projects from failing.) . . .
>
> 2. The life cycle concept perpetuates our failure so far, as an industry, to build an effective bridge across the communication gap between end-user and systems analyst. In many ways it constrains future thinking to fit the mold created in response to failures of the past. It ignores such factors as . . .
>
> -- An increasing awareness that systems requirements cannot ever be stated fully in advance, not even in principle, because the user doesn't know them in advance—not even in principle. To assert otherwise is to ignore the fact that the development process itself changes the user's perceptions of what is possible,

---

22. Swartout and Balzer, "On the Inevitable Intertwining of Specification and Implementation," 1982.
23. McCracken and Jackson, "Life Cycle Concept Considered Harmful," 1982. Italics added. Used with permission.

increases his or her insights into the applications environment, and indeed often changes that environment itself. We suggest an analogy with the Heisenberg Uncertainty Principle: *any system development activity inevitably changes the environment out of which the need for the system arose.* System development methodology must take into account that the user, and his or her needs and environment, change during the process.

3. The life cycle concept rigidifies thinking, and thus serves as poorly as possible the demand that systems be responsive to change. We all know that systems and their requirements inevitably change over time. In the past, severely limited by inadequate design and implementation tools as we were, there was little choice but to freeze designs much earlier than desirable and deal with changes only reluctantly and in large packets. . . . To impose the [life cycle] concept on emerging methods in which much greater responsiveness to change is possible, seems to us to be sadly shortsighted.

Evolutionary Development

In 1981, Tom Gilb published the article "Evolutionary Development."[24] He noted that there was a tremendous thirst for a theory of how to plan and develop evolutionary systems, but there was very little literature on the subject except that coming from Harlan Mills in IBM's Federal Systems Division. Gilb proposed that instead of developing detailed requirements, one should start with a short summary of the measurable business goals of the system (he called this Design by Objectives)[25] and proceed with incremental deliveries. He pointed out that incremental deliveries are not prototypes, but real software delivering real value to real people.

Meanwhile, While No One Was Paying Attention . . .

As Gilb noted, during the 1980s most of the computing literature was focused on languages and life cycles, while some of the most interesting advancements in software development were taking place almost unnoticed by corporate IT departments—in the world of ARPANET, Internet, and personal computers (see Table 2-1).

During the 1980s useful PC software exploded, fueled by newly available low-cost PCs and a favorable climate for entrepreneurship. Start-up companies found ways to maintain and upgrade software packages on a regular basis to generate more revenue. Since software packages were largely independent of each other, PC owners could pick and choose from a wide array of programs that could live in the same computer, mostly without destroying each other. A

---

24. Gilb, "Evolutionary Development," 1981.
25. Gilb, "Using Design by Objectives Tools (DBO)," 1984.

Table 2-1 *Some Milestones in the Evolution of Internet and PC Software*

Year	Milestone
1977	Apple II
1978	WordStar
1979	VisiCalc
1980	MTP (precursor of SMTP)
1981	IBM PC
1982	Lotus 1-2-3
1983	TCP/IP standardized
1984	POP (Post Office Protocol)
1985	PageMaker
1986	LISTSERV
1987	HyperCard
1988	First Internet virus
1989	http (World Wide Web)
1990	Internet goes commercial
1991	Initial release of Linux

wildly successful domain-specific language—the spreadsheet—was the killer application that brought PCs into many companies.

At the same time, Internet development was being driven by noncommercial forces; for two decades, government and academic bodies had joined forces to develop ARPANET as an academic and military communication platform. Only after commercial use was allowed in 1990 did commercial forces take over, and by then e-mail had been invented and ARPANET's low-dependency architecture had proven to be extremely robust.

"The Internet? That's not software!" we often heard in the late 1990s. Like any disruptive technology, the Internet was widely ignored by mainstream software development for a long time, because it broke prevailing paradigms about software. As Ward Cunningham, inventor of the Wiki, said, "The Internet really favors text. It doesn't want to send objects around, it wants to send text."[26] How could moving around pages of text be software?

Spreadsheets and e-mail were not considered software either, and open-source software was widely ignored for years. But while fourth-generation languages had largely failed in "making programming by professional programmers superfluous," the Internet, personal computing, and, in the 1990s, open-source software succeeded in turning a vast amount of programming over to users.

These are classic examples of disruptive technologies—technologies that do not solve prevailing problems but instead find an unmet need in a low-end niche where the existing technology is too expensive or cumbersome to be considered. After establishing a foothold in the low-end niche, disruptive technologies grow stronger and more powerful and eventually become capable of doing the job of the established technology, but at a lower cost, size, power consumption, complexity, or something like that. It is the nature of disruptive technologies to evolve over time; thus the Internet, PC software, and open-source software are all case studies in successful evolutionary development.

Why Did It Work?

What made it possible for PCs, the Internet, and open-source software to create an explosion of successful software almost under the radar of the mainstream software development?

Internet

1. *Technical vision:* Perhaps no one was more visionary than J. C. R. Licklider, who saw the computer as a way for people to communicate more effectively. He conceived of, found funding for, and managed the early development of ARPANET. And there were many other visionaries who worked alongside Licklider or followed in his footsteps.

2. *Robustness:* ARPANET's design goal was to provide reliable communication between computers of different types, even if any part of the network failed. The novel solution to this problem was to launch a packet of data from one computer and let it find its own way to another computer based on the packet address, without any administration or control.

3. *Emergent standards:* E-mail originated as a communication mechanism between administrators of various computers on ARPANET. As new

---

26. Cunningham, "Wiki Inventor Ward Cunningham with John Gage," 2006. You can find this informative video at www.youtube.com/watch?v=bx6nNqSASGo. The quote is located in the video at 1:02–1:05.

administrators with different types of computers joined the network, the mail protocol was modified to accommodate the newcomers. Over the years, the essential elements of e-mail headers emerged.

PCs

1. *Minimized dependencies:* Early PC software consisted of focused applications that had no dependencies on other applications, so programs had to coexist without doing harm to each other. The expectation rapidly developed that one should be able to add a new program to a PC without experiencing any unintended consequences.

2. *Staged deployment:* PCs were comparatively inexpensive, and the first vendors of PC programs were entrepreneurs with limited funds; therefore, early programs were rudimentary and aimed at generating revenue and getting feedback from the market. If software packages were successful, a new release followed in perhaps a year. Over time the expectation developed that useful software would have regular new releases.

3. *Experimentation:* The early PC software market was a vast experiment; for example, Intuit's popular Quicken software was the forty-seventh financial package to be released for PCs when it came to market in 1984. A decade later, the Internet experienced the same high level of commercial experimentation. James Surowiecki explains that all emerging markets act this way; he wrote, "No system seems to be all that good at picking winners in advance. . . . What makes the system successful is its ability to generate lots of losers and then to recognize them as such and kill them off."[27]

Open Source

1. *Personal investment:* People who write open-source software write it to solve a problem they are experiencing, as well as to contribute to the community. Developers understand their problem well and are personally invested in the integrity of their solution because they will use it. In addition, their work will be open for public scrutiny.

2. *Common purpose:* Open-source contributors care about their work because they are mutually committed to achieving a common purpose. They collaborate constantly, on a global basis, through simple text messaging tools, simple rules, and the code base itself.

---

27. Surowiecki, *The Wisdom of Crowds*, 2004, p. 29.

Today, each of these eight factors remains core to the creation of valuable software-intensive systems.

Distraction

By the mid-1990s PC software had grown up, the Internet was bursting with possibilities, and open-source software was beginning to be useful. But back in the corporate IT departments of the world, a serious threat started draining off vast amounts of attention and money; it was called Y2K. There was great fear that all of the software upon which the world had come to depend would fall apart as the date changed from 1999 to 2000. So instead of looking into emerging technologies, IT departments, especially in large companies, focused intense efforts on checking out the plumbing of existing applications, or replacing key software before the turn of the century. By the time Y2K was past and those same IT departments had time to come up for air, the world of software development had forever changed.

Y2K

I wrote a lot of code in the 1970s and '80s, most of it on minicomputers that controlled hardware. In those days, minicomputers did not have a reliable way of determining the date; when a minicomputer was powered up, you had to type in the date for the real-time clock, because it was not retained when power was off. Therefore, no programmer in her right mind would put a date dependency in the code; we used the clock only to establish relative, not absolute, time. So I was pretty sure that most of those old minicomputers would make it unscathed across the magic date line. I was a lot less worried than most.

Mary Poppendieck

The Future of Agile

As we look at the history of software development, we see a consistent goal: Avoid the high cost of discovering defects late in the development process by discovering them as early in the development process as possible. However, we see a big difference of opinion on how to go about achieving this goal. On the one hand we have people like Dijkstra and Mills, who framed establishing correctness as an ongoing activity of system development. On the other hand, we have the life cycle concept, which framed establishing correctness as a project management activity. We recall what Daniel McCracken and Michael Jackson said in 1982: "Any form of life cycle is a project management structure imposed on system development." Historically, we have seen that these two were often confused (see Table 2-2).

Table 2-2 *A Lesson from History*

Let Us Not Confuse	
System Development	**Project Management**
Success = accomplishing the system's overall objective	Success = achieving planned cost, schedule, and scope
Learning/feedback cycles	Phases with exit criteria
Quality by construction	Quality by inspection
Encapsulate complexity	Manage scope
Skilled technical leaders	Resource management
Technical disciplines	Maturity levels
Historically Robust	**Historically Fragile**

The history of software system development gives us technical concepts such as hierarchical layers, early integration (the precursor of continuous integration), information hiding (the precursor of object-oriented programming), and even constructive programming (the precursor of test-driven development) that are considered essential today. We see that simple, low-dependency architectures and skilled technical implementation are the never-changing ingredients of successful software development. We discover that solid technical leadership and incremental deliveries that provide feedback are essential. These technically focused practices for developing good software have never become less critical—although they may have occasionally been forgotten. When they are rediscovered, they prove just as effective as ever, and sometimes even more so with modern tools. The technical concepts have been robust over time.

On the other hand, when we look at the history of project management in software development, we find practices that have proven to be fragile over time. Ensuring that requirements are correct before proceeding ends up creating big batches of untested code. Phased systems that separate design from implementation don't work because they do not allow for feedback. When system development time is longer than the likelihood of change in the environment, or the system itself will change that environment, phased systems don't work. Waiting for testing at the end of phases violates the mandate that quality be built into the software in the first place. Maturity levels have not necessarily proven to be an indication of technical capability.

So where does agile software development fit into this picture? We suspect that the aspects of agile software development that reside in the project management frame are likely to change over time and are therefore a matter of choice. On the other hand, agile development has extended many practices from the system development frame. These technical practices have withstood the test of time and they will continue to be highly effective long into the future. So if you are using agile software development—or even if you are not—start with the system development frame. It is fundamental; it is not a fad.

Frame 5: Essential Complexity

The complexity of software is an essential property, not an accidental one. . . . The classic problems of developing software products derive from this essential complexity and its nonlinear increase with size.

—Fred Brooks[28]

The history of software development is a history of attempts to conquer its complexity. But in his landmark paper "No Silver Bullet," Fred Brooks claimed that no silver bullet will ever exist that can put an end to "the software crisis," because software is inherently complex. He wrote:[29]

Einstein repeatedly argued that there must be simplified explanations of nature, because God is not capricious or arbitrary. No such faith comforts the software engineer. Much of the complexity he must master is arbitrary and complex, forced without rhyme or reason by the many human institutions and systems to which his interfaces must conform. These differ from interface to interface, and from time to time, not because of necessity but only because they were designed by different people, rather than by God.

Divide and Conquer

There wasn't much argument, historically, about how to deal with software's inherent complexity; everyone agreed that the answer was to divide and conquer. The real question was "Along what lines should we divide software so as to conquer its complexity?"

---

28. Brooks, "No Silver Bullet: Essence and Accidents of Software Engineering," 1986.
29. Ibid.

Edsger Dijkstra believed that the best way to control complexity was by creating hierarchical ordering, creating layers that treated the next-lower layer as a virtual machine. We might call this *Divide by Structure*. Dave Parnas suggested that such a division might work to begin with but was not the right division criterion for maintaining software, so he advocated *Divide by Responsibility*. In the end, division by responsibility has proven to be the most valuable technique for designing maintainable code, although there certainly are many cases where layered architectures are used as the essential simplifying technique.

Barry Boehm recommended that we *Divide by Process*, with verification steps after each process. However, this approach has not effectively dealt with the internal complexity of software. Tom Gilb recommended that we *Divide by Value* instead, an approach that has withstood the test of time.

The strategy of *divide and conquer* is fundamental, but in practice, determining the best axes of division is not so simple. It is essential to devise an architecture that will effectively deal with the complexity *in the context of the domain*, and not all domains are alike. Thus the starting point for conquering complexity over the long term is an architecture that appropriately fits the domain. Consider, for example, the architecture of the Internet.

The Internet Architecture Emerges

On January 1, 1983, the 12-year-old ARPANET architecture was declared obsolete; any of the 200 sites that wanted to stay on the network had to switch to the new TCP/IP protocol. The initial ARPANET architecture depended on interface message processors (IMPs)—by then aging computers—and a network control protocol (NCP) that was being strained to its limits. To overcome limitations of the original protocol, TCP/IP was aimed at creating a network of networks—thus the name "Internet." The new protocol had four main design goals:[30]

- *Network connectivity:* Each distinct network had to stand on its own, and no internal changes could be required of any such network before being connected to the Internet.

- *Error recovery:* Communications would be on a best-effort basis. If a packet didn't make it to the final destination, it would quickly be retransmitted from the source.

- *Black box design:* Black boxes (later called gateways and routers) would be used to connect the networks. No information would be retained by the

---

30. Leiner et al., "The Past and Future History of the Internet," 1997.

gateways about individual flows of packets passing through them, keeping them simple and avoiding complicated adaptation and recovery from various failure modes.

- *Distribution:* There would be no global control at the operations level.

These design goals were brilliant in their breadth and simplicity; fundamentally, the underlying architecture of the Internet is expressed in these four design goals. At first the designers—Robert Kahn and Vinton Cerf—thought of TCP/IP as a prototype that would eventually be reengineered. But once it was developed and deployed, "it just continued to spread without stopping."[31] And the rest, as they say, is history.

Low-Dependency Architecture

As the software industry has grown, it has become apparent that the vast majority of the money spent on software is for maintenance—that is, making changes to existing systems. The logical conclusion to draw from this is that good software architecture[32] must support change over time. This means, as Dave Parnas first observed in 1972, that a good architecture has a partitioning scheme that puts things that are likely to change together into the same subsystem (high cohesiveness) and insulates subsystems from changes in other subsystems (loose coupling). Over time it has become abundantly clear that change is easiest and least expensive when these rules are followed; a good architecture is necessarily low-dependency.

There is no substitute for low-dependency architecture; no amount of planning or foresight can take its place. Minimizing (or breaking) dependencies should be a top technical priority, especially in organizations that wish to use agile software development. We have often found companies trying to employ agile practices to maintain a monolithic code base with massive interdependencies, but we have rarely seen this work well. Why? In agile development, change is encouraged rather than avoided. But with a tightly coupled architecture, change is both risky and expensive. Thus, attempting agile development in a

---

31. Stewart, *The Living Internet,* www.livinginternet.com/i/ii_cerf.htm, n.d.
32. "'Architecture' is a term that lots of people try to define, with little agreement. There are two common elements: One is the highest-level breakdown of a system into its parts; the other, decisions that are hard to change." Fowler, *Patterns of Enterprise Application Architecture,* 2003, p. 1. "Architecture represents the significant design decisions that shape a system, where significant is measured by cost of change." Grady Booch, www.handbookofsoftwarearchitecture.com/index.jsp?page=Blog&part =2006.

large system with a tightly coupled architecture creates a dissonance that cannot be easily reconciled.

The classic rationale for a tightly coupled architecture has been efficiency: Fewer interfaces should mean fewer instructions to execute and less jumping around in the code. David Parnas noted in his 1972 paper that information hiding would demand a lot more processing power as the program flow transferred frequently between modules.[33] But when you compare the skyrocketing cost of maintenance with the relentless increase in processing power and its decrease in price, the rationale for tightly coupled architectures makes little sense. These days there is rarely an excuse to sacrifice ease of change for execution speed, with the exception of some embedded or network-intensive software.

If you are struggling with a tightly coupled architecture, take a leaf out of the Internet playbook and work to pay off this technical debt.[34] However, do not spend large amounts of time defining a new architecture in great detail; after all, the underlying architecture of the Internet can be expressed in four well thought-out rules. If you spend a lot of time developing an architectural framework, the world will pass you by long before it's implemented. Settle on a solid, low-dependency technical vision and evolve in that direction.

If You Need to Reach Agreement—You're Lost

Amazon.com[35] is all about growth. Back in the late 1990s, when the company was getting started, it didn't worry much about scale. So Amazon's systems grew into a massive front end and a massive back end—an architecture that was considered best practice at the time. But every holiday season, things nearly fell off a cliff. Around the year 2000, the company realized that its current architecture would severely limit growth. Something different would have to be done.

So Amazon changed its *architecture*. There is no such thing, really, as a database anymore; there are only services that encapsulate both data and business logic. There is no direct database access from outside a service, and

---

33. Parnas, "On the Criteria to Be Used in Decomposing Systems into Modules," 1972.
34. The classic reference on design is Evans, *Domain-Driven Design: Tackling Complexity in the Heart of Software*, 2003. The classic reference for dealing with legacy code is Feathers, *Working Effectively with Legacy Code*, 2004.
35. Information in this sidebar is from these sources: Vogels, "A Conversation with Werner Vogels," 2006; Roseman, "Working Backwards & 2-Pizza Teams," 2006; Vogels, "The Amazon.com Technology Platform: Building Blocks for Innovation," 2007; Vogels, "Availability & Consistency," 2007; Vogels, Keynote, 2008.

there's no data sharing among the services. There are hundreds of services, and many application servers that aggregate data from services.

In order for this to work (=scale), services had to be decomposed into small, autonomous building blocks. Much like the Internet, there is no central control to fail, and services run locally. They make decisions based solely on local information so they can keep on running no matter what is going on in the overall system. The reason for this distributed architecture is simple: CTO Werner Vogels says that "if you need to do something under high load with failures occurring and you need to reach agreement—you're lost."

And guess what. Because the architecture is distributed, the organization can also be distributed. Amazon found that each service could have its own autonomous team that does it all—customer interaction, decisions on what to develop, choice of tools, programming, testing, deployment, operations, support. *Everything*. There are no handovers. Services interact with other services through well-documented interfaces and agreed-upon demand levels.

CEO Jeff Bezos feels that team size should be limited to the number of people who can be fed with two pizzas—maybe eight or ten people. Amazon.com has many, many two-pizza teams, each completely owning a service, cradle to grave. If an architectural feature is too big for a two-pizza team, Amazon's bias is to break the feature into smaller pieces, because the effectiveness of the team is as important as architectural consistency. Teams stay together over time—a two-year minimum commitment is expected of members—and own long-term responsibility for everything about their services.

It took several years for Amazon.com to evolve to the new architecture and learn how to make it work. Dependencies still exist, of course, and the company has developed some well-honed dependency management tools. Configuration management is a challenge, as is testing. But these challenges are creating opportunities for novel solutions. All things considered, the low-dependency architecture—both technical and organizational—works amazingly well.

Mary Poppendieck

Conway's Law

"Organizations which design systems are constrained to produce designs which are copies of the communication structures of these organizations," Mel Conway wrote in 1968.[36] He went on to say that the architecture that first occurs to designers is almost never the best possible design, so companies should be prepared to change both their product architecture and their organizational structure.

---

36. Conway, "How Do Committees Invent?," 1968.

One of the reasons why high-dependency architectures seem so intractable is that they usually reflect the organization's structure, and changing the organizational structure is often not considered an option. But it should be. We regularly find companies struggling to implement agile practices with functional teams, that is, teams organized along technology lines. For example, there might be a database team, a mainframe team, a Web server team, even a testing team. Invariably these technology (or functional) teams find that they are dependent on the work of several other teams, so delivering even a small feature set requires a large amount of communication and coordination. The complexity of the communication adds time and increases the likelihood of error, and the added overhead cost makes small incremental releases impractical.[37]

"Our Architecture Is Too Complicated for Cross-Functional Teams"

"I am a product owner of a Scrum team," she said. "We have a couple dozen teams, and each one has its own product owner. Each sprint I decide what my team should do, but invariably, I need some work done by three or four other Scrum teams in order to complete my stories. I go to those product owners, but they have their own commitments and they don't have time to help me out. I have to put my request into their backlog, and it can take three or four sprints for them to get around to it. I have to do this for three or four different teams, so basically, I can't get anything done in a sprint. In fact, getting anything useful done at all can take months."

"It sounds like your teams are organized along technology layers," I responded.

"That's true," she said. "Each team owns a part of a technology layer. So if I need some little thing from another layer—which always happens—I have to get another team to do it. And the way we're structured, other teams don't have any incentive to help me out."

"Have you considered cross-functional teams? Could you conceive of a team with all the skills necessary to implement a complete feature?" I asked.

"Oh, no, that's impossible." It was her boss who answered my question. "Our architecture is much too complicated for cross-functional teams. And many parts of our code are understood by only a couple people. We simply couldn't spread those people across all of the teams."

"Could you have those experts provide consulting to help people on the teams who could change their code under their watchful eye? That way you

---

37. See Larman and Vodde, *Scaling Lean and Agile Development*, 2009, Chapter 3, Feature Teams, for an in-depth discussion of this topic.

would spread their knowledge around and speed things up at the same time," I suggested.

"No, that's impossible. Our system grew up over time and now it's a complex web of interlocking applications," he said. And so was his organization's structure, apparently.

Implementing Scrum in this organization was not helping much. The managers had been hoping Scrum would be an easy way to speed up development, but they had ignored the underlying need to rationalize their complex technical and organizational architecture. I suspected that until they addressed the high-dependency architecture, they would not be able to form feature teams that could rapidly and independently deliver customer-focused features.

Mary Poppendieck

It is difficult for agile development to flourish in a highly interdependent environment, because teams cannot independently make and meet commitments. Agile development works best with cross-functional teams in which a single team or small group of teams has the skill and authority necessary to deliver useful feature sets to customers independent of other teams. This means that whenever possible, teams should be formed along the lines of features or services. Of course, this is most useful if those features or services are relatively small and have clean interfaces. Conway's Law is difficult to escape.

Another big mistake we see in organizational structures is the separation of software development from the larger system supported by the software. For example, when hardware and software are involved, we often find separate hardware and software (and sometimes firmware) teams. This is similar to forming teams along technology layer lines. Conway's Law says that it might be better to organize teams (or groups of teams) that are responsible for both the hardware *and* the software of a subsystem of the product.

Consider, for example, a digital camera with a picture-capture subsystem to set exposure, capture, and process pictures; a storage subsystem to store and retrieve pictures to a memory card; an electronic interface subsystem to transfer pictures to a computer; and possibly a smart lens subsystem. Each subsystem is software-intensive, but the camera should not be divided into a hardware subsystem and a software subsystem. Why? Suppose there were a change to the camera's focusing system. With subsystem teams, only the picture-capture team would be involved in the change. With hardware and software teams, both teams would be involved and the change would not be obviously limited to a few people. When changes can be limited to a smaller subsystem, the cost and risk of change are significantly reduced.

Similarly, when business processes are being changed, it is often best to place software developers on the business process redesign team, rather than have separate software development teams. This is not to imply that the software developers would no longer have a technical home with technical colleagues and management. As we will see later, maintaining technical competencies and good technical leadership is essential. The organizational challenge is to provide people with a technical base even as they work on cross-functional teams. We will take up this challenge again at the end of the chapter.

Frame 6: Quality by Construction

If you want more effective programmers, you will discover that they should not waste their time debugging—they should not introduce bugs to start with.[38]

—*Edsger W. Dijkstra*

Virtually all software development methodologies share the same objective: Lower the cost of correcting mistakes by discovering them as soon as they are made and correcting them immediately. However, as we demonstrated earlier, various methodologies differ dramatically in the way they frame this goal. The sequential life cycle approach is to create a complete, detailed design so as to find defects by inspection before any coding happens—because fixing design defects before coding is supposedly less expensive than fixing design defects later on. This theory has a fundamental problem: It separates design from implementation. A careful reading of the 1968 NATO conference minutes shows that separating design from implementation was regarded as a bad idea even as the term *software engineering* was coined.[39]

But it gets worse. Sequential development leaves testing until the end of the development process—exactly the wrong time to find defects. There is no question that finding and fixing defects late in the development cycle is very expensive; this is a premise of sequential development in the first place. And yet, sequential approaches have brought about exactly the result they are trying to prevent: They delay testing until long after defects are injected into the code. In fact, people working in sequential processes *expect* to discover defects during final testing; often a third or more of a software release cycle is reserved to find

---

38. Dijkstra, "The Humble Programmer," 1972.
39. Naur and Randell, *Software Engineering: Report on a Conference Sponsored by the NATO Science Committee*, 1968.

and fix defects after coding is theoretically "complete." The irony is that sequential processes are designed to find and fix defects early, but in most cases they end up finding and fixing defects much later than necessary.

Where did we get the idea that finding and fixing defects at the end of the development process is appropriate? Just about every quality approach we know of teaches exactly the opposite. We should know that it is best to avoid defects in the first place, or at least to find defects immediately after they have been inserted into the code. It's the same as losing your keys: If you lost your keys a few seconds ago, look down. If you lost them a few minutes ago, retrace your steps. If you lost them a week ago, change the locks.[40] And yet we wait until the end of the development process to test our code, and by that time we need a lot of locksmiths. Why do we do this?

Part of the reason why we delay testing is because testing has historically been labor-intensive and difficult to perform on an incomplete system. With a lean frame of mind, we can no longer accept this historical mental model; we must change it. In fact, changing the historical mindset regarding testing is probably the most important characteristic we have seen in successful agile development initiatives. You can put all of the agile project management practices you want in place, but if you ignore the disciplines of test-driven development and continuous integration, your chances of success are greatly diminished. These so-called engineering disciplines *are not optional* and should not be left to chance.

Test-Driven Development

So how do you keep from introducing defects into code? Dijkstra was clear on that; you have to construct programs "from the point of view of provability." This means that you start by stating the conditions that must hold if the program is to perform correctly. Then you write the code that makes the conditions come true.[41] In fact, formal methods for constructing correct code have been around a long time, but they have been historically difficult to use and have not found practical widespread application. So what has changed?

xUnit Frameworks

In 1994, Kent Beck published "Simple Smalltalk Testing" in the *Smalltalk Report*.[42] In three pages he outlined a framework for testing Smalltalk code along with suggestions for how to use the testing framework. In 1997, Kent

---

40. Thanks to Tomo Lennox for this analogy.
41. Freeman, *Software Systems Principles: A Survey,* 1975, p. 489.
42. Beck, "Simple Smalltalk Testing," 1994, pp. 16–18.

Beck and Erich Gamma wrote a version of the same testing framework for Java and called it JUnit. Many more xUnit frameworks have been written for other languages, and these have become the first widely used—and practical—tools for constructing correct programs.

How can testing be considered a tool for constructing a correct program? Isn't testing after-the-fact? It is a bit of a misnomer to call the xUnit frameworks testing frameworks, because the recommended approach is to use these frameworks to write design specifications for the code. xUnit "tests" state what the code must do in order to perform correctly; then the code is written that makes these "tests" pass. While specifications written in xUnit frameworks may be less rigorous than formal methods such as Design by Contract, their simplicity and flexibility have led to widespread adoption. A well-considered xUnit test harness, developed and run wisely, makes quality by construction an achievable goal.

xUnit "tests," or their equivalent using some other tool, are the software specification; they specify, from a technical perspective, how the smallest units of code will work, and how these units will interact with each other to form a component. These specifications are written by developers as a tool for designing the software. They are not—*ever*—written in a big batch that is completed before (or after) the code is written. They are written one test at a time, just before the code is written, by the developer writing the code.

There are tools to measure what percentage of a code base is covered by xUnit tests, but 100% code coverage is not the point; good design is the point. You should experiment to find out what level of code coverage generates good design in your environment. On the other hand, 100% of the xUnit tests you have in a harness should *always* pass. If they don't pass, the policy must be: *Stop*. Find and fix the problem, or else back out the code that caused the failure. A unit test harness with tests that always pass means that when there is a failure, the fault was triggered by the last code checked into the system. This eliminates large amounts of time wasted on debugging; Dijkstra's challenge has been met.

Unit tests are not universally applicable. For example, code produced by code generators—perhaps fourth-generation languages or domain-specific languages—is often not amenable to unit testing; you will probably have to use some form of acceptance testing instead. In addition, it is usually not practical to write unit tests for existing code bases, except for code that you are changing.

For new code, or for changes to existing code, xUnit tests or their equivalent should be considered *mandatory*. Why? Because writing tests first, then writing the code to pass the tests, means that the code will be *testable* code. If you want to change the code in the future, you will want testable code so you can make changes with confidence. Of course, this means that the tests have to be maintained over time, just like other code.

Acceptance Tests

In many organizations, a relatively detailed specification of what software is supposed to do from a customer's perspective is written before code is written. This specification should be written by people who truly understand the details of what the system is supposed to do, assisted by the members of the development team who will implement the features. The details of the specification should not be written long before the code; no doubt they will change, and the effort will be wasted. The detailed specification should be written iteratively, in a just-in-time manner.

There are traditionally two uses of a software specification: Developers write code to meet the specification, and testers create various types of tests and write test scripts to assure that the code meets the specification. The problem is, the two groups usually work separately, and worse, the testers don't write the tests until after the code is written. Under this scenario, the developers invariably interpret the details of the specification somewhat differently than the testers, so the code and tests do not match. Well after the code is written, the tests are run and these discrepancies are discovered. This is not a mistake-proofing process; this is a defect-injection process (see Figure 2-3).

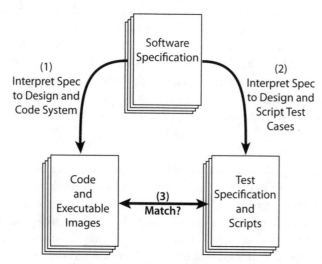

Figure 2-3   *A defect-injection process*

To mistake-proof this process, the order of development needs to be changed. Tests should be created first—before the code is written. Either the tests are derived from the specification, or better yet, the tests *are* the specification. In either case, coding is not done until the tests for that section of code are available, because then developers know what it is they are supposed to code. This is not cheating; it is mistake-proofing the process (see Figure 2-4).

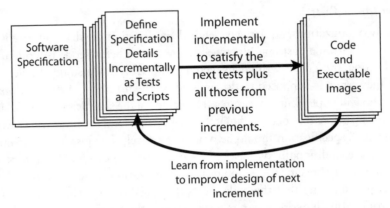

Figure 2-4   *A mistake-proofed process*

The preferred approach to specifying the details of a software product or application is to write acceptance tests. These tests are end-to-end tests that specify what the application is supposed to do from a business perspective, so they are quite different from unit tests. When the specification is written as executable tests, it can be run repeatedly as small parts of the code are written, and defects can thus be detected and fixed the moment they are injected into the system.

Of course, not all specifications can be written as automated tests, and automated tests must be created with insight or they will become a complex burden just as fast as any other software. However, creating an intelligent harness for testing that the code does what it is supposed to do is the best way we know of to produce code that—by definition—meets the specification.

Test Automation

Executable tests (specifications, actually), whether they are acceptance tests or xUnit tests or other tests, are the building blocks of mistake-proofing the software development process. These tests are put into a test harness, and then every time new code is written, the code is added to the system and the test harness is run. If the tests pass, you know not only that the new code works, but also that everything that used to work is still working. If the tests don't pass, it's clear that the last code you added has a problem or at least has exposed a problem, so it's backed out and the problem is immediately addressed.

If this sounds easy, rest assured that it is not. Deciding what to automate, writing good tests, automating them, running them at the right time, and maintaining them is every bit as challenging as writing good code. It requires a good test architecture, sensible choices as to what to include in various test suites, and ongoing updating of tests so that they always match the current code.

Automation scripts need to be developed to support running tests early and often, and the discipline to stop and fix defects the moment they are discovered must be adopted. And although methods to do all of these things exist, they are new and have a serious learning curve. If you are going to spend money for training and tools for agile development (and you should), this is the first place to invest.[43]

The Presentation Layer In most cases automated tests should not be run through the user interface, because this interface usually executes slowly; and it invariably changes very frequently, making the maintenance of such tests almost impossible. Just as it is a good idea to separate the user interaction layer from the layer that performs the business functions, it is also a good idea to test the presentation layer separately from the rest of the code. With a thin presentation layer, the presentation layer tests can be a simple verification that a screen action sends the correct result to the next layer of code. Other tests that are automated can then be run beneath the user interface, rather than through it.

Testing to Failure

The constructionist approach to developing software assures you that the software will do what it is supposed to do. However, you cannot be so sure that the software will not do what it is *not* supposed to do. In fact, you can't even list all of the things that you do not want the software to do—no matter how hard you try, software will always find another way to surprise you. The classic approach to assuring that a system is robust is to push it to failure on all fronts that can be imagined, and then design the system to operate *well inside* the failure envelope.

Exploratory Testing Make sure your organization has some testers with devious minds who love to break systems. When they are successful, everyone should be pleased that they have found a weakness, and a test should be devised so that the failure mode will be detected by normal testing in the future. In addition, the cause of the failure should be examined to see if a better design approach can be used to avoid such a failure in the future, or if there is a boundary condition to steer clear of. Exploratory testing should be done early and often during development because it often uncovers design flaws, and the earlier a design flaw is found, the easier it is to remedy.

---

43. We highly recommend Crispin and Gregory, *Agile Testing: A Practical Guide for Testers and Agile Teams*, 2009, for a lot more detail on test automation and on testing in general.

Usability Testing If a system is behaving exactly the way it was specified, but users can't figure out how to use it effectively, the system is not going to be very useful. High training costs, low productivity, and high user error rates are all signs of poor interaction design. Human-interaction capabilities should be validated through usability testing. This validation is often done initially with simple paper models, then perhaps prototypes, and in the end with the actual system—again, the earlier, the better.

Stress Testing Performance, load, scalability, security, resilience, stability, reliability, compatibility, interoperability, maintainability—these are various aspects of stress testing that should be done as appropriate in your world. Generally you want to push your system over a cliff during this testing so that you know where the cliff is, and then stay away from that cliff in normal operation. Once again: Do these tests as early and as often as possible.

Figure 2-5 summarizes the various types of application testing we have discussed in this section.

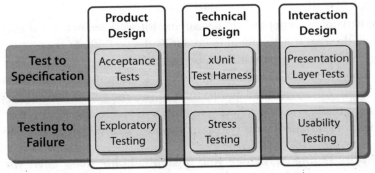

Figure 2-5   *Application testing*

Continuous Integration

Code does not exist in a vacuum; if it did, software development would be easy. Code exists in a social setting, and arguably the biggest problem we have in software development is that code isn't always a good neighbor. Thus integration is often the biggest problem with software, and when it is, leaving integration to the end of development is another example of a defect-injection process. Harlan Mills figured this out in 1970—and he found a solution. First he developed a skeleton of a system, and then he added small programs one at a time and made sure each of them worked before adding the next program. He called this *top down programming*, but somehow the underlying idea got lost in translation and few people really understood what Mills meant by the term.

Today our term for what Mills called top down programming would be *stepwise integration*. And with the test harness frameworks that we have available today, we can go further and integrate more or less continuously. We can use the same criterion for judging its effectiveness as Harlan Mills used: If you have a big-bang integration problem—or even a little-bang integration problem—you are not doing continuous integration very effectively.

Where did we get the idea that we should wait until the end of development to put the pieces of the system together? This is just another example of saving up all of our hidden defects and not trying to find them until the end of development. This violates every known good testing practice in the book. How can we possibly think it makes sense? Why do we do this?

The explanation lies partly in the distorted logic of the sequential frame of reference, but mainly in the sheer difficulty of testing software after every tiny integration step. In the past, testing has been mostly manual and therefore laborious, and moreover, testing partially done code has an annoying tendency to raise false negatives. In addition, as we raise the level of integration to larger system environments, the testing becomes all the more complex, because we have to test across a wider span of programs. And finally, it is impossible, really, to find everything that could go wrong, and testing for even a subset of the possibilities can be a long process, and thus one that cannot be undertaken very frequently.

So it should come as no surprise that continuous integration is not easy, and as integration escalates to higher system levels, it becomes a huge challenge. But consider the benefits: Many companies set aside 30% or more of each release cycle for a series of integration tests and the associated repairs necessary when the tests uncover defects. On the other hand, the best companies budget no more than 10% of a release cycle for final verification, and they do this with increasingly short release cycles. They can do this because the defects have been uncovered earlier in the development process; if they find defects at final verification, they are surprised and work to discover ways to keep those defects from escaping to the final verification step in the future.

Quite often, additional integration testing is required after a product is delivered. This is appropriate, as long as the integration flows smoothly and does not uncover defects. However, if customers have problems integrating the software you deliver, there is work to do to make your product more consumable. Integration problems anywhere in the value chain should challenge you to find and fix the true cause of the problem, so that such problems don't occur in the future.

Enabling continuous integration for complex systems constrains architectural choices. Easily testable, low-dependency choices are much preferred.

How Often Is "Continuous"?

Over the past decade, many tools and techniques have been developed to make early and frequent integration possible at the unit, application, and system levels. But it is not always practical to integrate all of the code all of the time. Furthermore, with a low-dependency architecture, it may not be necessary to run integration tests on truly independent parts of the code. How often you integrate and test depends on what it takes to find defects as soon as they are injected into the code, including defects that will affect other parts of the system once integration occurs. So the proof that you are integrating frequently enough lies in your ability to integrate rapidly at any time, without finding defects. That being said, there are some commonly used integration cadences that you might consider.

Every Few Minutes It is a common practice for agile developers to check their code into a configuration management system very frequently. Before they check in code, they download the most recent build and run a test harness locally. Then they check in their code, which triggers an automatic build and test cycle, which can be expected to pass. On the rare occasions when the build and test fail, the developer who checked in the code backs it out immediately and remedies the problem locally. With this discipline, the cause of defects should be easy to spot, because only a small amount of code is changed before a test harness is run; thus if a problem arises, it's clear that the latest code has introduced the problem. This is about as easy as debugging gets, but it requires the absolute discipline of always maintaining a test harness where 100% of the tests pass.

It is very important for a test harness that is used this often to run quickly, or else developers will delay check-in (it takes too much time), which means that more time elapses before any defects are uncovered—and this creates a vicious circle. Therefore, wise decisions on the structure and content of this test harness are essential, because a fast-running test harness cannot cover the entire application.

Every Day At the end of the day, it's time to run tests that are too lengthy to run continuously. This may mean running an acceptance test harness. Acceptance testing tools differ from xUnit testing tools in several ways. First, the tool must be able to distinguish between tests that should pass and tests that are not expected to pass because the code is not yet done. Second, acceptance tests often require the capability to set up a scenario in the database, or perhaps to run on a real database. Third, these tests will take longer—often they run overnight—and when developers come in the next day, the first order of business should be to *stop* and fix anything that went wrong overnight. If everything was working the day before and something went wrong overnight, only yesterday's code could be the culprit. The failed test may be in some unexpected portion of the code, but the failure was most likely caused by something exposed by yesterday's code.

Acceptance testing is often done with a "clean" database. In practice, the production database is going to be messy, so acceptance tests run on a clean database are inadequate for finding all of the problems. Nevertheless, running an acceptance test harness every day and fixing whatever is wrong (as far as practical) will bring great benefits. But sooner rather than later, the system should be tested on a more reasonable facsimile of the actual production database.

Every Iteration When software is ready for release, there are generally some staging activities that take place. For example, system testing—including such things as end-to-end scenario testing, running the system on a copy of the production database, and running in a user environment—is done to make sure that the code is ready for release. In general, it is a mistake to delay all staging activity until the system is ready for release. It is far better, for example, to run system tests as early as possible and find the problems when they are introduced, not later. On the other hand, system testing a partially done application can be a real problem. The complexity of setting up system tests can be large, they can take a very long time to run, and incomplete features that give false failure indications can waste a lot of time. But it is well worthwhile to try to change this reality and find ways to do valid system tests on partially done applications. Consider improving the architecture of systems that make setting up system testing difficult.

At the end of every iteration[44]—or even sooner—the development team should strive to produce a *system-testable* application. The application may not be done from a user perspective, but features should be complete enough to stage into a system test and successfully pass this test. Of course, this may not be practical unless much of the system testing is automated, especially if the tests are lengthy. Therefore, test automation is important, including test setup, test execution, and defect reporting. Finally, a clear mechanism to determine what features should work and what features are not yet complete must be a part of any system testing done before the application is complete.

Stress testing at the system level is also important. There will no doubt be an assortment of stress tests to run. It is a good idea to start running these at the end of each iteration so that if anything is wrong, you will find it earlier rather

---

44. An iteration might be two to four weeks. When kanban scheduling is being used, as described in Chapter 3, system testing would, at minimum, occur prior to a release. Even if releases are not close together, system testing should still be done more frequently.

than later. This is particularly true because failure of these tests is quite often expensive to rectify later in the development process.

User acceptance tests (UATs) are also good candidates for running early and often—but getting cooperation from users can be problematic. However, if early UATs mean much faster delivery with many fewer defects, the benefits can be significant. Even if users are not willing to allow you into their environment for early UATs, creating a simulated user environment can go a long way toward helping to find the defects that will otherwise be revealed much later in the process.

After Deployment

Despite your best efforts, defects will occasionally escape into production. If you have done all of the testing we just mentioned, this should happen much less frequently than before. But when defects do escape, look upon it as a good opportunity for the development team to discover what it is about its design approach and development process that caused the defects and allowed them to escape. We recommend that developers, or at least representatives of the development team, follow their system to production and work with the people responsible for supporting the system to find the root causes of problems. This will help to give developers insight into how the system is used, as well as help them to improve their designs so that the same kind of problems will not escape in the future.[45] There is wisdom in the approach of Amazon.com (see the sidebar "If You Need to Reach Agreement—You're Lost"), where each service team is responsible for operations as well as development.

Code Clarity

The final ingredient of quality by construction is simplicity. In a nutshell, mistakes hide in complexity, and they are exposed in simple, well-factored code. The time and effort it takes to deliver, maintain, and extend software are directly related to the clarity of the code. Lack of clarity is technical debt that will eventually have to be paid off with interest, debt that can overwhelm your ability to develop new features. Failure to pay off technical debt often results in bankruptcy: The system must be abandoned because it is no longer worth maintaining. It is far better not to go into debt in the first place. Keep it simple, keep it clear, and keep it clean.

---

45. See Zeller, *Why Programs Fail*, 2006; Zeller, "Predicting Bugs from History," 2008; and Nygard, *Release It! Design and Deploy Production-Ready Software*, 2007.

In the book *Clean Code*, Robert Martin interviewed several world-class programming experts and asked them how they recognize clean code.[46]

Bjarne Stroustrup, inventor of C++:

I like my code to be elegant and efficient. The logic should be straightforward and make it hard for bugs to hide, the dependencies minimal to ease maintenance, error handling complete according to an articulated strategy, and performance close to optimal so as not to tempt people to make the code messy with unprincipled optimizations. Clean code does one thing well.

Grady Booch, author of Object-Oriented Analysis and Design with Applications:

Clean code is simple and direct. Clean code reads like well-written prose. Clean code never obscures the designers' intent but rather is full of crisp abstractions and straightforward lines of control.

"Big" Dave Thomas, founder of OTI and godfather of the Eclipse strategy:

Clean code can be read, and enhanced by a developer other than its original author. It has unit and acceptance tests. It has meaningful names. It provides one way rather than many ways for doing one thing. It has minimal dependencies, which are explicitly defined, and provides a clear and minimal API. Code should be literate since, depending on the language, not all necessary information can be expressed clearly in code alone.

Michael Feathers, author of Working Effectively with Legacy Code:

I could list all of the qualities that I notice in clean code, but there is one overarching quality that leads to all of them. Clean code always looks like it was written by someone who cares. There is nothing obvious that you can do to make it better. All of those things were thought about by the code's author, and if you try to imagine improvements, you are led back to where you are, sitting in appreciation of the code someone left for you—code written by someone who cared deeply about the craft.

Ward Cunningham, inventor of Wiki and Fit, co-inventor of Extreme Programming. The force behind Design Patterns. Smalltalk and OO thought leader. The godfather of all those who care about code.

You know you are working with clean code when each routine you read turns out to be pretty much what you expected. You can call it beautiful code when the code also makes it look like the language was made for the problem.

---

46. These quotes are from Martin, *Clean Code: A Handbook of Agile Software Craftsmanship*, 2009, and are used with permission. If you are looking for an in-depth discussion of the best techniques for creating simple, readable code, we highly recommend this book.

The Secret History of Information Hiding

David Parnas was on sabbatical in 1969 and was surprised to discover that the clear, simple designs prized in academic settings were not considered useful in industry. He tells the story of Johan, a database expert, and Jan, who was building a compiler. Over a lunch, Parnas watched with concern as Johan drew the details of the "open file" command on a napkin, so Jan could write code to open a file in the compiler. Dave didn't know exactly what was wrong, but his instincts said that the code base would suffer.

The napkin was copied and used by other members of the compiler team, and various instances of file-opening code found their way into many areas of the compiler. Months later, Johan forgot about the napkin and changed the file structure. Back on the compiler team, no one realized that the details of opening a file had changed, so the compiler stopped working. It took a long time to find out what had gone wrong with the compiler, and even longer to fix it.

Parnas realized that if the file-handling module had been structured to hide its inner workings from outsiders, the problem would never have occurred. This is why he called his approach "information hiding." And he finally understood how to explain that good design was commercially important: Clear, simple design would lead to a system that was much easier to maintain when something changed.

Mary Poppendieck, using Information from Parnas,
The Secret History of Information Hiding, 2002

Refactoring

No one expects the first draft of a book to be perfect, and you should not expect the first draft of code be perfect either. More important, virtually all useful code bases will eventually need to be changed (and this is good, not bad). Code must be kept simple and clear, even as developers understand the problem more clearly and as the problem itself undergoes change. Therefore, code must be continuously refactored to deal with any duplication or ambiguities that were discovered through deeper understanding or introduced by the latest change. An increasing number of tools are available to assist with refactoring, but tools are not usually the issue here. The important thing is that developers must *expect* refactoring to be a normal part of their work. Like continuous testing, continuous refactoring *is not optional*. Choosing not to refactor is choosing not to pay down technical debt that will eventually show up as increased failure demand.

Frame 7: Evolutionary Development

Peter Denning has been around software for a long time. He contributed to the understanding of operating system principles and has held just about every leadership position at ACM.[47] In 2008 he and two colleagues wrote a position paper about why very large system development projects—the kind that are dealt with at the Navy Postgraduate School of Computer Science where the authors work—are so often unsuccessful. They said:[48]

> If development time is shorter than the environment change time, the delivered system is likely to satisfy its customers. If, however, the development time is long compared to the environment change time, the delivered system becomes obsolete, and perhaps unusable, before it is finished. In government and large organizations, the bureaucratic acquisition process for large systems can often take a decade or more, whereas the using environments often change significantly in as little as 18 months (Moore's Law). . . .
>
> The traditional acquisition process tries to avoid risk and control costs by careful preplanning, anticipation, and analysis. For complex systems, this process usually takes a decade or more. Are there any alternatives that would take much less time and still be fit for use? Yes. Evolutionary system development produces large systems within dynamic social networks. The Internet, World Wide Web, and Linux are prominent examples. These successes had no central, preplanning process, only a general notion of the system's architecture, which provided a framework for cooperative innovation. . . . The astonishing success of evolutionary development challenges our common sense about developing large systems. . . .
>
> Evolutionary development is a mature idea that . . . could enable us to build large critical systems successfully. Evolutionary approaches deliver value incrementally. They continually refine earlier successes to deliver more value. The chain of increasing value sustains successful systems through multiple short generations.

Denning and his colleagues talk about two kinds of evolution. First there is the evolution of a system as it goes through a series of releases. This can work, they say, as long as the releases are close together. When releases stretch out beyond the environment change time, this strategy does not work. A second kind of evolution occurs when multiple systems that compete with each other are created and only the fittest survive.[49] To test the multiple-options approach, two projects were launched by the World Wide Consortium for the Grid (W2COG) to develop a secure service-oriented architecture system; one used a standard

---

47. ACM is the Association for Computing Machinery. www.acm.org.
48. Denning, Gunderson, and Hayes-Roth, "Evolutionary System Development," 2008. Reprinted with permission. Many of the ideas in this section come from this letter.
49. This is also called *set-based development*.

procurement and development process, and the other project ran as a limited technology experiment (LTE) using an evolutionary development process.

> Both received the same government-furnished software for an initial baseline. Eighteen months later, the LTE's process delivered a prototype open architecture that addressed 80% of the government requirements, at a cost of $100K, with all embedded software current, and a plan to transition to full COTS software within six months. In contrast, after 18 months, the standard process delivered only a concept document that did not provide a functional architecture, had no working prototype, deployment plan, or timeline, and cost $1.5M.[50]

Evolutionary development is not new. As we have seen, it was named by Tom Gilb in 1981 and has been the primary framework for developing PC, Internet, and open-source software. Evolutionary development is the preferred approach for reducing risk, because it confronts risk rather than avoiding it. Evolutionary development attempts to discover the systems that are best able to handle risk, either by rapidly adapting the current system to handle risks as they present themselves, or by fielding multiple systems and selecting the best alternative.

At the heart of the evolutionary approach is an ongoing series of short cycles of discovery, each cycle delivering one or more "experiments." The experiments are constructed so as to fail fast, that is, to quickly indicate any weaknesses to the development team so team members can improve the system based on this feedback. Each cycle of discovery has three phases: ethnography, collaborative modeling, and quick experimentation (see Figure 2-6).

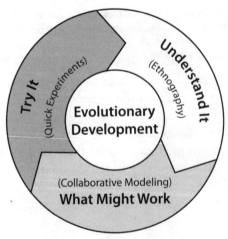

Figure 2-6   *Cycles of discovery*

---

50. Denning, Gunderson, and Hayes-Roth, "Evolutionary System Development," 2008. Reprinted by permission.

Ethnography

Ethnography "brings new learning and insights into the organization by observing human behavior and developing a deep understanding of how people interact physically and emotionally with products, services, and spaces,"[51] writes Tom Kelley, IDEO general manager. He insists that fieldwork is the most important step in design. Various members of the development team—people with different backgrounds and jobs—spend time observing people grappling with the problem that their system is supposed to solve. They look, with a beginner's mind, for things that annoy people, things that get in their way as they try to do the job. They create a bug list of everything that is wrong about the current experience.

Ethnography is not about gathering requirements or holding focus groups. It's not about a product owner or product manager telling the development team what the system should do. It's about several development team members with diverse backgrounds going to the place where the system will be used and talking to the people who will use it. It's about observing firsthand how those people do their job now, what annoyances they have—even the little unspoken ones—and how they cope. Ethnography is about focusing on what works and what doesn't. And it's about constantly asking *why*? Why do people behave the way they do? Why are they annoyed by the way things work? Why are products and services designed the way they are? Why are they difficult (or easy) to use? It pays to observe outliers—people who don't follow the rules and use a product in an unusual way, people who either love or hate a product and aren't afraid to talk about why.

Follow Me Home

It's fair to say that ethnographic research in software development was pioneered by Intuit, the maker of Quicken, QuickBooks, and TurboTax, popular software for managing home finances in the United States. In 1989 Intuit began its "Follow Me Home" program, to help keep the growing company in touch with customers. The book *Inside Intuit* describes how the program worked:[52]

> Members of the marketing and engineering staffs followed willing, first-time customers home from software stores to watch them install and use

---

51. Kelley and Littman, *The Ten Faces of Innovation*, 2005, p. 8. Many ideas in this section are from Chapter 1 , "The Anthropologist."
52. Taylor and Schroeder, *Inside Intuit*, 2003, p. 72. Italics in the original.

Quicken. The Intuit escorts solicited feedback and answered questions. The powerful experience of watching new customers in their own homes taught engineers and marketers the precept *We Are Not Our Customers* and the critical corollary *We Have To Make Quicken Even Easier To Use.*

"I did a 'Follow Me Home,'" a manager said in one of our workshops. "I used to work for Intuit." This was a bit of a surprise since we were a long way from Intuit's headquarters.

"What was it like?" I asked.

"I was a developer at the time. We went to a customer's home and watched how she used our software. Several people came, with different backgrounds, so we saw different things and asked different kinds of questions. It was amazing," he said. "We learned so much about things we had never thought of. It really changed the way I look at software."

Mary Poppendieck

The biggest cause of failure in software-intensive systems is not technical failure; it's building the wrong thing. We know this. Study after study confirms it. And yet we continue to put intermediaries between the development team and its customers. We might call these intermediaries systems analysts or product owners, but all too often they represent a handover of information. Second-hand information about the problem to be solved handicaps the people making the detailed decisions about how the system will behave. A critical role for product managers and product owners is to build bridges between customers and development team members, so they can talk to each other.

Collaborative Modeling

The information gained from ethnography should be digested by a thoughtful team which then works out what to do with it. This is the time for imagination, brainstorming, and storytelling. The team needs to develop a model of what the next step toward improving the customers' experience might be. They might write some use cases and then break them down into stories with tests. They might update the product road map or create a mind map.

Quick prototypes are useful during modeling. Team members might sketch a picture or create a paper prototype that everyone can see, move around, modify, improve. Developers might try development spikes to investigate risky technical problems. Some team members might prototype part of a new business process or run database load projections through a simulator to see how the system might respond.

In the book *The Elegant Solution*,[53] Matthew May says that one of the 12 practices of great innovators is to *think in pictures*. This is very useful in software development, because software is invisible to anyone who doesn't read the code. By making mental models visible with pictures, diagrams, charts, and so on, the development team members can more easily communicate with one another, with customers, and with others who are interested in their work. For example, use paper prototypes instead of computer-generated ones to model a user interface. The only caution is not to invest too heavily in drawing the picture. If a model is too perfect or too laborious to produce, it will discourage change—and the purpose of a model is to encourage discussion and change.

Quick Experimentation

Experimentation goes beyond creating prototypes for modeling; in this phase you actually implement portions of the real system. In other words, experimentation is implementation with the acknowledgment that what is implemented is probably going to change, or that another solution may prove to be superior. TCP/IP was considered an experiment, for example, although it turned out to be so good that we are still using it 30 years later. Even TCP/IP has evolved through several versions over the years.

In software development, there are two general approaches to experimentation. The more common approach is to develop in iterations, implementing the highest-risk and highest-priority software first. With the iterative approach, it is important to think of the software developed in early iterations as an experiment and make that code easy to change as the system grows to include more and more features. Software design should be focused on making change easy in any case, so low-dependency architecture and test harnesses should be part of the iterative process.

However, it is important not to make critical, expensive-to-change design decisions early in the iterative development process; difficult-to-change decisions should be handled with a set-based approach. Set-based design is often used in hardware development, where change is typically more difficult than in software development. With set-based design, decisions are scheduled for the last responsible moment—the point in time when the decision must be made or it will be made by default—and several options are developed at the same time. Typically the options being developed cover as much of the design space as possible, so as to allow experimentation with several significantly different approaches. When the time for the decision arrives, the choice is made based on which is best from a system perspective.

---

53. May, *The Elegant Solution: Toyota's Formula for Mastering Innovation*, 2007.

Both iterative development and set-based development are low-risk approaches that add predictability to the development process, as counterintuitive as that may sound. With iterative development, you develop the high-risk and high-value features first, all the while gaining a lot of knowledge about the capability and capacity of the development team as well as obtaining customer feedback. It is then much easier to predict when the system will be ready or to stop development at any time and still have a very useful system. With set-based development, decision points are scheduled and there is always an option that will work when the decision time arrives, again, reducing risk and protecting the schedule. We recommend that you consider a combination of both approaches to evolutionary development.

Cycles of Discovery

With the experiments done, it's time to repeat the cycle: Try the experiments out in the field to discover how well they really work, then use ethnography, collaborative modeling, and experimentation again. We realize that full deployment of every experiment is not always possible or necessarily desirable, but come as close as you can. We also realize that ethnography is not always possible, especially in contracting situations. We understand that sometimes an intermediary is required instead of having the team connect directly with customers. If your world doesn't allow each phase to be completed the way we describe, come as close as you can to the principles:

1. Work in cross-functional teams.

2. Be sure the team deeply understands the customer's situation.

3. Have the team work together to come up with solutions.

4. Model the solution in some way—text, diagrams, sketches, prototypes, whatever works—to produce a shared direction.

5. Try out solutions quickly in an environment that is as close to the real one as is practical.

6. Think of the solutions as experiments and expect to modify them.

7. Work in small steps, preferably at a regular cadence.

8. Do it again.

The bottom line of evolutionary development is this: You cannot afford to develop systems of a size and timeline that stretch beyond your environment change time. If you are using lengthy planning processes to increase predictability, you can confidently predict this: If the system development time is greater than the environment change time, the system will fail.

Frame 8: Deep Expertise

Is a programmer an author or a translator?
Is code written for a machine or for a person?

Some people frame programming as a job of translation: Take a text-based specification and translate it into a language that a machine can understand. But is this the correct mental model? Two programmers working independently will create very different solutions to the same problem, often with large differences in interpretation. Similarly, two authors will produce widely different interpretations of the same topic, often with large differences in interpretation. However, two translators will produce relatively similar interpretations of the same work. If you think of programming as translating specifications into software, you probably aren't a programmer. Very few people who "write code" think of themselves as translators; they think of themselves as authors of the code they write.

Some people, especially those who have never written code, assume that programmers write code for machines to read. Nothing could be farther from the truth; programmers write code for *people* to read. Programmers write initially for themselves, but more important, they write for the people who must interact with or change their code in the future. Good programmers work hard to clarify their intent as they write; they want their audience, the people who read their code, to know what they intended the code to do.

When you read something written in your native language, you can quickly tell what's being said, but when you look at writing in a language you don't understand, you have no clue what it's all about. Programmers write in a peculiar language, and they write for people who understand that language; those who can't read the language aren't part of the audience. Sometimes we see demands for documentation from people who can't read the code, but we know that anyone who seriously expects to change the code is going to have to read it. We believe that for most purposes, it is much more important for code to speak for itself than for documentation to translate its meaning.

Writing Is Very Much Like Programming

I write books these days, but I was a programmer for many years, and I wrote a lot of code. I find writing a book to be very much like programming; I use the same thought processes and even the same approach to writing.

In order to write software, I had to get inside the heads of the people who would be using the system and imagine how they would use it. I needed a clear idea of what others working on the system were expecting of my code. I wrote the code in small, logical chunks and checked out each bit of code in a simulator as soon as it was written. And after code was written, I spent quite a bit of time revising it to make it work well and cleaning it up so that it was clear and readable. I knew that without readable code, even I wouldn't be able to figure out what the code was supposed to do in a day or two, let alone those who would be changing it in the distant future.

In order to write a book, I need to get inside the heads of the people who might be reading the book and imagine what they would be interested in reading about. I need a clear idea of what others have said about the topics I'm writing about. I know by now that the first draft is only the starting point; the text will go through plenty of reviews and revisions before it becomes a book. I have come to really appreciate how invaluable the insights of reviewers can be. I spend a lot of time refactoring a book to make sure that my intent is clear, to remove duplication, and to be sure that the book flows smoothly.

Mary Poppendieck

Expertise Is Important

"Software construction is a *creative* process,"[54] Fred Brooks wrote. "Great designs come from great designers. . . . Study after study shows that the very best designers produce structures that are faster, smaller, simpler, cleaner, and produced with less effort. The differences between the great and the average approach an order of magnitude."

If writing software were a translation process, you could hire a couple of great designers, have them design a great system, give the design to a team of translators, and expect excellent results. But attempts to do this have a dismal track record. By now we should have learned that in software development, we *cannot separate design from implementation*. Why? Because writing code is a creative process. People who write code are authors, not translators; they make design decisions constantly. "How do I handle a buffer to prevent overflow? What is the best way to group these ten things? How do I spot subtle duplication and remove it? How do I make a remote call that will never hang the system under any circumstances? Oops! That's what caused a customer's system to crash a couple of years ago; better not use it here." And so on. Just about every ten minutes another design decision is made.

---

54. Brooks, "No Silver Bullet: Essence and Accidents of Software Engineering," 1986. Italics in the original.

Expertise is needed at *every level* of a development organization. Sure, you should have a few great designers, but they must share their vision and their expertise with the people implementing the system. Otherwise, their great designs will never be realized and their expertise will not find its way into the software. If you want systems that are "faster, smaller, simpler, cleaner, and produced with less effort"; systems that delight customers; systems that are easy to maintain and extend—then you must have design expertise at the point where design decisions are actually made. Technical excellence comes from a conscious and well-planned effort to develop and sustain expertise at every level of the organization.

Developing Expertise[55]

If you were a passenger on U.S. Airways flight 1549 as it lost power in both engines on take-off from LaGuardia Airport on January 15, 2009, you couldn't have chosen a better pilot. Captain Chesley B. Sullenberger III, age 58, got his pilot's license when he was 14. For seven years he flew F-4 Phantoms for the air force where he was a flight leader and training officer. He started flying commercial aircraft in 1980 and had accumulated 19,000 hours of flight experience by 2009. He worked with federal aviation officials investigating aircraft crashes and devised improved methods for handling emergencies. He even flew gliders; and on that cold January day, he glided his powerless Airbus to a perfect landing in the Hudson River.

The biggest danger in water landings is that the aircraft will flip or break up if water catches the aircraft unevenly, so the landing has to be perfect. In this landing, one engine (below the wing) sheared off, but the wings remained intact and the plane floated while 150 passengers congregated on the wings or huddled in life rafts. Nearby ferries rushed to the rescue, and within minutes everyone was safe. When the pilot was congratulated on his amazing landing, he replied, "That's what we're trained to do."

There is an interesting number in this story: 19,000. People who study expertise have learned that it doesn't matter if we are talking about pilots, musicians, lawyers, golfers, or software designers; the evidence is clear: It takes elite performers a minimum of 10,000 hours of deliberate, focused practice to become experts. That means it takes about ten years just to arrive at the top level. And world-class performers don't stop practicing once they reach the top; they keep

---

55. The information in this section comes from Ericsson et al., *The Cambridge Handbook of Expertise and Expert Performance*, 2006; Colvin, *Talent Is Overrated*, 2008; and Gladwell, *Outliers: The Story of Success*, 2008.

up their deliberate practice, continually putting effort into getting better than others in their field. Elite performers make their own luck. The passengers of flight 1549 were indeed lucky; they were lucky that Captain Sullenberger was in the cockpit, paired with Jeffrey Skiles, a 49-year-old copilot who had 26 years of commercial aviation experience and had been a pilot since he was 15. And then there were the three flight attendants, who among them had a total of 92 years of experience. It was the skill of these experts that brought the plane down and evacuated it safely.

You do not want to trust your software systems to luck. Technical excellence is not a matter of luck; it is a matter of skill, and that skill takes time to develop. If you are developing systems—and if you want excellent systems—focus on growing a cadre of skilled developers. Everyone does not have to be an expert; you should have some experts, some on their way to expertise, and some beginners. You need to be sure they are all continually increasing their expertise, especially in a technology area that changes as rapidly as software.

Deliberate Practice

There is broad consensus among researchers of expert performance that inborn talent does not account for much more than a threshold; you have to have a minimum amount of natural ability to get started in a sport or profession. After that, the people who excel are the ones who work the hardest. They have to put in a good ten years of deliberate practice to become experts. Deliberate practice is not about putting in hours; it's about deliberately working to improve performance. Deliberate practice works like this:

1. Identify a specific skill that needs improvement.

2. Devise—or learn from a teacher—an exercise designed to improve the skill.

3. Practice repeatedly.

4. Obtain immediate feedback on the results of each effort and adjust accordingly.

5. Concentrate on pushing the limits, and expect repeated failures.

6. Practice regularly and intensely, perhaps three hours a day.

Deliberate practice does not mean doing what you are good at; it means challenging yourself, doing what you are not—yet—good at. So it's not necessarily fun. Keeping up this kind of practice day in and day out requires passion on the part of the participant. It also requires encouragement from people who matter (parents and peers, for example) and a teacher who can identify the skills to be improved and knows the latest practice techniques (at least at first).

Unfortunately, our organizations are not set up to develop experts. First of all, work assignments are rarely structured to provide challenges so developers can push the limits of their competence. Instead we tend to assign people things to do that they are already good at. Second, we rarely provide managers with the technical depth to understand the work they manage and provide regular, focused feedback so developers can improve. Nor do we provide an alternate way to generate this kind of feedback, for example, by providing technical mentors or experienced teammates and a thoughtful review process. Finally, we tend to keep developers at arm's length from their customers, rather than allowing them to get immediate feedback and become deeply engaged in the overall success of their efforts.

The Ten-Year Rule

You don't want an inexperienced developer working without guidance on critical software any more than you want an inexperienced captain piloting your airplane. You can hire experienced developers, but if their experience is not in your domain, it's probably not sufficient. Degrees and certifications are indications that the person has met the threshold to become an expert, but developing true expertise still takes years.

The ten-year rule has been found to hold in almost every complex domain investigated; it takes that much deliberate practice to become an elite performer in any field. In half as much time, you get competent but not brilliant performance. Expertise is domain-specific; people who move to a similar domain may have a head start, but they will not immediately be top performers. And ten years of experience doing the same thing does not necessarily indicate expertise; if the experience didn't involve deliberate efforts to improve weaknesses and try new things, it probably doesn't count toward developing expertise.

So it's unlikely that new college graduates are going to be great designers or great programmers, unless they have been writing software for many years before college. In order to become great, those new hires right out of school need time, mentors, and ongoing focused practice. Just writing code is not sufficient. Learning happens through writing code that solves a problem in an effective manner, code with elegant style and clarity, code that is better than the last attempt. In order to make this happen, new developers need teachers or mentors, challenging work assignments, immediate feedback, and, most of all, work they can become engaged in. You need some experts to guide those developing their programming prowess. And you have to have a way for those who are practicing to know when they have done a good job and where they can improve.

Retention

"Right," you say. "Have you ever heard about turnover? How am I going to keep anyone around for ten years?" Turnover comes in two flavors; there is systemic turnover that you probably can't control, and there is turnover that might be reduced if your organization were a more attractive place to work. Let's start with systemic turnover. Military organizations experience very high turnover; most recruits join the military for a couple of years and then move on to other careers. Certain countries—India comes to mind—experience similarly high turnover among new software development recruits. If this is your situation, investigate the way in which top military organizations handle high turnover. First of all, they build the capability to rapidly bring new recruits up to speed through focused training and carefully designed work assignments. Second, they maintain a core of leaders who stay in the organization over many years, and their programs for developing expertise are concentrated on these medium- and long-term members.

With the exception of systemic turnover, we observe that retention is often a matter of a self-fulfilling prophecy: If you don't think retention is important or achievable, it won't be. But if you work to provide a place where people are challenged and helped to reach their full potential, it will be a place where passionate people prefer to work.

Why do people working on open-source projects contribute so much effort for free? In part it is because open-source work provides exactly the kind of deliberate practice that is not available in most companies. Developers take on challenging assignments and submit code that is reviewed by an expert committer, who provides immediate feedback. If the code is committed, more—sometimes harsh—feedback is provided by the open-source community—exactly what a person who passionately wants to become an expert really needs. Open-source developers care deeply about their work, as do expert authors, pilots, and trumpet players. We believe that one of the best ways to retain people who are growing their expertise is to provide them with the opportunity to improve their skills and to become passionate about their work. We will discuss this further in Chapter 5.

Standards

Standards are the baseline of current good practice in an organization that everyone is expected to achieve. They are sort of like learning the scales in music. One of the roles of experts is to make sure that standards are in place. Those who have learned through hard experience the best way of doing things in their environment should make sure that others don't have to reinvent the wheel. But standards are never perfect and need to be constantly challenged and improved. So once someone has mastered a standard practice, a good learning exercise would be for a mentor to help that person challenge aspects of the standard that need improvement and come up with a better way of doing things. We will discuss this at length in Chapter 4.

Code Reviews

Code reviews are a good way of turning programming into deliberate practice. Having code reviewed by an expert (equivalent to a committer) or a colleague (for example, in pair programming) provides immediate feedback on style, clarity, robustness—whatever is important in your domain. This feedback is often accompanied by ideas for improvement. Anyone who views programming as a skill to be constantly improved will appreciate the feedback that comes from reviews that focus on developing expertise. Common code ownership also contributes to the feedback and improvement process, because those who write code knowing that colleagues will read and change it will pay attention to code style and clarity. Junior people can not only see but also work with examples of code written by more experienced colleagues.

The way to develop expertise throughout your organization is to provide the environment that nurtures expertise and helps people reach their full potential:

1. Create time and space for wise experts to act as mentors for those who are learning.

2. Provide many opportunities for deliberate practice with interesting challenges and effective feedback.

3. Make it possible for people to be passionate about their work.

Portrait: Competency Leader

In 2006, Jeff Immelt talked about the five traits he is looking for in leaders at GE: external focus, clear thinking, imagination, inclusiveness, and domain expertise.[56] "Why domain expertise?" he was asked. "The most successful parts of GE are places where leaders have stayed in place a long time. . . . The places where we've churned people . . . are where we've failed." Immelt explained that leaders with domain expertise make the important decisions correctly because they can rely on their deep knowledge of the business. We think the same principle applies to competency leaders: The best decisions and the best guidance come from leaders with solid expertise in the technical fields for which they are responsible.

---

56. Immelt and Stewart, "Growth as a Process," 2006.

What do competency leaders actually do? First and foremost, they are committed to developing excellent technology in their organization. They begin by framing good software development in terms of an enabling architecture, mistake-proofed processes, evolutionary development, and technical expertise. They ensure that a low-dependency architecture is in place. They make sure that test-driven development and continuous integration are used effectively. They provide for cycles of learning with iterative development and set-based design, and they advise when each is appropriate. They set standards, insist on code clarity, and make sure code reviews are focused on enhancing learning.

"Oh, You Mean the Maestro!"

We were on a conference call to a growing company in Brazil. The four-person start-up had grown to 20, and the founders realized they needed a way to provide consistent quality by teaching everyone about good practice in software development. They were creating a position of technical (competency) leader and were trying to find a way to define the role so that team leaders knew what they were responsible for and the technical leader also had clear responsibilities.

I said, "Well, think of music. You have a conductor for every performance, but musicians have their own teacher, who works with them to be good on their particular instrument. The technical leader is like a music teacher, while the product champion is like the conductor."

"Oh, you mean the Maestro!" I could hear the light bulb click on across the Skype conference call. "The champion is like the Maestro. The technical managers are the teachers."

"My brother-in-law is a Maestro," Samuel said. "Observing his work, I noticed that he acts like the one who conducts the orchestra. Moreover, he does the arrangements for all musicians of the orchestra and generally he delivers a score containing the details and the tempo that each musician will play on their instrument. When they decide to play a new song, the maestro will work on the scores in order to define how the orchestra will play that song. Then, each musician will train with the provided score at home separately and when they get together, generally, they start playing the new song smoothly. The interesting thing in this part is that they have never done it together before and still they can play it very harmoniously."

Mary Poppendieck, with a quote from
Samuel Crescêncio, OnCast Technologies

Growing Technical Expertise

Probably the most important role of a competency leader is that of a teacher who guides the purposeful practice necessary to develop expertise. The role of teacher is considered essential in developing musical and athletic expertise, and it is also found in education: Graduate students work under the guidance of a major professor in their field. Teachers provide goals, challenging work, and immediate feedback. They help their students get better by providing opportunities for them to test their developing expertise. Teachers may not be elite performers in their field, but they are aware of the best techniques and training methods and use these to guide their students.

If you want the people in your organization to develop their expertise to its full potential, you have to provide teachers. Not just training, but teachers—teachers who match the work to the person, who find challenging assignments so that each individual can improve, who pay close attention to the work being done and provide feedback. You might call these people mentors or managers, but in this book we will call them *competency leaders*.

Competency leaders are often line managers, but line managers are not always competency leaders. Sometimes we find line managers with 50 or 60 people reporting to them. It's hard to imagine how these managers can play the role of teacher. Who will watch out for the technical development of all these people, care about their career paths, make sure they are developing to their full potential? And who is watching out for the core technologies that constitute the company's competitive advantage?

Critical technologies need leaders. Someone has to train new people in the technology, set and improve standards, make sure the technology is expanded to keep ahead of the competition. Assume that you have the fastest Web response time in your market niche, or a superb capability to develop ultra-secure transactions, or some similar competitive advantage. What's going to keep you ahead of the competition over time? Your current expertise resides in people who need to see where their future lies, and your future expertise lies with new people who need to be recruited and mentored. This is the job of the competency leader. It is a critically important and very challenging job. And unfortunately, it is all too often absent in our organizations.

Your Shot

1. What percentage of your release cycle is spent in "hardening," system testing, user acceptance testing, and similar activities? What is the average age of a defect when it is first discovered? What are you doing to drive these numbers toward zero?

2. Is Conway's Law—organizations that design systems are constrained to produce designs that are copies of the communication structures of these organizations—evident in your organization?

3. Would you consider your basic system architecture low-dependency or tightly coupled? If it is *not* low-dependency, answer the following questions:

   a. How many people have to get involved in delivering a new medium-sized feature?

   b. How many teams have to get involved? How do they communicate with each other?

   c. How rapidly do you implement a new medium-sized feature using a normal process?

   d. Do you have any competitors who routinely implement new features significantly faster?

4. Watch the video "The Yawning Crevasse of Doom" by Martin Fowler and Dan North (www.infoq.com/news/2008/08/Fowler-North-Crevasse-of-Doom). This video discusses the pitfalls of separating developers from customers. How many handovers separate developers from customers in your organization?

5. Review the following list of basic disciplines and give yourself/your team a score of 0 to 5 on each discipline. (0 means you've never heard of it; 5 means you could teach a course on it.) Look at any score of 3 or below and consider how to improve in that discipline.

   a. Coding standards (for code clarity)

   b. Design/code reviews

   c. Configuration/version management

   d. One-click build (private and public)

   e. Continuous integration

   f. Automated unit tests

   g. Automated acceptance tests

   h. *Stop* if the tests don't pass

   i. System testing with each iteration

   j. Stress testing (application- and system-level)

   k. Automated release/install packaging

   l. Escaped defect analysis and feedback

6. Every year SANS Institute publishes the 25 most dangerous programming errors. The following list was published in January 2009 (see www.sans.org/top25errors/#s4). Which of the errors do your developers recognize? Which errors does everyone know how to prevent? Who is making sure that your organization does not make any of these errors? What kind of training or mentoring program exists, and what coding standards are in place to prevent these (and similar) errors?

   CATEGORY: Insecure Interaction Between Components

   1. Improper Input Validation

2. Improper Encoding or Escaping of Output

3. Failure to Preserve SQL Query Structure (aka "SQL Injection")

4. Failure to Preserve Web Page Structure (aka "Cross-site Scripting")

5. Failure to Preserve OS Command Structure (aka "OS Command Injection")

6. Cleartext Transmission of Sensitive Information

7. Cross-Site Request Forgery (CSRF)

8. Race Condition

9. Error Message Information Leak

CATEGORY: Risky Resource Management

10. Failure to Constrain Operations within the Bounds of a Memory Buffer

11. External Control of Critical State Data

12. External Control of File Name or Path

13. Untrusted Search Path

14. Failure to Control Generation of Code (aka "Code Injection")

15. Download of Code Without Integrity Check

16. Improper Resource Shutdown or Release

17. Improper Initialization

18. Incorrect Calculation

CATEGORY: Porous Defenses

19. Improper Access Control (Authorization)

20. Use of a Broken or Risky Cryptographic Algorithm

21. Hard-Coded Password

22. Insecure Permission Assignment for Critical Resource

23. Use of Insufficiently Random Values

24. Execution with Unnecessary Privileges

25. Client-Side Enforcement of Server-Side Security

7. What are the three most important technical competencies in your organization, for example, competencies that create a competitive advantage for your company? Who is responsible for ensuring that each of those competencies is being used well, preserved, and expanded? Who hires and mentors new people in these competencies?

Chapter 3

Reliable Delivery

Snapshot

It's hard to imagine how the Empire State Building—all 85 stories plus a dirigible mooring dock—could have been built in a year. In the spring of 1930, there was nothing but a hole in the ground, and by fall, the building looked pretty much the way it looks today. The mooring dock was added a couple of months later to push the building to record heights, but no one seemed to notice that it was never actually used. The building itself was also a commercial failure for quite a while, because it was built in a bad location. But if you get past those two shortcomings, it's an amazing story.

There are lessons to be learned from the story of meeting an impossible deadline while building the tallest building in the world, lessons that can be applied to system development. First, the owners managed risk by hiring a builder who had a proven track record of building skyscrapers in a year. Second, the builders managed the workflow instead of scheduling tasks. Third, pull scheduling was used to successfully deal with an immovable deadline. Finally, the people who created the vision remained at the helm, leading the effort during the hard and detailed work of actually constructing the building and delivering it on time.

The frame we look through in this chapter is quite different from the typical sequential development frame of reference. It presumes a level of expertise and a management approach that you may not be prepared to support. But for those who are looking for new ideas and can look away from their familiar frame for a while, this chapter is bound to challenge you with some new ideas.

Race to the Sky

In 1930 the Empire State Building captured the record for being the tallest building in the world and held it for over 40 years. At 85 usable stories, this skyscraper is not just tall; it is massive, boasting twice the girth of other sky-scrapers of the period. Over time, other buildings passed the Empire State Building in height and cross section, but none has come close to its most remarkable record: This enormous building was built in a year.

At the end of August in 1929, the Empire State Building was just a gleam in the eyes of a handful of speculators. They had no plans, just a couple of adjacent lots with four huge abandoned buildings, a stack of financial projections, and an absolute deadline: May 1, 1931—20 months away. In New York City at the time, all office leases started on May 1, so missing the deadline was not an option.

Three weeks later the financiers had hired an architectural firm (Shreve, Lamb, and Harmon) and a construction firm (Starrett Brothers and Eken), and on September 22 demolition of the existing buildings started. Throughout the winter as the site was prepared, drawings were drawn, logistics were planned, materials were ordered. On April 7, 1930, the first steel column was bolted in place. By May the building was growing at the rate of 20 stories a month, one story a day. About 15 stories below the top on any given day, metal window columns were already installed, and another 15 stories below, the limestone was in place. "When we were in full swing going up the main tower, things clicked with such precision that once we erected fourteen and a half floors in ten working days—steel, concrete, stone and all. We always thought of it as a parade in which each marcher kept pace and the parade marched out of the top of the building, still in perfect step," said architect Richmond Shreve.[1]

Six months after steel construction started, the frame was topped off at the eighty-fifth floor. A month later the exterior was complete except for the deco-rative mast. Eleven months after construction started, the interior systems were in place: elevators, electricity, plumbing, heating, and ventilating. The Empire State Building was open for business on schedule: May 1, 1931.

How Did They Do It?

This amazing speed seems almost impossible today, but it wasn't so unusual at the time. When they got the job in 1929, the Starrett Brothers and Eken were completing the 66-story Manhattan Company Building (40 Wall Street), which

---

1. Tauranac, *Empire State Building: The Making of a Landmark*, 1995, p. 204.

they built in a year, including demolition of the existing building. Although the Empire State Building was higher and enclosed twice the floor space, at least they had time to demolish the existing buildings before they started on the new one. The Chrysler Building was vying with the Manhattan Company Building to be the tallest building in the world, and it took only 18 months to build. In New York City at the time, you started a building in spring, completed the exterior in the fall, and finished the interior over the winter so it would be ready to rent on May 1.

How did they do it? Fundamentally, they framed the problem differently from the way we would today. Their mental model—which dictated what was important and what was not—would not be recognized in today's commercial world, except perhaps by those who understand lean thinking. Let's take a look at the world through the eyes of the Starrett Brothers, Paul and William (Bill). By 1930, Paul had been building skyscrapers for 40 years, and Bill for 30. During World War I, Bill had worked with the War Industries Board, constructing bases, hospitals, and flying fields with astounding speed. With that kind of background, the builders framed their work exactly orthogonal to the way projects are framed today.[2]

Team Design

The team approach to the design of the Empire State Building was universally praised by its members and has always been cited as one of the most important factors in the speed of its construction. There is no question that the success of the Empire State Building was due largely to the team who designed the building and put it together—and it was a team. Builder Paul Starrett wrote, "I doubt that there was ever a more harmonious combination than that which existed between owners, architects, and builder. We were in constant consultation with both of the others; all the details of the building were gone over in advance and decided upon before incorporation into the plans."[3]

Not only was there genuine respect and trust among all members of the design team, but if the team did not have the answers, they didn't guess; they called in subcontractors—including fabricators, installers, and inspectors—for advice on the design and to nail down agreements among all parties on the spot. For example, the building design was greatly influenced by meetings with mechanical engineers and Otis, the elevator manufacturer. Bassett Jones, principal mechanical engineer, wrote, "The proper simultaneous development of building,

---

2. Most of the ideas in this section come from Willis and Friedman, *Building the Empire State*, 1998.
3. Starrett, *Changing the Skyline: An Autobiography*, 1938, p. 293.

steel and elevator plans avoided the common error of attempting to fit an elevator plant into a previously fixed building arrangement and steel layout."[4]

Because the builders had enormous influence on the design of the building, it was specifically designed to be built quickly. Starrett wrote, "Never before in the history of building had there been, and probably never again will there be an architectural design so magnificently adapted to speed in construction."[5]

Flow

Paul and Bill Starrett were keenly aware of the biggest constraint they were facing. It was not money. It was not labor. The real issue was how to get all of the material necessary to build a massive building onto a small site in the middle of a very busy city. How then would they get it to the place in the building where it was needed, exactly when it was needed? And how would they get 3000 workers to the right location? Finally, how would they get rid of 30,000 loads of material from demolition and excavation?

"Our job was that of repetition—the purchase, transport to the site, and placing of the same materials in the same relationship, over and over. It was . . . like an assembly line—an assembly line of standard parts," Paul Starrett wrote.[6] Since the building couldn't move along the assembly line, the assembly line flowed through the building. Managing the flow of that assembly line was essentially all the builders focused on. They did not think of the world in terms of input-process-output. They did not break down the job into tasks. If they could just get the right materials and the right people in the right place at the right time every day for a year, the building would get built. Even the slightest turbulence in that flow would jeopardize the completion date.

Schedule

There were no computers in 1930, which may have been a good thing. The Starrett Brothers started by disconnecting the workflows as much as possible, to simplify their job and reduce the risk of cascading delays. Then they created a separate schedule for each workflow, concentrating on what they called the "four pacemakers": structural steel, concrete floors, metal window columns, and exterior limestone.

Each of the four pacemakers was designed so that it could be scheduled separately from any other work, although, of course, the structural steel had to be in place first. To see how these pacemakers were scheduled, look at Figure 3-1, which shows the structural steel schedule.

---

4. Jones, "The Empire State Building. VIII. Elevators," 1931.
5. Starrett, *Changing the Skyline: An Autobiography*, 1938.
6. Ibid., p. 296.

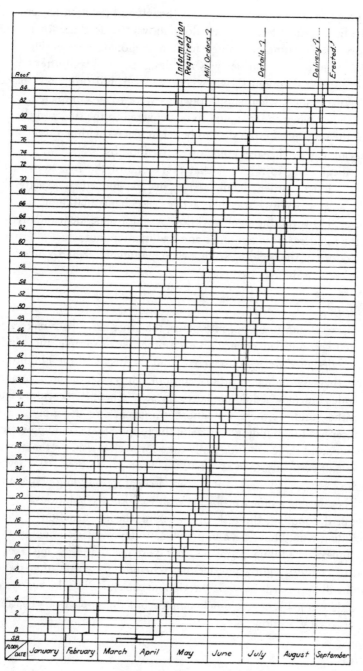

Figure 3-1   *Structural steel schedule for the Empire State Building (From Shreve, "The Economic Design of Office Buildings," 1930, p. 346.)*

This schedule shows the 85 stories on the left and the months across the bottom. The first vertical line for each floor shows the deadline for the design of each story; the accumulated lines form a diagonal representing the design schedule. Note that the top tier was not designed until well after construction started. The next diagonal shows when the steel mill order was placed. The third diagonal shows when shop drawings were to be completed. The fourth diagonal shows when the steel was to be delivered to the site, and the last diagonal was the schedule for the steel to be set in place—within a week after delivery. You can just see the steel going up in five months.

The critical thing to notice is that every one of the five steps in the steel workflow—design, order, detail, arrive, install—moved at exactly the same pace; the steel workflow was like a five-piece band marching together to a steady beat. However, the steel workflow was not dependent on anything else. In fact, the builders chose two mills and had them manufacture alternating horizontal sections of the building so that each manufacturer had a bit of a cushion to help it keep up the required pace.

Decoupling

After the steel began to be put into place, the other three pacemakers could be constructed without dependence on each other. For example, the window columns were designed to be constructed from the inside of the building without need for either scaffolding or a finished floor. Thus each of the pacemakers had its own independent schedule similar to the steel schedule shown in Figure 3-1.

Inside the building, there was another approach to decoupling. Supplying electrical service to a building the size of the Empire State Building would break new ground, and there was not really time for such a risk. So the building was broken in half vertically, then each half was broken into three 30-story sections, and each section was wired as if it were a separate building. Thus a complex problem became six simpler problems with well-known solutions.

Without decoupling, the task of managing the construction of the Empire State Building would have been impossible. Today we use computers to help us with complex scheduling problems, but perhaps that is a mistake. We are tempted to create a tightly interlocking schedule, forgetting that the slightest deviation will necessarily cascade throughout the entire interlocked system. Not only is a decoupled schedule much simpler, but the impact of variation is isolated to its own workflow.

Logistics

On a busy day, some 500 trucks dropped off material during the day—often more than one a minute! The trucks were tightly scheduled, as was the material

on them. The material was moved to the location for installation almost immediately, because there was no place to store it. Steel was delivered outside and
installed within a week. Finally, there was the problem of getting skilled workers to the place where the material was waiting to be installed.

Every morning, 3000 people, give or take a few dozen, were hired by trade
foremen and sent to work. They had to get to the right location in the building,
work for a half day, break for lunch, and go back to work for the rest of the
day. A complex system of elevators was put in place: The top 30 floors or so
used construction cages, the next approximately 30 floors used elevators
reclaimed from one of the demolished buildings, and as the building rose, the
lowest floors used permanent elevators lined with protective wood for the dura-
tion of construction.

A local restaurant was contracted to set up restaurants every dozen or so
floors throughout the building. The owners did not pay for the privilege but
instead agreed to serve the same food as their street-level restaurant at lower
prices. This made it attractive for workers to eat on-site instead of creating a
bottleneck at the elevators as thousands of people tried to leave and then reen-
ter the work site at midday.

Cash Flow Thinking

In the early 1930s, time was money. Just the running costs of interest and taxes
while the Empire State Building was under construction were about $10,000 a
day.[7] So if you could shave off a day by spending $5000, that was a good
investment. For example, the builders bought larger (and thus more expensive)
electrical boxes so that electrical conduit could be put in place without bending,
which saved both bending and wire-pulling time. Industrial rail tracks were laid
on floors as they were constructed and materials were placed in carts, hoisted
through shafts inside the building, and then pushed on the rails to the place
where they were needed. The expense of the rail tracks was not usually justifi-
able in smaller buildings, but it was considered money well spent in constructing the Empire State Building. Throughout construction, the builders made
decisions based on a cash flow, rather than a balance sheet, perspective.

The Empire State Building was not framed by cost, schedule, and scope. It
was constrained by two acres of land, New York City's zoning ordinances, $35
million of capital, the laws of physics, and May 1, 1931.[8] It was constructed by
deeply experienced leaders who framed the issues they faced in terms of flow—
the flow of materials, the flow of people, and the flow of cash.

---

7. Willis and Friedman, *Building the Empire State*, 1998, p. 18. 10,000 USD in 1929
   would be approximately 120,000 USD in 2009.
8. Anonymous, "Skyscrapers: The Paper Spires," 1930.

Frame 9: Proven Experience

When you absolutely, positively have to deliver on time, the Empire State Building holds some important lessons. Of course, system development is not the same as building a building, so the analogy has limitations. But the stark contrast between the best logistics practices of the 1930s and typical construction project management practices today gives us food for thought.

The first thing to notice is that the owners did not start out with specifications or with bids; they did not even start out with a design. They started out by hiring two highly experienced firms, each with the proven capability to meet their aggressive cost and deadline constraints. These firms were able to commit to meeting the constraints by extrapolating from existing experience. In fact, the builders signed a fixed-price contract before there were any architectural drawings or building specifications.[9] The commitment to deliver on time and on budget was not made based on the details; the commitment was made based on *the ability to shape* the details. This is very important. *The schedule was not laid out based on the details of the building design; the building was designed based on the constraints of the schedule.*

When you absolutely have to have something done on time, or within a certain budget, or both, a reliable commitment can be made only by people with enough domain knowledge and proven experience to be confident that the deadline can somehow be met. They may not know how, but they know the problem is solvable in some manner within existing constraints because they have dealt successfully with problems like it before. If it is not possible to find people with the proven capability to deliver within a timeline and budget that they can be confident about meeting, you cannot expect reliable delivery. Either (1) the people do not have the domain expertise necessary to understand the problem and its likely solution, or (2) the problem is not understandable, cannot be solved, or will change. In either case you should use evolutionary development, and promises beyond what can be confidently projected should not be made.

You may think that this is cheating, but think about it. The only people who can reliably commit to deliver are those people who have developed a reliable capability to deliver. You don't want to sum up the estimates of dozens of people and assume that their estimates will add up to a reliable whole. They probably won't. You want people who have the demonstrated capability to reliably deliver whole systems to lead the effort; and you want them to figure out how to design the details of the system so that the constraints of the system are met

---

9. Willis and Friedman, *Building the Empire State*, 1998, p. 27.

in the best possible way. You do not work backward from the details of a system to its schedule; you start with a high-level schedule and design the details of the system to meet that schedule.

This strategy of designing the effort to fit the constraints, rather than computing the constraints from the design, is absolutely the most effective way to achieve reliable delivery.

Constraints Expose Risk

The deeply experienced builders of the Empire State Building knew immediately where to focus their attention; they knew that material flow was the main constraint and biggest risk of the system, so their efforts centered on minimizing the risk hidden in this constraint.

What is the biggest constraint in your system? Is it understanding the problem to be solved? Devising an effective solution? Implementing the solution? Access to skilled developers? Available testers? Complexity? Politics? You should start by identifying this constraint, and then focus your attention on dealing effectively with it. You may improve other areas, but that will do nothing to improve the overall system; you can improve the system only by dealing with its biggest constraint.

Two very common constraints affecting the on-time delivery of software are system design and implementation complexity, so we'll take a look at these in more detail. However, these are not the only constraints in system development, and they may not be your biggest constraint. Take a realistic inventory of your environment and make sure that you identify and address your major constraints and thereby mitigate your greatest risks.

System Design

Before system development starts, it is important to understand the overall goals and constraints of the system and to define the key measurements whereby you will know that those goals have been met (or not). Ideation, as discussed in Chapter 1, is the first step toward understanding your customer and the purpose of the system you are building. This is done under the guidance of a product champion, and the result might be, for example, an approved product concept. This step is critical for new systems, but it is often implicit for modifications to existing systems. Nevertheless, the purpose and goals of the system, as well as its key constraints, should always be clear to those who are working on it.

As Tom Gilb has preached for decades, you should always start system design with an agreement on measurable business goals, which may include, but certainly are not limited to, valid time and cost constraints.[10] These measurable business goals are the authentic "requirements" of the system. Based on these goals, system design will generally produce a high-level architecture and a high-level feature road map. The features in this road map are pointedly *not* requirements; they are the chosen framework in which the business goals (the real requirements) are expected to be achieved. For ongoing feature development and maintenance of an existing system, these goals should already exist, but they may be expanded upon.

The second step in system development is to create a high-level system design under the guidance of clearly articulated design goals. In our example of the Empire State Building, the high-level design was created by a small design team during intense meetings over the course of the first two months of work. They set a design goal that a person could reach any floor with a single elevator trip. Achieving this goal locked in both the floor plan and the exact height of the building. They wanted the windows to be a notable architectural feature and the window columns to be decoupled from other construction and built from the inside of the building. Achieving this goal through detailed discussions with metal fabricators resulted in very innovative construction techniques that produced an elegant architectural feature. To avoid design loopbacks, the lower columns of structural steel were the initial focus of the design. To speed construction, the concept of dividing the building into six segments for electrical construction was adopted. These are the kinds of goals and design decisions that make up system design.

Design Loopbacks

Unplanned design loopbacks due to design mistakes are probably the biggest threat to on-time delivery of new technology. There were virtually no unplanned loopbacks in the construction of the Empire State Building, even though it was commissioned with practically no design at all. This remarkable achievement is widely attributed to its team design approach. The team of owners, architects, and builders rapidly pulled together an overall design and quickly drilled down to the technical details of every area that was new and unproven. This worked because there was a vast amount of technical expertise coupled with deep professional respect among the members of the team. This teamwork and respect were extended to subcontractors whenever the architects and builders dealt with an area where they did not feel competent to develop specifications on their own.

---

10. See Gilb, "Multidimensional Quantified Goals Should Direct Software Design Processes," 1978.

When contracts are used in software development, a similar broadly cross-functional team approach to design is rare. With a typical contract, one party decides what should be done and hands over the design to another party to implement and often to a third party to deploy and support. Although it may be unavoidable, such a contractual approach is far from ideal; it increases costs and decreases flexibility. Unfortunately, organizational policies often create contractual relationships between departments inside a single company that produce the same effect. Sequential development methods, derived from contracting practices, encourage over-the-wall handovers, even though it has been demonstrated many times that concurrent engineering—engaging experts from all steps of the workflow in the initial design—is one of the best ways to eliminate design loopbacks.

If you do not involve the people who understand the details of the system early in the process, you will not discover the pitfalls that await you until much later, when their discovery often results in costly redesigns and cascading delays. The solution to this well-known problem is *not* to complete the entire design and get sign-offs. The solution is to involve those who will have to implement and live with the design early in the process and drill down as much as is necessary to be sure that lurking problems have been uncovered and addressed. It takes expertise to identify these areas and trust to turn over design decisions to downstream experts. But in the end, concurrent engineering is a lot less expensive than wishful thinking.

Design mistakes are not only technical. A very common mistake in developing systems is building the wrong thing, because of unrealistic or unarticulated goals, badly defined system specifications, or poor communication among customers, developers, and production support.[11] In fact, the Empire State Building was a commercial failure for almost 15 years, most likely because the owners built on a poor location for a commercial building. Timing didn't help; a massive oversupply of office space hit New York as the building was completed, along with the Depression. As effective as the design team was, it contained no expertise in commercial real estate, and that was where the mistakes were made. Do not make this mistake in your design team: Don't trust second-hand information about what customers really want. In Chapter 1 we discussed *ideation* and in Chapter 2 we discussed *ethnography*. These are important concepts that can help you avoid the kind of mistake that was made in the building of the Empire State Building.

---

11. See Charette, "Why Software Fails," 2005.

Implementation Complexity

The builders of the Empire State Building worked aggressively to reduce the complexity of their job by decoupling building subsystems, workflows, and schedules. Reducing complexity by decomposition is hardly a new idea. The problem is that the lines of decomposition are not intuitively obvious and thus are often drawn incorrectly. One of the biggest advantages of engaging experts in the system delivery process is that they know where to draw the decoupling lines. Experts have a keenly developed sense of what's important and what can be ignored. They know the domain well enough to understand what the essential groupings are and what decompositions will work to simplify the problem. In addition, experts can pick up an anomaly in an apparently working system long before a novice has any idea that something is wrong.

The most essential decomposition of the Empire State Building was allowing *schedules* to be decoupled (e.g., the four pacemakers), preventing any delay from impacting other schedules and effectively parallelizing rather than serializing delay. The second most important decomposition was assigning areas of responsibility to subcontractors (e.g., the elevator subcontractor) and involving them in the design of the work from the start. The third important decomposition was dividing the work into repetitive patterns (e.g., the electrical work was organized into six smaller buildings) rather than a monolithic whole.

Three Ways to Reduce Schedule Complexity

If you want to go fast and meet deadlines, you have to figure out a way to simplify and decouple schedules. Unfortunately, many common scheduling practices decompose system development in a way that will almost certainly *increase*, rather than decrease, coupling. Let's take a look at three areas where common scheduling practices can be self-defeating: (1) dependencies, (2) utilization, and (3) critical path.

Dependencies Most scheduling approaches include methods to deal with dependencies. Few, if any, work first and foremost to *remove* dependencies. But schedules should be decoupled; a delay in one schedule should have minimal impact on other schedules, and this works only when dependencies are removed. As with the Empire State Building, decoupled schedules are not really practical unless the architecture is also decoupled, which makes the low-dependency architecture discussed in Chapter 2 all the more important.

Does your scheduling approach result in spending a lot of time and effort dealing with dependencies, or do you divert that energy toward removing dependencies?

Utilization Most schedule coupling that we see in software development does not come from the architectural dependencies; it is the direct result of trying to achieve a high utilization of people. It seems that many companies don't ever want to see idle workers, so they use scheduling systems to enable them to fully use workers' available time. This creates tight coupling of multiple schedules and invariably leads to cascading delays. The inevitable delays decrease utilization to a far lower point than what can be achieved with a decoupled scheduling system. As we have demonstrated in previous books,[12] queuing theory makes it clear that attempting to maximize utilization is a self-defeating process. Optimal utilization can be achieved only by concentrating on flow.

Do you measure utilization in a way that encourages people to focus on maximizing it? Is one of the important purposes of your scheduling or portfolio management system to increase utilization? Or do you realize that trying to drive utilization beyond its natural limit will almost certainly *decrease* utilization?

Critical Path Another way to tightly couple schedules is to find a critical path and schedule it without slack; this approach also tends to be self-defeating. Instead of focusing on the critical path, consider the possibility of *not having a critical path*. For example, the builders of the Empire State Building used two steel mills so they always had a backup supplier and the mills always had slack time to catch up.

If your schedule is mission-critical, every element of the so-called critical path should have at least one and preferably two alternate approaches, insofar as that is possible. This is called *set-based design*, a practice we have covered in previous books.[13] The idea of set-based design is to develop multiple alternatives for every critical design decision and make the decision as late as possible—when you have the most information. At decision time, you must be sure that at least one of the alternatives will work. You might develop a good approach that will work for sure, a better approach that has a bit more risk, and an aggressive approach that pushes the limits but would be the best approach if it works out. Developing multiple options may seem more expensive than developing a single approach, but for critical decisions it is almost always cheaper and gives better results.

---

12. See Poppendieck, *Lean Software Development: An Agile Toolkit*, 2003, Chapter 4; and Poppendieck, *Implementing Lean Software Development: From Concept to Cash*, 2006, Chapter 5.

13. See Poppendieck, *Lean Software Development: An Agile Toolkit*, 2003, pp. 38–45; and Poppendieck, *Implementing Lean Software Development: From Concept to Cash*, 2006, pp. 160–64.

An important benefit of set-based design is that you always have an alternative; you don't really have a critical path. Instead, you have unmovable deadlines that you have confidence you can meet, because at each deadline you know there will be at least one viable way to move forward. This allows you to eliminate design loopbacks while maintaining the ability to make innovative decisions and respond quickly to market changes without compromising the schedule.

Frame 10: Level Workflow

Let's take another look at the structural steel workflow of the Empire State Building, as shown in Figure 3-1. The steps in the workflow are shown as diagonals going from the first floor to the top. The five diagonals are the due dates for each of the five workflow steps: design, mill order, milling details, delivery, and construction. Design was completed in batches of varying size, because many sections of the building looked exactly the same for several stories. Starting with the second step, mill order, work flowed in batches of two stories at a time, because steel columns were (and still are) two stories high, and every two-story column had different specifications because of load-bearing considerations. This technique of breaking work into small (in this case two-story) batches and moving each batch through the workflow independently is what allowed the steel structure to be built so quickly.

Small Batches

One of the biggest contributions of agile software development is the use of iterations. If you think of an iteration as a two-story batch of work moving through the development workflow, you can see why iterations are so effective. Before iterations became common, development was done in much bigger batches, usually a complete release at a time. The introduction of iterations—all by itself—usually has an immediate positive effect on both speed and quality in the development process. Why is this?

Iterations cause small batches of work to move through a development process, and small batches of work have all sorts of good effects. In almost every domain where lean is applied, small batch sizes lead to a surprising increase in both speed and quality, because they provide rapid feedback and signaling of incipient problems before they grow large. The surprise comes because the cost of operating blindly—without feedback—is hidden and almost always underestimated. When high-quality rapid feedback is used to develop a system, quality does not get out of control, schedules are less likely to slip, and risk is greatly reduced.

In his book *The Principles of Product Development Flow*[14] Donald Reinertsen lists multiple benefits of reducing batch size in product development: reduced cycle time, reduced variability in flow, accelerated feedback, reduced risk, reduced overhead, increased efficiency, dramatically improved ability to meet plans, and, finally, higher motivation and a greater sense of urgency. This is a pretty impressive list of benefits, and it is a good match to the early benefits reported by many organizations that have adopted agile development.

The principle of small batches can be applied beyond iterations; there are other batching mechanisms in a development process, each one creating its own batch size. Projects are a batching mechanism, and so are release cycles. In many organizations, iterative development has not changed the size of these batches; just because the software is ready to deploy doesn't mean it will be released. But if short iterations have so many good effects, can we assume that short release cycles might bring about similar benefits? And if so, what is the limit? Can a release cycle be too short?

As you move work from development to release, you have to do a certain amount of staging—things such as system testing, user acceptance testing, packaging, installation, training, updating support information, and so on. On the one hand, this staging can be expensive and time-consuming. On the other hand, there is a real cost in waiting: Defects build up undetected, competitors may beat you to market, customers may change their minds. So how do you trade off the costs of each release against the benefits of frequent releases?

Reinertsen points out that the economic lot size calculation used in inventory control can be applied to product development. Figure 3-2 shows how this might work. Here we see a curve of release overhead costs, that is, the cost of staging a release, which is usually considered a fixed cost for each release. As the release size gets larger, the overhead cost can be spread across more development effort, so the cost per unit of development effort decreases. But there is a second curve that accounts for costs that increase because of delaying a release—costs such as finding and fixing hidden defects and integrating ever larger batches of code; these costs tend to increase nonlinearly with batch size. The total cost is the sum of the two costs, which is a U-curve. The lowest cost is at the bottom of the U-curve, and this spot indicates the economic batch size.

There was a time when the choice of batch size was made by creating a graph like the one in Figure 3-2 and finding out where the two lines crossed.

---

14. See Reinertsen, *The Principles of Product Development Flow: Second Generation Lean Product Development*, 2009, Chapter 5, Batch Size.

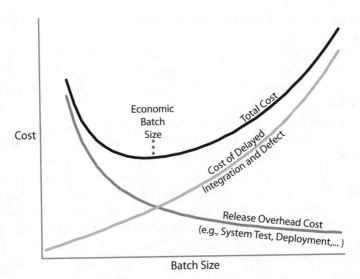

Figure 3-2   *Economic batch size*

The crossover point was the economic batch size, so you could compute, for example, how far apart to schedule releases. But that result is based on an assumption: *Overhead costs are fixed*. What if overhead costs are not fixed? What if you could dramatically reduce the time and expense of running the system test? What if training costs could be eliminated with a more intuitive interface and smaller batches? Then the graph would give a different answer. As Figure 3-3 shows, batches can be much smaller—releases can be much closer together—when overhead costs are reduced.

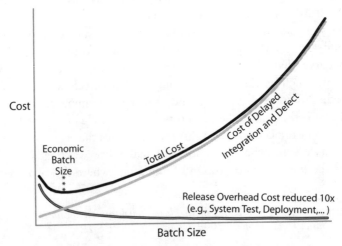

Figure 3-3   *Drive down overhead costs to drive down batch size.*

The idea of reducing batch size works throughout the development workflow; use the good technical practices we covered in Chapter 2 to reduce the cost of moving work to the next step in the workflow and you can move smaller amounts of work more frequently to downstream processes. The value of the feedback you get will far outweigh the cost of each transfer.

Iterations

The structural steel workflow chart shown in Figure 3-1 was a very useful tool for visualizing the building of the Empire State Building. We wondered if we could create a similar workflow chart to visualize a software system being developed, using an iteration as the basic batching mechanism. How would such a workflow chart look? In order to find out, we will take an example problem and work through a few scenarios.

Assume for the sake of this example that you want to develop an application. You take a week to document the overall goals of the application and decide that there will be about a dozen features, and you can complete about two features per iteration. For the first scenario, assume that you decide to start with one-month iterations, and you select the features for each release just before you start working on it. Prior to each release, you need two weeks to stage the software for release by running a system test. Laying this out on a chart similar to the one used for the Empire State Building, we get Figure 3-4.

In this scenario, releases are eight weeks apart, starting at the end of week 11. Staging takes two weeks, or 25% of the eight-week release cycle. Ten weeks elapse between the time features are selected and their actual release.

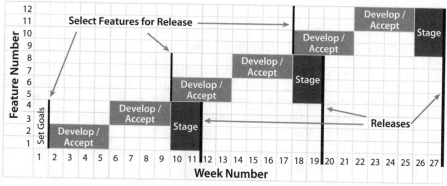

Figure 3-4 *Software workflow chart: Scenario 1*

Making Work Ready

There is a problem with this scenario: The features are too big. It can take a great deal of time to decide exactly what it means—in detail—to implement each feature. A tremendous amount of work and risk can be encountered while figuring this out, and a great deal of expertise is usually required to do it well. So our recommendation is to break features down into smaller elements that we call *stories* shortly before the development of each feature is likely to begin. We can see that this step is missing from the workflow in scenario 1; let's call this missing step *make work ready to code*.

Work is made ready by people who do the hard work of understanding what customers really need, probably a mix of business analysts, testers, technical writers, and others. Developers should also be involved, providing technical insight, but for the majority of their time, they may be working on development while the next set of stories is being prepared. If this is the case, future work can be made ready at the same time that current work is being developed— although it should not happen too much in advance. A good approach is to make work ready one iteration before it will be developed, although this timing is context-dependent.

Classic analysis techniques such as use cases, business rule matrices, scenario diagrams, UI prototypes, and so on can be used to understand a feature in detail and divide it into stories that will take perhaps one to three days to implement. Each story should include tests that specify its conditions of satisfaction. When it is time for the development team to commit to what will be done in the next iteration, the stories have been prepared, the definition of *done* is clear, and therefore reliable estimates are possible.

Ready-Ready to Be Done-Done

Systematic was established in 1985 and employs more than 450 people worldwide with offices in Denmark, Finland, the United States, and the UK. It is an independent software and systems company focusing on complex and critical IT solutions. Often these systems are mission-critical with high demands for reliability, safety, accuracy, and usability.

Solutions developed by Systematic are used by tens of thousands of people in the defense, health care, manufacturing, and service industries. Systematic was appraised in November 2005 using the SCAMPI method and found to be CMMI level 5 compliant. During 2006, Systematic adopted Scrum and a story-based early testing approach to software development and achieved significant positive results.

In a CMMI context all development processes are monitored for effectiveness and efficiency. Therefore, measures were also established on the Scrum process. The choice of measures was highly inspired by lean. At Systematic, we wanted a measure to help establish focus on a "stop the line" mindset toward defects, to ensure that defects are addressed immediately after they are identified. We also wanted insight into the flow of story implementation, that is, how much waiting time is incurred when a story is implemented.

These considerations led to a number of measures; the two most important are

1. Fix time after a failed build: Are problems proactively handled?

   The main reason to measure how long it takes from a build failure on the shared build server until the next successful build has to do with speed and quality. If a defect or a problem is not addressed immediately after it is identified, rework will accumulate and it will be difficult to deliver a sprint with high quality and maintain a high velocity.

2. Flow in implementation of a story: Is a story implemented without breaks in calendar time and context shift?

   In lean, a steady flow is desired from the time a customer requests a service until that request is fulfilled. From a lean perspective, we want to eliminate the waste associated with context shift or waiting. Therefore we strive to ensure that when work is started on a story, it is implemented without any interruption or waiting time.

   Assume a story is estimated to be three workdays of effort. However, for various reasons it takes nine workdays to implement the story. The flow of this story implementation is then defined as three days' calendar time of work implemented over nine calendar days, a flow of 3/9 or 33%. This is measured for all stories.

   When we started measuring flow, it was around 30%, but from 2007 to 2008 we have increased this to 59% for Q4 2008.

   Efficient flow eliminates the waste associated with context shifts and handovers. In addition, the team members find it more satisfying that when work is initiated in a sprint, it is sufficiently clarified to allow for a smooth implementation during the sprint.

Two teams added the following objectives to their projects:

1. Bring the fix time after a failed build in control with an average of less than a working day.

2. Increase the flow of implementation of a story to greater than 60%.

None of the projects met these two objectives initially, but Systematic was committed to continually improve toward the objectives.

A comparison of the productivity of two of these projects to other projects in Systematic in August 2008 showed their productivity to be 140% and 360% better than the average. There is some uncertainty related to the productivity numbers because they are based on a new size measure (cosmic function point) that was introduced in early 2008. However, these measures were consistent with the gut feeling of the management team, who believed that these two projects showed characteristics of hyper-productive teams.

The two projects had focused on the flow measure through 2008, and they quickly understood that in order to establish a good flow within sprints, the product backlog has to be maintained continuously and concurrent with delivering of sprints. Inspired by the common use of the term *done-done* to express that a story is fully completed, Systematic introduced the term *ready-ready*, to express that work from the product backlog has been sufficiently elaborated to be allocated to a sprint for implementation.

The product owner is asked, "Are you ready-ready?" and the team is asked, "Are you done-done?" —or in short to all, "Are you ready-ready to be done-done?" When your project is ready-ready to be done-done, you can deliver value at high velocity.

Carsten Jakobsen[15]

One of the ways to improve workflow is to overlap steps in the workflow, so that when it is time for an iteration to start, features for that iteration have been *made ready to code* and development can begin immediately. When teams concurrently make work ready for the next iteration during development, we find that quite often they can cut the iteration length in half. So for scenario 2, let's assume that the iterations are now two weeks long, and during the week before the start of each iteration, the work is made ready to code. We assume that we can still do two features in each of the shorter iterations, because the work has been made ready ahead of time, which was half of the work. The new workflow is diagrammed in Figure 3-5.

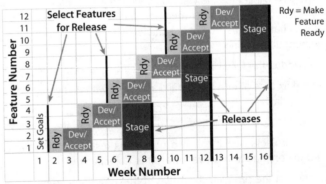

Figure 3-5   *Software workflow chart: Scenario 2*

15. Adapted from Jakobsen and Sutherland, "Scrum and CMMI—Going from Good to Great: Are You Ready-Ready to be Done-Done," 2009. Used with permission.

In scenario 2, releases are now four weeks apart instead of eight, and they start at the end of week 8 instead of week 11. In addition, seven weeks, instead of ten, elapse between the time features are finalized and their actual release. But notice: Staging now takes up 50% of the four-week release cycle.

At this point, many companies are tempted to question whether the shorter release cycle is worth the 50% overhead. But as we mentioned earlier, the correct questions to ask are "How can we reduce staging time? What if we were to run staging after each iteration?" To do this and keep costs reasonable, staging time should probably be cut in half. Part of the time reduction can come from staging after each iteration, so that the problems introduced by one iteration can be found and fixed while the next iteration is under way. But more work is usually necessary to reduce staging time—and this is where automation can be very useful. While we're making improvements, let's delay the decision on which features to implement until it is really necessary. The resulting workflow is depicted in Figure 3-6.

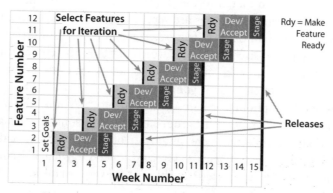

Figure 3-6 *Software workflow chart: Scenario 3*

In scenario 3, releases are still four weeks apart, and they start one week earlier. But now there are only four weeks, instead of seven, between the time features are selected and their actual release. Better yet, staging takes up 25% of the four-week release cycle, instead of 50%.

The next question that comes to mind might be "Why not release the application after every iteration?" This might be a good choice for the next scenario; it would give a release every two weeks, with the first release starting at week 5. The downside is that staging would again take up 50% of a release cycle, so you would want to further shorten staging. See Figure 3-7.

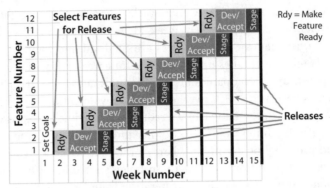

Figure 3-7   *Software workflow chart: Scenario 4*

Kanban

Iterations use a timebox as a batching mechanism. But feature size may not always be such a good match to the timebox as we depicted in the preceding four scenarios. Sometimes features are very short; it may take a couple of hours to make a change to an existing feature. Sometimes features are not as easily divisible into iteration-sized chunks as we would like. Sometimes features vary widely in size relative to each other. Thus sometimes it can be difficult to find the perfect timebox to choose for your batch size.

There is another option. You can say to yourself, "What if I did not use time to determine batch size? What if I grouped features in some other manner—for example, what if I collected a minimum set of useful features, called that a batch, and released them when the set was done? Or what if I could release each feature as it was completed?" (This can be very useful in a maintenance environment.)

In the Empire State Building, the steel construction batch size was based on a single column, two stories high; work moved through the workflow one set of two-story columns at a time. Similarly, you can create flow by having one feature flow through the system at a time. This approach is often called *kanban*, the name of a manufacturing technique that has been applied to software development.[16]

How Kanban Works

Let's revisit our example and see how it would work in a kanban system. The word *kanban* means "card," and in manufacturing, a *kanban card* is used to

---

16. See Hiranabe, "Kanban Applied to Software Development: From Agile to Lean," 2008, for a history of kanban in manufacturing and an introduction to its application to software development.

signal that work needs to be done. We would like a similar way to use cards to signal that work needs to be done on a feature. To do this, we set up a *kanban board* to track each feature as it flows through the workflow. We will have one column for each step in the workflow. We will put features, and later the stories derived from each feature, on Post-it Cards and put these in the column on the kanban board that represents their current position in the workflow.

All kanban systems are designed to limit work-in-process, because the more work-in-process, the slower the flow. That's one of the reasons kanban systems were invented in the first place—to limit work-in-process and thus increase flow. The mechanism for limiting work-in-process in software kanban is to limit the number of items in each step of the workflow.

Figure 3-8 shows a possible layout for a kanban board. In this example, work arrives at the board on the left side, in the "Next Features" column. No more than three features may be awaiting action in this column. When there is room, a feature moves to the right, into the make work ready column. It is then decomposed into stories, which are placed in the next column. The stories move to the right, through development and unit test, then to acceptance test. Once stories pass their acceptance test, they are reassembled into features, which move through a feature-level acceptance test and staging. Finally, a feature moves into the "Ready to Release" column.

As work moves through the workflow, cards representing the work are moved downstream (to the right). Team members can work on any step of the workflow they have the skills to address; the general practice is to expect people to be able to work effectively in at least two steps in the workflow. Then if a bottleneck occurs downstream, people from the upstream step can help out in the downstream process. Every day the team meets briefly to discuss how things are going and to see what is needed to keep work flowing.

Finally, when a feature is complete, we record the time it took to move across the board. The date it was posted in the "Next Features" column is subtracted from the date it moved into the "Ready to Release" column, and the result is entered on the "Days to Complete Feature" graph. Over time, this graph will give a good view of the *throughput* of the kanban process.

Note that we are using the same workflow steps that we used in our scenarios example, although we have broken down the develop/accept step into more detail. There are many variations on the theme of kanban boards.[17] The workflow

---

17. There are many different ways to lay out a kanban board. See Scotland, "Kanban, Flow, and Cadence," 2009, for a good introduction to kanban boards. See Ladas, *Scrumban: Essays on Kanban Systems for Lean Software Development*, 2008, for much more detail on kanban boards.

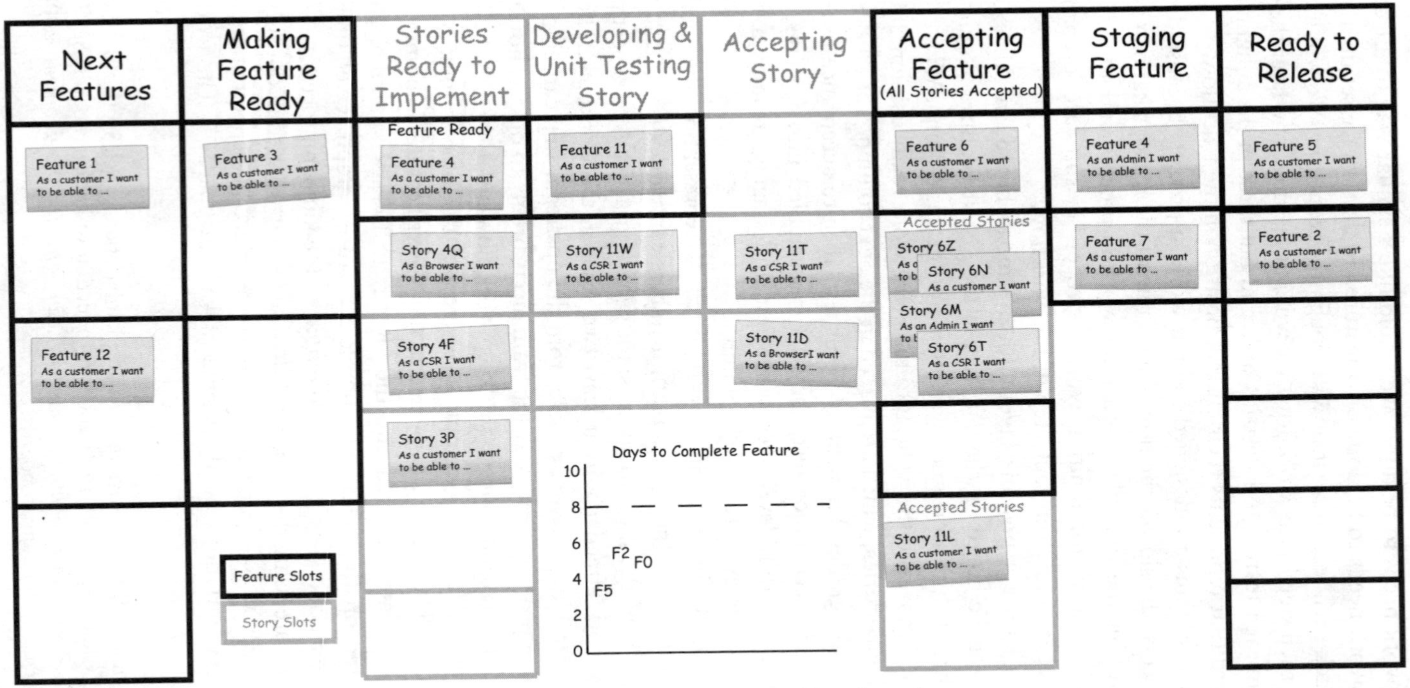

Figure 3-8 Example of a kanban board

step represented in each column, as well as the "proper" number of cards (indicated in this case by boxes) allowed in each column, should be the subject of experimentation. The goal is to balance the work so that there is an even flow. Start with a few extra boxes, allowing more work-in-process, and gradually reduce the number of boxes until unevenness or blockages occur. This gives the team an opportunity to find the cause of the variation or constraint and remedy it, and then perhaps more boxes can be removed.

Figure 3-9 shows what a kanban scenario might look like for the example we have been charting.

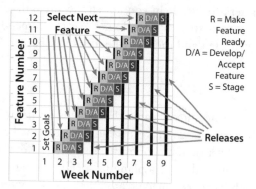

Figure 3-9 *Software workflow chart: Scenario 5 (kanban)*

In scenario 5, we maintain the assumption that each feature will take a half week to make ready and a week to complete, and that we select features as late as possible. However, we assume that we are able to cut the staging time from one week to half a week, and that we can release as often as once a week. With these assumptions, we release two features a week for six weeks, starting in the middle of week 4 and ending in the middle of week 9. Note that at any one time, two features are under development; this was also true in the earlier scenarios, but in this scenario the batch size is one feature rather than one iteration's worth of features.

Since all of the features are the same size in this theoretical example, scenario 5 could have been done with an iteration (timeboxed) system, but that would not have allowed for any variation in the size of features. In practice, features vary in size, and thus they will not always be done at even time intervals. We have two choices about how to deal with this reality: We could choose to have a release each time a feature is done, in which case the releases would not be exactly evenly spaced; or we could maintain a cadence of weekly releases. In that case there would be times when there is only one feature to release, whereas the next week might have three features. Either of these approaches is quite all right in a kanban system; the overall flow should not suffer from variations in feature size or even release size.

Iterations or Kanban?

There is no one best way to develop software. Every approach has its strong and weak points, and every context makes different use of those strong and weak points. Iterations and kanban are certainly not the only ways to manage workflow in software development, but both are quite good at promoting a smooth and rapid flow of small batches of work. In this section we will compare kanban and iterations to help you match the strengths and weaknesses of each one against your particular situation.[18] We recommend that you choose one of them to get started and then use the ideas in Chapter 4 to keep improving your process.

Commitment

You can monitor the health of teams that are using iterations by observing whether or not they are able to make a commitment at the beginning of an iteration and reliably deliver on that commitment at the end of the iteration. At the beginning of the iteration there is a planning meeting at which a team commits to the stories (which have been made ready) that it will complete. This commitment is influenced by the team's established velocity. By the end of the iteration, the team should be able to meet that commitment.

In a kanban system, on the other hand, work is done on a best-effort basis, and you monitor the health of a team by tracking the average time for a feature to be completed. Each approach has its place; the dynamic of how work gets done is different depending on whether the constraint of a deadline is present or not. On the one hand, there is the student syndrome—students often wait until an assignment is due before they work on it. Iteration deadlines can counteract the student syndrome and cause things to get done at a regular cadence. The constraint of a commitment to a deadline can generate energy and focus the team on meeting the deadline. On the other hand, inappropriate deadlines are similar to inappropriate targets; they create dissonance and often cause people to stop trying to meet the deadlines. Moreover, the limited work-in-process and the visibility of flow on a kanban chart are just as capable of generating energy and focus as an iteration deadline. Experiment and see what works better in your situation.

---

18. A good comparison of Scrum and kanban systems can be found in Kniberg, "Kanban vs Scrum," 2009.

Teamwork

In an iteration system, everyone on the team needs to work together and help each other out to be sure that the team commitment is met. There should be no partial credit; stories are not done until they are truly *done*, that is, tested, integrated, documented, and ready to deploy (if not deployed). Anything less gets zero credit. If you need the "no partial credit" rule to encourage teamwork, then iterations, with their team commitment, tend to require more teamwork. In a kanban system, each person is more likely to work in his or her individual area and move to work on a downstream bottleneck should one develop.

However, the dynamics of teamwork are not necessarily determined by which workflow practice is used. There are many teams using iterations in which individuals focus on their specialties, and there are plenty of organizations using kanban where colleagues eagerly help each other out. Different types of work and different organizational cultures experience the benefits of each approach differently. We know of one organization in which the creative front-end work is done with iterations, and the more routine later work is done using a kanban approach.

Batch Size

In theory, a batch size of one feature is better than a relatively arbitrary time-based batch size. As you saw in scenario 5, the workflow was (theoretically) quite a bit faster when using a batch size of one. There are additional reasons to use a batch size of one feature rather than an iteration timebox. In many environments it can be difficult to fit features neatly into small timeboxes, and attempts to do so may generate unnecessary waste. In other environments, there may be a wide variation in size of features, and moving features through the system one at a time can make this variation easier to manage.

On the other hand, timeboxes are very useful mechanisms to force the details of a feature to be limited in scope so as to finish the feature within an appropriate amount of time, as we will discuss in Frame 11: Pull Scheduling. The "right" approach depends upon the kind of work being done.

Cadence

A timebox approach to development has a regular cadence, a drumbeat of work getting done. Cadence is good. Although kanban systems do not inherently have a cadence, it is a common practice to establish a cadence in a kanban system by having regular releases—for example, once a week—and releasing everything that is ready when the release date arrives.

Don't limit yourself to one tool. As Miyamoto Musashi, a famous seventeenth-century samurai, once said, "Do not develop an attachment to any one weapon or any one school of fighting."[19]

Capacity

In order for work to flow, it is very important to limit the amount of work to capacity; do not try to force more work through your development organization than it has the capacity to deliver. Trying to force a system to work beyond its capacity invariably causes turbulence and slows things down. It is rather difficult to limit work to capacity, however, if you do not know what your capacity is. Whether you use iterations or kanban, it is important to generate a useful measurement of your capacity, so you know how much work your system is capable of handling.

Iterations: Velocity

The measurement of capacity in an iteration system is velocity, that is, how many ideal-sized stories can a team regularly deliver during its chosen iteration timebox? Since all stories are not an ideal size, we measure velocity in terms of story points, and then assign a point score to each story based on its estimated level of difficulty. A story might be 1 story point or 3 story points or maybe 6 points, but not much more. (Larger stories are broken down into smaller stories.) Over time, a team should begin to complete approximately the same number of story points per iteration. That number is called *velocity*, which describes the *capacity* of the team.[20] For example, if a team can be counted on to deliver about 50 story points every iteration, you begin to have a handle on the team's capacity. Remember that *velocity is a measure of capacity*; it is not a measure of performance.

When a group of teams delivers reliably based on the teams' velocity, you begin to get a good feel for the capacity of the organization. This is a relatively rough estimate, and it pretty much falls apart if you reorganize teams frequently. Velocity varies from one team to another, and it changes when the team makeup changes or when the team moves to a different class of problems.

---

19. Credit goes to Henrik Kniberg for this quote. It can be found in Kniberg (ibid.).
20. This assumes long-lived teams that have the needed skills to deliver the feature without dependence on other teams.

Kanban: Throughput

You know you have a stable kanban system when you have a stable flow, that is, when the average cycle time of features moving through the workflow is relatively stable. This time is generally measured from the time a feature is accepted into the "Next Features" column until it is either "Ready to Release" or actually released. Arriving at a stable cycle time is easiest if the features are more or less the same size (or at least the same average size) and the development team is relatively stable. Once you stabilize cycle time, you have a service level measurement that can be used to provide an estimated delivery date when you accept work. Your goal is to say to customers either "No, we really do not have the capacity to do that," or "Yes, we can do that and you can expect it within a week [day, month, or whatever the service level is]."

Once a team has established a reliable cycle time, two things happen. First, the team is able to reduce the cycle time by reducing work-in-process, that is, reducing the number of available boxes on the kanban board. This is a simple application of Little's Law from queuing theory: Time through the system is directly proportional to the amount of work-in-process. Second, a reliable cycle time establishes the average number of features that move through the system in a set period—average number of features per week, for example. This is the throughput of the system, and *throughput is a measure of capacity*.

Frame 11: Pull Scheduling

Returning to the Empire State Building, we noted in Frame 9: Proven Experience that the builders' commitment to deliver on time and on budget was not made based on the details; details didn't exist. Their commitment was based on the *ability to shape* the details. The builders did not lay out a detailed schedule of the building based on its design; the building was designed based on the constraints of the schedule. In other words, the builders did not work backward from the details of the building to arrive at its schedule; we would call this *push scheduling*. Instead, they started with the constraints of the system and developed the schedule to accommodate those constraints; we call this *pull scheduling*.

Perhaps pull scheduling does not sound comfortable to you, and even if it does, you may be wondering exactly how you would go about using it. In this section we will discuss the theory behind pull scheduling, so that you can figure out how you might apply it in your situation.

Why do we need schedules in the first place? We schedule things because we want them to happen, and we believe that the best way to make sure they happen is to arrange for them in advance. For example, we, the authors, travel extensively, and we usually book airplanes and hotels quite far in advance. We are sure that if we don't buy airplane tickets and obtain hotel reservations in advance, it will be either expensive or difficult to get a desirable flight or hotel at the last minute. Our trips are rather complicated, and the arrangements we make in advance give us confidence that we will be able to meet our commitments.

What if we could be convinced that if we showed up without prior arrangements, we could still get the flight and hotel we wanted at the same or even less cost than if we had reserved and paid for them in advance? Well, we still would plan the trip—decide on the flights we might want and maybe choose a few desirable hotels. But if we were assured of availability at equivalent or lower cost, you can be sure we would stop locking in the details of our trips by buying tickets in advance.

In fact, there are many cases when we do not schedule trip details very far in advance. We don't reserve taxis or most train trips in advance; we can generally show up at the train station, buy a ticket at a reasonable price, and get on the next train. Similarly, when we are driving a car, we don't reserve a hotel when we are confident that we can drive up to just about any hotel on our route and have a nice, reasonably priced place to stay. Being able to change plans at the last minute is very convenient!

While we haven't been convinced that we can stop booking airplane trips in advance, we suggest that much of that detailed scheduling you may have been doing in system development could be unnecessary. You can usually get what you want to happen when you need it to happen, without committing to the details in advance—and it will probably cost you less. Now you may be saying to yourself, "Wait a minute! My situation is much too complex or changeable for that." But in fact, the more complex and changeable the situation, the more likely it is that pull scheduling will result in a significant improvement over push scheduling.

Push systems are managed by "pushing" a predetermined plan to the operating environment and tracking task completion against that plan. Since the plan is fixed in advance, a push system is ill equipped to handle variety or variation. And since all work has variation—the more complexity and change, the more variation—it is impossible to follow a detailed plan exactly unless it has enough slack to absorb the variation. For example, let's say we need to fly from Copenhagen to Stockholm after a closing panel of a conference. For what flight time should we buy tickets? Typically, we need to buy such tickets weeks in advance, so we will purchase tickets for a later flight, to give ourselves extra time to get from the conference to the airport. We allow for variation with slack.

Pull systems are managed by managing the queue of things that should happen next; when people want to know what to do next, they pull an item off the top of a queue. Since these queues can be changed dynamically, pull systems are naturally capable of handling variety and variation. Therefore, it is not really necessary to add slack to absorb variation, because the system creates the necessary slack when necessary—and *only* when necessary.

To see how a pull system works with our travel example, let's say the panel is canceled and the conference is over early. The next item in our queue of things to do is go to the airport and fly to Stockholm. If we have purchased the airplane tickets in advance, changing the flight time is likely to cost more than the ticket itself. So instead we wait for the later flight, which gives us a lot more slack than we need in our schedule. But let's assume we are assured that all the flights will have some spare room and we have coupons that will get us on any flight. Then it is certainly better to decide on the exact flight *just in time*, rather than to wait for the late flight that we scheduled *just in case*.[21] Pull systems lock in details *just in time* and therefore use no more slack than is necessary. Alternatively, if we are traveling from Copenhagen to Aarhus, we would travel by train, so we can simply show up at the train station and get on the next train, because trains run frequently and there is always room.

Scheduling Medium-Sized Systems

In the last section we looked at five scenarios for using pull scheduling on a medium-sized system—one that had about a dozen features that might take a couple of weeks each to develop and could be worked on by a single team or a small number of collaborating teams. What makes these scenarios pull systems? For one thing, the features are not scheduled at the beginning of development; they are identified at a high level and perhaps given an initial prioritization. Detailed analysis of each feature is delayed until immediately before it is developed, so the schedule of one feature per week is simply a rough estimate. Because early investment in each feature is low, features can be easily rearranged, dropped, added, or modified based on knowledge that is accumulated during development or obtained through feedback from customers.

Iteration systems are inherently pull systems as long as the development team is not told what to do at the beginning of each iteration; instead, the team decides what it is capable of doing, based on its velocity. Kanban systems are also inherently pull systems; features are pulled into the system only when there

---

21. If this scenario seems far-fetched, it would be exactly the approach we would use to take a train to Aarhus.

is an empty box on the kanban board. In both cases, demonstrated capacity—velocity or throughput—is the primary scheduling mechanism. For the initial schedule of the 12-feature system we examined in the last section, a rough estimate was made: A team can probably complete about two features per one-month iteration. This estimate came from an understanding of the difficulty of each feature, the proven capability of the team, and the stability of its velocity or throughput. After two or three features are completed, the initial estimate is validated—or invalidated as the case may be—and adjusted as necessary.

You manage a pull system by managing the queues, instead of by scheduling the details of the work. At any time before a feature is selected for development, you can change its order, modify its description, even delete it entirely. You can add a new feature that becomes important and put it at the top of the queue. Pull scheduling is a bit like taking a train; features show up at the top of the queue when it makes sense for them to be implemented, and they catch the next train through the workflow. Trains don't fill up until they are about to depart, and there are a lot of trains with frequent departures. When this approach to scheduling works, it works very well.

Decouple

Iteration and kanban systems have good pull mechanisms for small to medium-sized systems. What about large systems? The way the Empire State Building handled its massive size was to divide all large problems into medium-sized problems with known solutions. We recommend that you try very hard to do the same. Try to divide a large system into smaller batches that can be decoupled from each other, and if possible, run each batch through the system separately. Even if you are developing a large system, you should try to release its features in small batches. Often customer needs can be decoupled into relatively small sets of features that are independently useful. Your goal is to decouple demand into minimum useful feature sets (MUFs),[22] prioritize them, and work on one MUF at a time.

Decoupling also applies to teams; teams work better if they can operate independently, without significant dependencies on other teams. We recommend using *feature teams*,[23] that is, relatively small, long-lived, cross-functional teams

---

22. This term is a modification of the term *minimum marketable features* (MMFs) from Denne and Cleland-Huang, *Software by Numbers*, 2004. We use the term *useful* instead of *marketable* because some development organizations we know of do not serve markets.

23. See Chapter 7 in Larman and Vodde, *Scaling Lean & Agile Development: Thinking and Organizational Tools for Large-Scale Scrum*, 2009, for an in-depth discussion of feature teams.

that complete end-to-end customer features. Feature teams stay together over time, moving features through the workflow as a team, accepting new features when others are finished. The ability of feature teams to act independently is related to the dependencies in your architecture, so we reemphasize the need for low-dependency architectures.

When decoupling of teams is not practical, there must be a clear way to coordinate work across teams. This can be relatively simple for a small group of teams working on a single feature, especially if the teams have the same planning horizon. Things are much more complicated when teams must coordinate work across a large number of other teams in order to get things done. The most difficult situation, however, occurs when agile teams are dependent on teams that have much longer planning time frames. Dissonance between teams with different planning horizons is common and can be difficult to resolve.

Scheduling Small, Frequent Requests

In software development, there always seem to be more requests coming in than you can possibly deal with. We rarely see a situation where there is more capacity than demand; instead, we usually find that requests come pouring in a lot faster than they are closed out, as we depict in Figure 3-10.

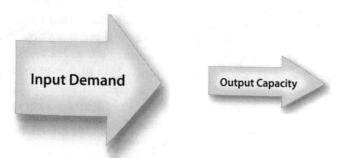

Figure 3-10 *Demand exceeding capacity*

One of the most important requirements of flow systems—whether iteration or kanban or even large batch systems—is that the work must be limited to the capacity of the system. This is not optional; it is essential. Pushing a flow system beyond its capacity creates turbulence and causes it to slow down. This happens with highways at rush hour, it happens at airport security lines, and it will happen to your development system if you try to push more work through the system than it has the capacity to deliver.

Managing capacity is a fundamental management responsibility. Development teams will find it almost impossible to deliver reliably if the demand is not

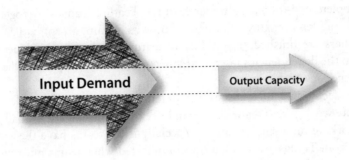

Figure 3-11   *Limiting demand to capacity*

managed so that it is limited to the proven capacity of the teams. You may be able to increase the capacity of your organization by adding people, but you cannot sustainably increase the output of your organization by overloading people. It is essential that you limit demand to capacity (see Figure 3-11).

Arbitrate with Value

In order to limit demand to capacity, you need to make decisions about which requests to accept and which to reject. You should have some sort of customer-focused goals—preferably measurable—to use to arbitrate demand. In order to decide whether a request is important, someone usually estimates how much it will improve customer outcomes, and someone else estimates how much it will cost to achieve those improvements. A decision about which items to work on can be made, at least in part, based on a *ratio of the benefit to the cost.* Notice that *the cost estimate does not need to be any more accurate than the benefit estimate,* because a ratio is no more accurate than its least accurate number.[24] Striving for a precise cost estimate does not reduce the uncertainty of the benefit/cost ratio enough to lead to a better decision.

If you are subject to an oversupply of requests, you should not spend much time on the initial evaluation of a request, because many of the requests will never get done. The initial value estimate for a request need only be accurate enough to compare it to other opportunities. The idea is to figure out which things you are not going to do as inexpensively as possible and discard them as quickly as possible.

---

24. If the estimated return is plus or minus 50%, the ROI will have at least a 50% uncertainty. If the uncertainty cost is also 50%, the uncertainty in ROI will be plus or minus 70%, assuming the uncertainties are normal and independent.

Limit Queues

The typical response to excess demand is to put all incoming requests on a list—which we will call a queue—and occasionally look at the queue and decide which items are the most important things to do next. This seems like a pull system, right? The problem is, if demand continues to exceed capacity, the queue keeps growing longer and longer. Occasionally an admission is made that not everything will get done and old stuff may be dropped from the bottom of the queue, but still the queue can represent months or years of work. Meanwhile, those needing the work done often have no idea when, or whether, it will happen.

This kind of queue between a development organization and its customers serves almost no useful purpose; instead, the queue is a buffer that keeps people from having to talk to each other. In a lean environment, a queue may be used as a buffer to absorb variation in demand, but not to keep people from communicating. Therefore we recommend that a queue for small regular requests should be no longer than needed to absorb the variation in demand (see Figure 3-12).

When a small request system[25] is served by a single team, you can use the

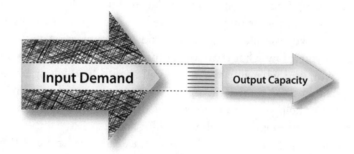

Figure 3-12   *Using a limited queue to limit demand to capacity*

team's velocity or throughput measurement to determine the size of the queue needed to absorb variation. When variation is moderate and velocity is stable in an iteration system, two or three iterations are often a long enough queue for small requests. In a kanban system, resist the temptation to build up a long queue of demand that is waiting for one of the limited slots on the kanban board. In either case, if dead items collect at the bottom of a queue, assume that the queue is too long; it is doing more than absorbing variation.

---

25. For example, a small request system may include simple upgrade and/or maintenance requests.

Let's say that you have set up a limited queue and it fills up (of course). When a new request arrives, there is no room in the queue. So what do you do? If the queue is full, the value of the new request should be compared against the value of existing requests in the queue, and *one of them should be discarded*, based on their relative value, combined with good judgment. The decision should ideally be an immediate decision; it should not need to wait for a committee meeting.[26]

"But," you protest, "our customers won't tolerate that!" Or "How will we learn what customers want if we turn down their requests?" Or "How will we keep track of what has been discarded?" Or "Won't customers simply keep their own queue?" Or "What do we do with the list we have now?" These are all good questions, and you should search for good answers. But answer them in this context: You do not have the capacity to do the work in your current situation, so work is, in fact, not going to get done. If your customers don't already know that, they will figure it out for themselves pretty soon at a negative cost to your relationship with them.

If you are able to make promises that you can keep and let your customers know promptly when you will not be able to accommodate a request, they will usually appreciate your honesty and be glad to know what will happen with their request sooner rather than later. Moreover, even though you have to turn down requests, you should maintain a good communication path with your customers so you know what is annoying them about your products and development system, and what improvements you should be thinking about. However, it's hard to imagine that accepting every request and ignoring most of them is going to help you gain more knowledge about how you can serve your customers better. Ethnography will work a lot better.

When a queue gets too long and develops a dead area at the bottom, some development organizations move the dead items to a secondary queue of ideas. Work in this queue is not "accepted" work, and in our experience it probably will never get done. But it can be useful for statistical analysis and to remind yourself of the kinds of things you don't have time to do. As for your current queue, clean it out as much as possible, put what fits into a limited queue, and then find a sensible way to deal with what's left, while admitting that in all probability it will never get done.

---

26. Corey Ladas suggests using a progressive priority filter—a kanban board with three priority columns. Priority 1 items are strictly limited; priority 2 is limited to twice as many items; priority 3 has a higher limit. This cushions the decision to throw things out, but when all three columns are full, you still have to discard requests. See Ladas, *Scrumban: Essays on Kanban Systems for Lean Software Development*, 2008, pp. 163–70.

"We Now Have a 'Never' List"

It was about three months after the executive had attended our class. He was showing us the improvements the company had made, which were impressive.

"But do you know the best thing that's happened?" he asked? We couldn't guess.

"We now have a 'Never' List! It was like a breath of fresh air throughout the company."

I could believe it. The development team now had reasonable expectations from management and honest communications with the marketing department. Everyone knew what to expect and when it would be delivered. Furthermore, because there were far fewer requests on the list, the time from request to delivery of those requests that were on the list was dramatically shortened.

Mary Poppendieck

Scheduling Larger Systems

Suppose that you need to develop a very large system, and efforts to decouple the system into smaller systems are not practical. This is particularly likely when software is part of a much larger physical system—maybe an air traffic control system or an airplane. What does a pull system look like for large systems?

We recommend that you do *not* start out by breaking down the work into detailed tasks, getting estimates on each task, and then laying out the tasks in a schedule. Why? The tasks have probably not been vetted; you are not sure they are what the customers really need, or what other parts of the system will actually require. And since this is a large system, you can be sure that it will be complex and will take a long time to develop. Therefore, you can be sure that the customer needs and available technology will change over that time. Complexity and change usually make it impossible to create a detailed list of features that will be valid over time, let alone tasks derived from these features.

In addition, just about every software system we know of has a lot more features than it needs.[27] That extra scope is the result of the way our industry usually plans work: We determine scope at the beginning of system development, put a

---

27. Jim Johnson, chairman of the Standish Group, first called this to our attention in his keynote talk at XP 2002 in Sardinia. Since then we have often asked the groups we address if the majority of features in the software they work on are frequently used or essential to the system. We rarely find people who think their systems pass this criterion.

box around it, and figure out how long that scope will take to develop. This is the wrong approach. A better approach was used in the Empire State Building: Start with the valid constraints of the system, and then design the system to fit within those constraints.

The constraints exist. Deadlines are usually very important to a business. The amount of money that can be invested to achieve a benefit has valid economic limits. On the other hand, in the overwhelming majority of cases, scope in a software system is not only expendable; it is usually overblown and selected by people who do not accept accountability for, or have the knowledge needed for, fitting the work within the constraints. Let's be honest; customers do not need scope. They need to have business goals accomplished within some constraints of time and cost. So it is imperative that the real constraints of time and cost be used to limit scope, and this imperative holds true in almost every situation we have encountered in software development.

Timebox—Don't Scopebox

So how is this done? How are constraints used to limit scope? We recommend that you think of scheduling as an exercise in timeboxing, rather than an exercise in scopeboxing. Lay out a timeline to match the valid constraints established during concept development. Establish deadlines along that timeline—preferably at even intervals not more than three months apart. Each deadline should be meaningful; it should be either a release date or, for larger systems, a synchronization point for making critical decisions. Each deadline defines when a general capability will be finished. These deadlines constitute a set of intermediate timeboxes.

As we mentioned in Frame 9: Proven Experience, the team laying out this timeline must have the knowledge necessary to be confident that the goals can be met within the constraints, the proven capability to solve similar problems, and the responsibility to make it happen. If this is not possible, do not commit to a schedule that is beyond what you have the proven capability to deliver. Use evolutionary development and commit only to the immediate deadlines that you are confident can be met.

Assuming that an experienced team can confidently establish a reasonable series of deadlines or synchronization points, scheduling is done backward from each deadline. If possible there should be different workflows that can be decoupled and planned separately, although it is a good idea to synchronize workflows at the deadlines. For most cases, it is adequate to limit detailed planning to the next deadline; for example, one of the activities at a synchronization meeting might be to create a more detailed schedule for work due at the next deadline. Of course, some look-ahead to long-lead-time items needed at future deadlines may also be necessary.

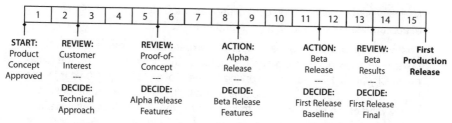

Figure 3-13 *A 15-month schedule for a software product*

A schedule for a software product that takes 15 months might look like Figure 3-13.

Notice that in this schedule there is no commitment to what features will be in the first production release until four months before that release, and the complete list of features is not finalized until two months prior to the first production release. It is very important to defer public commitment to exactly which features will be in the product, because this makes it possible to reliably release the product on time. The release date is guaranteed, but the exact features are not. *Timebox—don't scopebox.*

The key imperative of this kind of scheduling is that *the deadline should always be met.* Unfortunately, many people in our industry have become accustomed to not meeting deadlines because they have been given impossible deadlines or impossible push scheduling processes to work with. Push scheduling rarely works; you cannot break down scope in detail, lay it out on a timeline, then push this detailed schedule out to an organization and expect it to be followed. This deterministic approach does not take variation or learning into account and thus is almost guaranteed to fail at any scale, unless considerable slack is built into the process. On the other hand, scheduling approaches that pull work from sound intermediate deadlines have a good track record of success.

Case Study: Large System

In 1980 I was a process control engineer; my boss was Roland Reyers, who managed I&CS—Instrumentation and Control Systems. This was a group of about 20 very seasoned engineers who knew everything there was to know about how to build control systems for 3M tape-making processes. I was the new kid on the block; I could program these new things called minicomputers.

The Oklahoma City plant had commissioned a new process line to be built, and Roland wanted to experiment with a new computer control system. A few of my colleagues from Roland's group would design the process control equipment, using a PLC (programmable logic controller) for the digital logic.

My job was to provide analog control and operator interface, including transfer of appropriate control information to and from the PLC.

The project manager was George, a very experienced engineer who worked upstairs in an engineering group dedicated to the division that ran the Oklahoma City plant. He had been working on the project for maybe a year by the time I was assigned to the project. He had handled the architectural design of a new wing of the plant and saw to its construction. His colleagues were well along in designing the process equipment. Roland had known about the project all along, and he also knew that the time for his group to get involved was about a year before the scheduled plant start-up.

George set the milestones: date to ship to plant, date to be on-site for start-up, and actual start-up a month later. From those deadlines our I&CS team scheduled backward: We allowed perhaps six months before shipping to build and bench-test the control system, which meant we had to order equipment perhaps two months before that. We had our equipment set up in a room near our offices, and we tested our interfaces there. When we needed information from the engineers designing the process equipment, we went upstairs and talked to them.

We knew the deadline for plant start-up, and it went without saying that it would be met. But it was not George's job to worry about what the I&CS team was doing; it was Roland's job to be sure we got the control system done on time. And he certainly was not going to let us be late; that would be much too expensive for the division and a career-limiting event for him. In fact, Roland's group was never late. He was a very experienced process engineer, and he kept his two top engineers unassigned to projects so they could jump in whenever there was an emergency or help us whenever we needed it. At the beginning of most days, the senior engineers in Roland's group gathered in his office for a cup of coffee. At those informal meetings, we solved the problems of the world and the problems of the company, and occasionally we talked about our projects. That was about all Roland needed to keep up to speed on what everyone was doing.

And that was how the project was managed. No tasks, no Gantt charts, no critical path. 3M had developed this process over the years; it was reliable and repeatable. New plants, complete with complex processes and the latest technology, were routinely on time, and the new manufacturing processes produced superb products. Every project had a budget and schedule that were generated from experience. It had a contingency based on the level of risk of new technology—and there was a strong bias in favor of trying out risky new technology. There was no attempt to put together a detailed spec at the beginning because the technology was going to change. There was no work breakdown structure except in the heads of the appropriate engineers, no tasks or task tracking. There were just very clear deadlines that were *always* met.

Mary Poppendieck

Portfolio Management

Managing medium and large development efforts is usually more complicated than using a limited queue as we recommend for small requests. There may be a significant amount of knowledge embedded in these larger efforts, and you need to find a way to capture and leverage that knowledge. Furthermore, larger efforts are often handled by several different teams, and there are probably multiple business objectives to take into consideration when scheduling this work. Therefore, many companies use some sort of portfolio management approach to manage larger, more important requests and initiatives. There are many ways to do this, and we certainly do not have the definitive answer on the subject. But we would like to suggest a novel approach that you might try.[28]

The first step in lean portfolio management is to classify development efforts by type. For example, you might have business feature upgrades, strategic business initiatives, and infrastructure upgrades; you may also need to leave some time for maintenance. The next thing to do is to determine the cycle time (timebox) that you will allow for each type of effort. It may seem strange to timebox strategic initiatives, but if the Empire State Building could be built in a year by creating a design based on the constraints of the schedule, you might be able to make this work also.

Once you have a timebox for each type of effort, lay out a schedule that shows how many initiatives of each type you have the capacity to do in a year (see Table 3-1).

The table shows that you are allocating two slots of six months each for strategic business initiatives, 12 two-month-long slots for business feature upgrades, and a full year for the ongoing infrastructure upgrade effort, and you are reserving 20% of your capacity for other efforts, including maintenance. You

Table 3-1 *Classification of Development Effort by Type*

Type	Timebox	Number per Year
Strategic business initiative	6 months	2 of these
Business feature upgrade	2 months	12 of these
Infrastructure upgrade	12 months	1 of these
Other (e.g., maintenance)	Ongoing	20% of capacity

---

28. This approach is recommended in Ward, *Lean Product and Process Development*, 2007.

now know how much capacity you need for the year for medium and large requests and initiatives, and you know the staffing levels you need to provide that capacity. You can wait to decide on *which* business features you will work on until just before you start them, but you know that you have the capacity for 24 of them. Similarly, you can select the second strategic business initiative half-way through the year.

We recommend that you create permanent cross-functional teams to carry out this work and assign work to teams, not teams to work. Why? There is incontrovertible evidence that teams are much more effective when they stay together over time.[29] It takes time for new teams to get used to working together effectively, so newly formed teams are the least productive and have the lowest quality.

There is another reason why teams should stay intact: This decouples the workflow of a team from that of most other teams. Thus if an intact team is a bit delayed on one business feature, it can absorb the variation by taking a bit less time on the next business feature. On the other hand, the constant re-forming of teams that is typical of many portfolio management systems creates tightly coupled workflows, so any variation in one team cascades to multiple subsequent efforts and across many teams. Any increase in productivity that you think you might gain from such tightly coupled workflows is largely illusory.

Of course, teams may need access to individuals outside the team who have deep expertise in specific areas, and you will have to give some thought to how you will assure that such expertise is available as needed. Nevertheless, teams should be asked to deliver specific business outcomes within a planned time-box, and they should have the capability and leadership needed to do so. Generally, scope should not be part of the objective; scope should be determined by informed and ongoing decisions—driven by short feedback loops—about what is necessary to deliver the desired customer outcomes.

---

29. See Hackman, "Why Teams Don't Work," 2009. An excerpt: "Consider crews flying commercial airplanes. The National Transportation Safety Board found that 73% of the incidents in its database occurred on a crew's first day of flying together, before people had the chance to learn through experience how best to operate as a team—and 44% of those took place on the crew's very first flight." When asked why airlines don't keep crews together, Hackman answered: "Because it isn't efficient from a financial perspective. Financially, you get the most from your capital equipment and labor by treating each airline and each pilot as an individual unit and then using an algorithm to maximize their utilization." Maximizing utilization is the same justification often given for constantly re-forming project teams. It's amazing how much damage has been done in the name of maximizing utilization.

Frame 12: Adaptive Control

You can try to get better all you want, but if you can't see the effects, two things will happen: You won't get any better and you'll stop caring.[30]

The most robust systems are designed to continually monitor their own performance, compare it to the ideal, and adapt their parameters based on this feedback, to move performance closer to the ideal. The essence of adaptive control is to put good feedback mechanisms in place and use the feedback effectively.

Customer Feedback Every Iteration

Feedback has a lot of advantages:

1. Feedback improves the system under development.

2. Feedback improves developers' technical capability.

3. Feedback improves the team's ability to deliver desirable customer outcomes.

4. Feedback increases motivation.

That's a rather good lineup of benefits for something that shouldn't cost very much more than a leader's attention. It would seem to be a good investment. So why doesn't feedback happen more often? In fact, why not have the team obtain direct feedback from customers every iteration? There can be many reasons why not, but it usually boils down to the fact that the development team or the customers or both do not see the value of frequent, direct feedback from customers when compared to the difficulty in obtaining it. Therefore, feedback at the end of an iteration is often provided by a customer proxy. We urge you to consider the multiple benefits of direct customer feedback and find ways to make it an essential part of every iteration.

Sometimes we hear that it is difficult to get feedback from customers because they are too busy. If this is true in your case, perhaps customers do not see the benefit of providing feedback; you have to create a feedback program that has something in it for them. We have found that customers are usually happy to give feedback when it means that they will get something they are interested in, that actually does a job they really need done. Of course, the system must be very simple to install and/or check out, and giving feedback must be extremely

---

30. Paraphrased from a quote of Steve Kerr in Colvin, *Talent Is Overrated: What Really Separates World-Class Performers from Everybody Else*, 2008, p. 70.

easy. How easy is it for your customers to check out your software and give meaningful feedback?

It is not necessarily practical to engage customers in providing feedback to developers in every situation. Furthermore, there are different types of customers for most systems. The people who support systems value different things from those who use the system. Those who pay for the system may also have different values. So depending on the environment, a development team will want to carefully consider how and from whom it should obtain feedback. But by all means, the team should search out as much direct customer feedback as is practical, as often as possible—preferably every iteration.

"Customer Feedback Won't Work for Me"

I was discussing the benefits of customer feedback when a colleague said, "That wouldn't work for us. We can't ask our users how to improve our software."

"Oh, why not?" I was curious.

"Well, their companies pay us for the information they get from our data repository, so the business owners are our most important customers, and they would rather not pay for too much use of our system."

"I see," I replied.

"We do spend a lot of time watching how our users interact with our system. We look for things that are inconvenient, and for ways to improve their productivity. We take that information and create new features and products. This can result in more use of the product, but we also have to be sure that the business owners feel like they get a good value for any increased use. It's a delicate balance."

In this case the important thing was to recognize that different stakeholders had different values; moreover, it was important to spend time keeping those values aligned.

Mary Poppendieck

Frequent Releases

Your objective should be to move work through your workflow in small batches, all the way through to release. You should be obtaining feedback every iteration, but there is really nothing like the feedback that you get through releasing a system for sale or to production. We have heard many variations on the theme: "We thought we knew what our customers wanted, but we were dead wrong." Some are able to add, "Luckily we were doing early releases so we could change course and develop the product they really wanted." If you want to know what customers really want, give them what you think they want and listen to what they have to say about it. And remember this principle: What they want will be changed by what you deliver. So the earlier you are in the development process when you get this feedback, the more useful the feedback will be. Leave time in your schedule to respond to the feedback!

Going live is also an excellent way to improve the team members' competence. In Frame 8: Deep Expertise, we talked about the role of deliberate practice, with competent feedback, in developing expertise. Deliberate practice in development might be summed up this way: *If something is hard, do it frequently and you'll become good at it.* The more often a team goes all the way through a release cycle, the more reliable they become at going all the way through the release cycle, quickly and without errors. Automation scripts will get developed, lists of recommended coding patterns to adopt and to avoid will grow, and previously tricky problems will be solved routinely.

Consumability

Release time may be a time for the development team to breathe a sigh of relief, but for customers, all too often a new release is the beginning of pain and expense. The setup time versus waiting time curve holds for customers as well as development teams: While there may be some minor benefits in the new release, these can easily be outweighed by the cost of switching to something new.

A development team should find out the answers to a few questions before they ask customers to deploy a release and provide feedback: "How easy is installation? Configuration? How intuitive is the system to use? How many 3:00 A.M. calls does the operations group get with a new release? How easy is support? Troubleshooting? How long does it take for the system to deliver the value?"

These are not questions that a typical development team can answer, but it is important to find out the answers. In Frame 7: Evolutionary Development we discuss how to use ethnography to obtain good feedback. The first kind of feedback you are looking for is "How consumable is our product?" The next step is to make it consumable enough that you have customers who are willing to accept frequent releases and are interested in helping you with even more feedback.

A new release may not be for everyone, so it's best not to push a release to all customers at the same time; release to customers who are eager for the release. To minimize your long-term support costs, create incentives for other customers to pull the latest release when they need support or new features, so you don't end up supporting multiple releases of your software in the field.

Escaped Defects

No matter how hard you try, an occasional defect will escape to production despite your best efforts. Ideally, this is a rare event. When it happens, the defect is likely to be a devious problem that causes strange things to happen in other systems you didn't know about during development. Because of a big security fence between development and production, you are unlikely to hear much about many of these defects, let alone participate in chasing them down and finding their root cause. Certainly not every operational problem is caused by software, but a lot of them are. And when they are, the development team should be keenly interested in discovering what it was about its design and testing practices that caused the defect and allowed it to escape. In our experience, this kind of feedback is usually not sought and generally not welcome. This is a mistake. The only way to prevent escaped defects in the future is to examine the ones that occur in the present, methodically find their root causes, and, one by one, eliminate them.[31]

Customer Outcomes

You have not closed the loop until the development team sees the impact of its work on the customer outcomes. How many days did the new business process shave off the order fulfillment process? How is the new product selling? Does the new payment system meet PCI standards?[32] How many additional customers signed up because of the features in the latest release? And so on. If the purpose of development is to drive these measurements, and decisions are made based on the ability to drive these measurements, the results have to be made visible so that the team can get feedback on the results of its decisions.

"We haven't taken your advice on customer outcome measurements seriously" is the frequent response. "It's too hard to decide what those measurements should be, our customers don't want to be pinned down, and anyway, they are lagging measurements. Besides, we don't want to hold the development teams responsible for what they can't control. So we leave those kinds of decisions to the product owner."

Wrong answer. Excuses like these mean that very smart developers have been confined to doing what they are told, rather than being asked to creatively solve real problems. The idea that developers should not be held responsible for what they cannot control implies—between the lines—that the system will fail.

---

31. We recommend Nygard, *Release It! Design and Deploy Production-Ready Software*, 2007, and Zeller, *Why Programs Fail*, 2006, for more insight in this area.

32. Payment Card Industry (PCI) standards are the security standards that keep credit card transactions safe. They are very difficult to meet.

Because if the system is successful, developers are not responsible either. If developers do not know whether or not their work is ultimately successful, they cannot learn how to improve, and they will probably stop caring. If you wonder why your best people just put in hours during the day and work enthusiastically on open-source projects at night, it's because open-source work provides constant, useful feedback as well as credit for their work over the long term. The feedback helps them get better, and the credit keeps them passionately interested in their work.

Portrait: Product Champion, Take 2

When we left the product champion in Chapter 1, a product concept had been approved and it was time to start implementation. Product champions don't just have good ideas; they are passionate about their ideas and so they shepherd them through implementation and make sure they get delivered. Our past attempts to list the characteristics of a good product champion have not done the role justice, so we decided to tell the story of an effective product champion instead.

The Story of a Product Champion[33]

Name: Chris Hughes
Born: November 26, 1983
Title: Online organizing guru
Product: MyBO

February 2004, Harvard University

Chris Hughes's roommate, Mark, was annoyed; Harvard had refused to put the facebooks online. (Facebooks were paper booklets with names, photos, and such that you got at freshman registration.) So Mark decided to create a Web site where students could post their own facebook entries, bypassing official concerns about confidentiality. In the first three weeks the site had 6000 entries. Within a month, the roommates decided to add Stanford, Columbia, and Yale to the site. Chris Hughes was adamant: Each school had to have its own site, its own facebook. He somehow knew that general-purpose networking wasn't the idea; connecting with the people you were likely to meet on campus was the important thing. His instincts were exactly correct. Facebook became a campus meet-up site tailored to each campus.

33. See "How Chris Hughes Helped Launch Facebook and the Barack Obama Campaign" by Ellen McGirt, *Fast Company,* March 2009.

June 2004, Palo Alto

With active users on a path to hit a million by the end of the year, the three roommates drove west in search of adventure and venture capital. Mark Zuckerberg and Dustin Moskovitz never returned to Boston. Hughes finished up his last two years at Harvard, working for Facebook in his spare time, guiding the details of how Facebook actually worked. He didn't write code; he was the people guy.

Fall 2006, Palo Alto

Chris Hughes was now working full-time at Facebook. For the first time, politicians who were running in the fall elections were invited to create Facebook pages. There was this senator from Illinois who wasn't running for election but asked for a page anyway. Chris Hughes was a founder and the idea person, and in a small company he would be the person to deal with such a request. He helped to set up Barack Obama's Facebook page, and he came to really like the senator. Hughes decided that he had to see if the tools he had helped invent at Facebook could be used to organize support in a political campaign.

February 2007, Chicago

Chris Hughes was 23 years old, and for three years he had been pouring his energy into helping students connect online. Now he wanted to see if he could use those same tools to help connect people who wanted to get Barack Obama elected with each other. The day Obama announced his candidacy, MyBarackObama.com (MyBO) went live. Hughes could imagine thousands of people out there who wanted to help in some way to elect Obama. If they went to MyBO, they could find the 900 other people in their zip code who also wanted to do something to get Obama elected. They could set up a fundraising page or join their neighbors in organizing a rally. They could get a list of doors to knock on, complete with scripts of what to say. Eventually the site had all of these tools and many more. But in February, most of the tools existed only in the mind of Chris Hughes, who didn't have nearly the help he needed to make the site what he dreamed it could be.

Summer 2007, Chicago

Learning all he could about politics was hard for Chris Hughes, but he had a vision of what could happen, so he kept at it. He got some funding—not as much as he wanted—and focused his efforts on developing the tools that he felt were most needed. And he was the person behind the site. If you hit the Help button, Hughes would get your e-mail and he would respond. Because of his deep involvement, Hughes could see what eager volunteers needed to keep them engaged—usually information, material, ideas from others, and local contacts. The ability of the site to easily answer volunteers' questions grew, if for no other reason than that Hughes could answer only so many e-mails in a day. He was desperate for funds to improve the site, but all the campaign resources were focused on winning the primary in Iowa.

January 2008, New Hampshire

Barack Obama won a surprise victory in Iowa; Hillary Clinton won a surprise victory in New Hampshire. Suddenly everyone realized it was going to be a long campaign, one that would require organizing in four dozen states. There wasn't time to set up that many organizations. But when the campaign workers arrived in state after state, they found that thousands of people were already organized, holding rallies, knocking on doors, raising money. Hughes became the center of attention. He reminded campaign organizers that he had been begging for help to improve the site. Suddenly he got all the help he needed. He oversaw a rapid expansion of tools for self-organizing campaign workers, and the campaign saw a rapid expansion of self-organized campaign workers. Hughes paid special attention to the site's carefully crafted look and feel; after all, he had spent the last year figuring out just exactly what would energize political volunteers.

June 2008, Denver

Barack Obama was nominated by the Democratic Party, and Chris Hughes became even more central to the campaign. Sophisticated voter registration drives were added to MyBO. Volunteers got lists of people to call on election day. Use of the site exploded. Chris Hughes remained at the helm, organizing just the right timing for e-mail campaigns, understanding exactly the right way to keep everyone engaged. Other campaigns tried to imitate the site, without much success. Hughes had been at this now for almost five years. He knew exactly what he had set out to accomplish, and it was working.

November 2008, Chicago

It was 10:00 P.M. on election night. The California polls had just closed. Two dozen members of the online crew pounded out the final e-mail messages and sent them off. Then they raced downstairs to catch a waiting trolley to Grant Park, to hear President-elect Obama's acceptance speech. But the MyBO product champion waited upstairs for just a bit longer, to be sure that all of the e-mails got out OK. That's what product champions do: They make sure their baby works above all else. When he got downstairs, the trolley had left. Chris Hughes ran all the way to Grant Park. He made it just in time.

Your Shot

1. We recommend that you start with system constraints (e.g., cost, delivery, business outcomes) and then design a system to fit within those constraints. Planning for a car at Toyota, for example, involves setting target costs for each component and challenging the designers to stay within the target; setting deadlines for development and expecting them to be met; determining overall vehicle selling points and deciding what that means in detail during development. The question is, Can you imagine using such an approach in your organization? Gather together a team and challenge the members to brainstorm the things that would have to change in order for you to use such a seemingly backward process.

2. Ask yourself/your team the following questions:
   a. Do you have a level flow of work through your organization, or is it characterized by surges of high demand and pressure? If you have uneven demand, what is causing it?
   b. Do you sort work into different queues depending on the size of the effort and handle it differently? Why or why not? How does that work for you?
   c. What is the ideal cadence for delivery of software to your customers if there were no defects, minimal test setup time, and no customer consumability issues or learning curve? How far away from the ideal are you? What is the biggest obstacle to the ideal cadence?

3. What areas of your organization are most suitable for iterations? For kanban? Why?

4. Design a kanban board to track and govern work as it flows through your organization:
   a. What are the steps of your workflow? Make one column for each step.
   b. What limits on work-in-process would you put on each step? Decide how many items you will allow in each step of the workflow and write it at the top of the column or draw in that number of boxes.
   c. Experiment with using the kanban board. Put cards for work-in-process in each column. When a workflow step is completed, move its card to the next column—but only if there is room. How would you handle the situation when there is no space in the next step of the workflow? How might you prevent that situation from occurring?
   d. How does the kanban board differ from an iteration board?

5. Do you reorganize teams on a regular basis? If so, what benefits do you believe you are getting from this? What drawbacks might these reorganizations have? Do the benefits outweigh the drawbacks? Gather data to prove your hunches are (or are not) correct.

6. We recommend a portfolio management approach that is quite different from typical portfolio management systems. First categorize the types of work you do, then establish a standard timebox for each type, and finally, lay out timeboxes on

a schedule. Later on, as the time approaches, you fill in the actual project that will be done in each timebox. Gather together a team and challenge the team to consider the practicality of such an approach in your environment. What are the advantages and disadvantages?

7. In the ideal situation, a development team should have a way to obtain feedback directly from customers every iteration. Do you have a way to do this? Is it expected? Routine? Not practical in your context? How does your organization provide development teams with the essential feedback that they need to be successful? Can you think of any ways to improve and increase this feedback? Are your teams passionate about achieving their objectives? Can you imagine ways in which feedback might help create passionate developers?

Chapter 4

Relentless Improvement

Snapshot

A hospital is a rather dangerous place these days. Very dedicated professionals are struggling with a system that has grown so complex it can defeat their best efforts. Gloria was a dedicated nurse who grew totally frustrated with solving the same problems every day for 20 years. We see what happens when she vows *"Nevermore!"* and sets out to solve problems once and for all from that day forth.

As president of Toyota Motor Corporation, Fujio Cho launched "The Toyota Way 2001" to serve as a guiding beacon for the people in Toyota as the company expanded globally. Two pillars form the foundation of "The Toyota Way 2001": *continuous improvement and respect for people.* Continuous improvement means "We are never satisfied with where we are and always improve our business by putting forth our best ideas and efforts. We form a long-term vision and meet challenges with courage and creativity to realize our dreams. We improve our business operations continuously, always driving for innovation and evolution. We believe in going to the source to find facts to make correct decisions, build consensus, and achieve goals at our best speed."[1]

Most organizations agree that continuous improvement is important, but few practice it as relentlessly as Toyota. Seeing problems is easy, but caring about them is not; creating an organizational consensus to truly improve the way work is done is yet more difficult. Effective leaders in cultures of relentless improvement act as mentors; they understand that their primary job—and the best way to meet their challenges—is to help everyone learn to see problems, solve problems, and share the knowledge.

Relentless Improvement

Visualize Perfection

Establish a Baseline

Expose Problems

Learn to Improve

Manager as Mentor

---

1. From Liker and Hoseus, *Toyota Culture: The Heart and Soul of the Toyota Way.* 2008, p. 15.

Sick Hospitals

"Complexity kills" isn't just a metaphor these days; it's the reality faced by hospitals around the world. Computer technology isn't the only technology to advance in giant leaps over the past few decades. A vast array of new drugs and treatments made their way into the health care system at the same time. People are recovering faster and living longer than ever, but on the flip side, hospitals are caring for patients who are older and sicker, with an ever-growing diversity of treatments. As the complexity of hospital treatment soars, the dangers of being a patient in a hospital increase.

Doctors, pharmacists, and nurses are highly educated, deeply committed people. They are extremely careful to do no harm. And yet, harm happens in a hospital. Medical and medication errors are estimated to cause almost 100,000 deaths a year in the United States alone, and a similar number of people die of hospital-acquired infections. Perhaps another million patients are injured annually but survive.

To take just one example, almost half of the people in an intensive care unit in the United States receive a central venous catheter (CVC) for diagnosis or infusion of treatments. For every day a CVC is in place, over a half percent of the patients will get an infection, which will be fatal 18% of the time. This means that there are perhaps 15,000 deaths per year in the United States due to CVCs alone, despite the fact that there are proven techniques to prevent most of these infections.[2]

The first reaction to these startling statistics is to search for someone to blame. But the real cause of sick hospitals is not the smart, dedicated people who work there; it is the complexity of the system that these people have to work within. The greatest breakthrough in health care improvement today can be found at hospitals where this simple fact is acknowledged and effectively acted upon.

The Checklist

In 1935—barely three decades after airplanes began to fly—Major Ployer P. Hill was killed while testing the plane that was to become the B-17 bomber. Although Hill was an extremely skilled test pilot, he had forgotten to release a new locking mechanism on the elevator and rudder controls. Airplanes had

---

2. See Spear, "Fixing Health Care from the Inside, Today," 2005; Spear, *Chasing the Rabbit*, 2009; and "100k Lives—Getting Started Kit: Prevent Central Line Infections," n.d. www.ihi.org/NR/rdonlyres/BF4CC102-C564-4436-AC3A-0C57B1202872/0/CentralLinesHowtoGuideFINAL720.pdf.

become so complicated that even the best pilots could no longer remember to do everything right, every time, even though their lives depended upon it. But the plane was important to the U.S. Army Air Corps, so a group of test pilots got together to figure out what to do about the complexity problem. It was clear that training was not the issue; no one had more expertise than Hill. So instead they came up with a simple mechanism, in use routinely to this day in airplanes around the world: the checklist.[3]

In 2001 Dr. Peter Pronovost, a critical-care specialist at Johns Hopkins Hospital, developed a five-step checklist for inserting CVCs:

1. Wash hands with soap.

2. Wear a sterile mask, hat, gown, and gloves.

3. Clean the patient's skin with chlorhexidine antiseptic.

4. Put sterile drapes over the entire patient.

5. Put a sterile dressing over the catheter site once the line is in.

Five simple steps that everyone knew should be done. For a month Pronovost had nurses check off these steps on a checklist for every CVC, and they found that about a third of the time, at least one step was omitted. So Pronovost persuaded hospital administrators to allow nurses to intervene if a doctor forgot a step. The results were astonishing: CVC infections dropped to zero almost immediately, and over the next two years the hospital saw only two such infections. It is estimated that over those two years, the checklist prevented 43 infections and eight deaths and saved $2 million in costs.

These results have been replicated in every hospital where the CVC checklist has been effectively implemented. An initiative in Michigan in 2004 and 2005 reduced intensive care unit infection rates by 60%, and some large hospitals effectively cut their infection rates to zero. But notice, the use of the checklist has to be effective. As simple as it sounds, implementing such a checklist requires a lot of work—and the devil is in the details. The specific antiseptic and the full drapes have to be readily available, because in an emergency there isn't time to go running around looking for supplies. Nurses have to become team members with doctors just as copilots are teammates with pilots, or their intervention will not be effective. And more items have been added to the checklist, as it has been discovered that, for example, the vein chosen for the catheter makes a difference, and removing lines as soon as they are no longer needed is also important.

---

3. Much information in this section comes from Gawande, "The Checklist," 2007.

The How-to Guide for CVCs from the Institute for Healthcare Improvement says:[4]

> Hospitals will not successfully implement the central line [checklist] overnight. If you do, chances are that you are doing something sub-optimally. A successful program involves careful planning, testing to determine if the process is successful, making modifications as needed, re-testing, and careful implementation. . . . All the stakeholders in the process must be included, in order to gain the buy-in and cooperation of all parties.

IHI recommends using the *Model for Improvement.* The model has two parts:

> Improvement teams should (1) set clear aims, (2) establish measures that will tell if changes are leading to improvement, and (3) identify changes that are likely to lead to improvement.

> Use the Plan-Do-Study-Act (PDSA) cycle to conduct small-scale tests of change in real work settings—by planning a test, trying it, observing the results, and acting on what is learned. This is the scientific method, used for action oriented learning.

No Work-arounds

Gloria[5] was a nurse in West Penn Allegheny Hospital who went to a talk by Alcoa CEO Paul O'Neill about Alcoa's goal of zero injuries. O'Neill said that the way to approach the goal was to *see problems, solve problems, and share the learning.* Gloria always thought of herself as a problem solver, but that day she realized that she had been solving the same problems over and over, every day, for the last 20 years. She decided to stop working around problems and get rid of them once and for all. Of course, she couldn't do everything all at once, so she announced to everyone in her unit that from then on, if anyone brought her a problem between 2:00 and 2:15 in the afternoon, she would make sure that problem never happened again. The next afternoon at 2:00, Gloria went to the center of the unit and waited. Nothing happened. She did it again the next day. Nothing. Finally, after a week, someone brought her a problem—a nurse was trying to take a patient's history and the chart was missing a form.

Gloria went to work. She met with the secretary who assembled patient charts and discussed how she knew what forms would be needed and how to make sure they were all in the chart. It took day after day of 15-minute sessions, but eventually Gloria and the secretary worked out a system that would

---

4. "100k Lives—Getting Started Kit: Prevent Central Line Infections," n.d., www.ihi.org/ NR/rdonlyres/BF4CC102-C564-4436-AC3A-0C57B1202872/0/CentralLinesHowto GuideFINAL720.pdf.
5. From Spear, *Chasing the Rabbit,* 2009, and Spear, "Fixing Health Care from the Inside, Today," 2005, pp. 341–46.

ensure that all of the charts would have the correct forms. The system worked so well that chart building took only two hours a day—it used to take nine. It was like having an extra secretary in the unit, and nurses no longer had to chase down missing forms, so they also had more time. Gloria could now take 30 minutes a day to solve problems permanently. The next problem to pop up was a registration problem, and when it was resolved, the unit had the equivalent of yet another secretary, and Gloria had more time to resolve problems because she had less firefighting to do.

There were plenty more problems to address. Patients in Gloria's presurgery unit could wait up to two hours between signing in and being registered, then they would have to put on flimsy gowns and wait in public for almost a half hour before being assigned a bed. Despite all of this time, a quarter of all patients had incomplete lab results by the time they went into surgery. Supplies were often unavailable, and others were overstocked and out of date. Gloria attacked the work-arounds for these problems by focusing on providing a better patient experience. As a result of her efforts, registration happened immediately upon sign-in, no one got in a gown until a bed was assigned, lab work was complete, and fresh supplies were always available. There was far more time to spend nursing patients, and everyone was less frustrated and stressed.

No Ambiguity

Consider a physician hurriedly writing up a medication prescription and then dashing off to see another patient. The prescription makes its way to the hospital pharmacy, where the pharmacist will fill the order. But this is not always simple. There can be ambiguous characters—a *u* (for unit) can look like a 4 or a 6. Leading and trailing decimal points can be missed. Doctors can miss the interaction of a medication with patient allergies or order an inappropriate dosage. So the pharmacist has to clarify the details of many prescriptions with the doctor who wrote them.

Shortly after Paul O'Neill[6] cofounded the Pittsburgh Regional Health Initiative in 1997, he asked a pharmacist to keep track for one day of how many of the prescriptions he received required follow-up with doctors before they could be filled with confidence. The next day the pharmacist reported that he had received 150 orders, and 148 of them required follow-up. The pharmacist thought this was a normal part of the job, not 148 errors and hours of wasted time. Eventually the pharmacy developed a standardized format and prescription

---

6. CEO of Alcoa at the time, later U.S. Treasury Secretary under George W. Bush.

form, eliminated ambiguous abbreviations and decimals, and reduced follow-up by 50%.[7]

Once a prescription is filled, nurses have to dispense the medicine, and opportunities for error abound when medicines are dispensed in similar-looking packages or names are difficult to read. Most complex systems fall apart at the boundaries between departments, where ambiguities as to what is needed by one department or what is to be done by another department create a series of small problems. When ignored, these small failures, over time, line up in just the wrong way and eventually produce a catastrophic failure. Given enough ambiguities between departments, mistakes grow into near misses that grow into medication errors, and eventually a lethal dose of medicine or a serious allergic reaction slips through.

Quick Experiments

In one hospital, the biggest problem the pharmacy faced was the fact that when nurses were supposed to administer medication, they could not find it. This triggered constant work-arounds for the nurses and pharmacists alike; it could consume hours of time. In the past, everyone in this hospital thought of these work-arounds as part of their job, but they came to think of each case of missing medication as a failure.

The pharmacists investigated the problem of missing medications in detail. They discovered that the root cause of the problem was that they were filling orders in batches, creating a 12- to 24-hour delay from the time the order was written to when it was filled. During that time, things would often change, and the orders would no longer be for the right medication. The pharmacists decided to establish a flow system to address this problem. To help design the system, they devised an experiment to establish customer demand and their capability to meet the demand. The first step in the experiment was to determine the rate of flow; they counted the orders from the day before and calculated that they would need to fill one order every three minutes to meet the demand. That led to the question of whether the pharmacy was capable of filling an order every three minutes.

To find the answer, the pharmacists created a simulation using the actual orders from the previous day; a pharmacist and a technician working as a team tried to fill one prescription every three minutes. (These simulated orders went into a box for restocking.) The pair filled the first two orders on time, but they

7. From Savary and Crawford-Mason, *The Nun and the Bureaucrat: How They Found an Unlikely Cure for America's Sick Hospitals,* 2006.

couldn't get the third order filled in three minutes. Why? The medicine could not be found quickly. The experiment resumed. Two more orders were filled on time. The sixth order took too long. Why? The label printer jammed. And so on. They did this all morning until they had a list of a dozen causes of delay. Then they tackled each one in turn, until they could fill every order in three minutes.

With these problems solved, the pharmacy was able to establish a flow system in which orders were filled and delivered in 2-hour batches rather than 24-hour batches. They found that not only did this reduce missing medications by 88%, but the new system was a great boon to the nurses who used to get perishable medications too early and had to store them in refrigerators at the nursing station.

A peer hospital learned about the improvement and tried to copy the tools and practices developed in the first hospital. But it didn't work—they could not take solutions for another hospital's problems and get them to work in a different environment. So they visited the first hospital and learned about their simulation process—their problem-solving process—and took *that* back to their hospital. The pharmacists in the second hospital developed a list of their own problems and developed solutions specific to their problems—solutions that were *different* from the ones used in the first hospital.[8] This is pretty typical; adopting "best practices" from other organizations means you are adopting their solutions to *their* problems. It is far more effective to learn how to devise your own solutions to *your* problems.

Frame 13: Visualize Perfection

Removing problems is important, but it's not the same as defining perfection and then removing what is preventing you from getting there.

—*Jason Yip*[9]

Shortly after Paul O'Neill became CEO of Alcoa in 1987, he met with his safety director, who was proud that Alcoa's safety record was the best in its industry of large machines, high heat, and dangerous chemical processes. O'Neill was not impressed. "From today onward our objective is perfect safety for all people who have anything to do with Alcoa." Why perfect? Because he wanted the

---

8. The pharmacy story is from Spear, "Fixing Health Care from the Inside, Today," 2005.
9. Thanks to Jason Yip for this insight. See http://jchyip.blogspot.com/2009/05/focus-on-efficacy-and-esteem-takes.html.

company to stop believing that accidents were inevitable and turn its attention to learning how to design and run processes that were safe. He wanted everyone in the company to learn how to *see problems, solve problems, and share the learning*.[10]

To make his goal effective, O'Neill required business unit presidents to inform him of any reportable accident within 24 hours. This guaranteed that every incident would be swarmed immediately, while the information was fresh. O'Neill required a plan for how to prevent similar accidents within 48 hours. Thus workers learned to take the time to develop countermeasures for each problem immediately after the problem occurred. Finally, leaders at all levels were expected to develop people who would see problems as they happened, address them immediately, and share the learning.

The results were impressive; in eight years Alcoa became the safest company in the world to work for, and it kept getting safer after Paul O'Neill left. Alcoa's lost-time accidents dropped by 96% in 20 years, while its productivity and financial results saw a remarkable improvement. At the same time, the company became a leader in cutting greenhouse gas emissions. Alcoa had learned how to learn.

The Theoretical Limit

Paul O'Neill had no use for benchmarking, because he didn't want people's aspirations to be limited by the best results achieved by others. Instead, he urged people, both at Alcoa and at the Pittsburgh Regional Health Initiative, to strive for the *theoretical limit*: no accidents, no harm, perfect patient care, delighted customers. Those were goals to inspire people, goals that were worth striving for.

Work systems will never be perfect, but the starting point for improving work is to establish a shared vision of what perfection looks like. At Toyota, for example, everyone knows that production and delivery should be[11]

Defect free—never compromising customer satisfaction.

On demand—only in response to real need.

One piece at a time—providing those who needed something exactly what they could put to use, not overburdening them with the obligation to hold things in anticipation of future need.

---

10. Information on Paul O'Neill and Alcoa is from Spear, *Chasing the Rabbit*, 2009, and Savary and Crawford-Mason, *The Nun and the Bureaucrat: How They Found an Unlikely Cure for America's Sick Hospitals*, 2006.
11. Spear, *Chasing the Rabbit*, 2009, pp. 195–96.

Immediate—providing those who needed something what they needed without any waiting time.

Without waste—never spending time, effort, creativity, and other efforts in ways that won't be valued by someone else.

Safe—so no one gets hurt physically or emotionally or is professionally threatened.

Secure—so that things go only to those intended and not to others.

A shared vision of the ideal keeps everyone heading in the same direction and keeps improvement relentlessly moving forward. Take the time to develop a shared vision of what success looks like in your organization, and challenge everyone to find a way to get there.

High-Velocity Organizations

In *Chasing the Rabbit*, Steven Spear calls companies that consistently lead their industries *high-velocity companies*.[12] He says these companies respond to changes faster than their competitors, so they are always ahead; this reminds him of the way rabbits quickly dart ahead of danger. High-velocity organizations, the rabbits, are characterized by their persistent ability to learn faster than their competitors.

Spear suggests that the main barrier to rapid learning does not lie within functions; it lies in the gaps between functions. He points out that the more complex the technology an organization must deal with, the deeper the technical capability it must develop. While most organizations—hospitals, manufacturers, system development organizations—have developed the capability to handle new technology in their industries, they have not developed the associated capability to coordinate this technology effectively across the increasingly deep technology silos. What sets high-velocity organizations apart from others is their ability to learn rapidly across an increasingly complex array of technical departments.

"High-velocity companies differ from low-velocity companies both structurally and dynamically," according to Spear. "Structurally, they insist that each piece of work be done with an eye to the larger process of which it is a part. Dynamically, they insist that each piece of work be done in such a way as to bring problems to the attention of those who can best analyze and solve them. . . . They do not encourage or admire workarounds, firefighting, and heroic measures. They want to solve problems, not put up with them."

Spear notes that high-velocity companies *do not try to predict* how to deal with complexity; they *focus on learning* about the complexity. This is a very

---

12. This section is from ibid., pp. 20–27.

important distinction. Consider a development schedule. A low-velocity company would think of a schedule as a plan and measure variance against that plan, engaging in the static process of *predicting* what it will take to meet the goal. High-velocity organizations are not in the business of making predictions; instead, they would regard a schedule as a *hypothesis* of what it might take to meet the goal. When there is a variance from schedule, the hypothesis would be disproved; *it would be obvious that the schedule isn't perfect.* A high-velocity organization *welcomes variance as a learning opportunity,* a way to discover more about the complexities of its work. High-velocity organizations do not focus on getting the work done; they focus on *learning how to get work done.* There is a huge difference.

Customer Focus

The way high-velocity organizations help their people learn across functional barriers is to focus everyone on customers, because customers span technology boundaries. For example, a patient in a hospital moves from one department to another and is served by many specialists. By focusing on each patient from the time he or she needs medical attention until the time the person is healthy, hospitals break down barriers between departments. When we sketch value stream maps of the system development process, we do the same thing—we look at customer demand from the time a customer has a need until that need is resolved; we observe the steps in our process that demand must traverse and how long it takes for the customer's problem to make this journey. Customers give us a boundary-spanning view of our work. By focusing on these end-to-end value streams and learning how to adapt them to meet customer-focused goals, we can become high-velocity organizations.

Focusing on the end customer is not enough, however. It is also necessary to focus on the way work flows across boundaries, especially in a complex organization. "One of the fundamental elements of TPS [the Toyota Production System] that management must be fully committed to is the 'customer first' philosophy," wrote Gary Convis, president of Toyota Motor Manufacturing Kentucky. "Typically, organizations envision the customer only in terms of the person who purchases the final product at the end of the process. TPS has a different view. Essentially, each succeeding process or workstation or department is the customer. In a Toyota plant, we work very hard to ensure that all team members and all departments realize their dual role: they are at once the customers of the previous operation and the suppliers to the next operation downstream."[13]

---

13. Convis, "Role of Management in a Lean Manufacturing Environment," 2001.

Frame 14: Establish a Baseline

If you think of the standard as the best you can do, it's all over.
The standard is only a baseline for doing further kaizen.

—*Taiichi Ohno*

Steven Spear believes (and many agree) that most of the problems faced by today's organizations originate in the complexity generated by the increasingly deep and specialized technology needed to make things work. Hospitals used to be much simpler. So did software. As complexity increases, so does the need for specialists. As specialists have to deal with more and more information, they frame the world through increasingly narrower frames, and the view of the overall system fades from view even as it grows more complex. Handovers between specialties are breeding grounds for ambiguities, work-arounds, and failures. If you look at the health care examples at the beginning of this chapter, you see that all of the problems were associated with spanning boundaries.

The first attack on boundary-spanning problems is usually to create cross-functional teams that work together, share and reconcile their mental models with teammates, and thus span the boundaries. This is an excellent approach. However, as complexity increases, cross-functional teams are not enough. There will be an increasing demand for deep specialties; people will be in different locations; customers will have a complex web of needs. In short, a single small team will not be able to handle the complexity; there will still be handovers. In all likelihood, the biggest problems with work flowing through a system development organization will be associated with those boundary-spanning handovers. Therefore, the place to start with work design is to look at the way in which work crosses boundaries.

Work Design

Consider a work stream that takes medium-sized customer requests for a software feature; approves or rejects them; develops, tests, and deploys software; and obtains feedback to see if the software is what the customer needed. Spear suggests that the design of this workflow can be broken down into four levels:

1. **Output:** How do (final) customers submit their requests? How do they find out whether the requests are accepted or rejected? How do they discover when the work is delivered and available? How do you obtain feedback that what is delivered meets the customers' needs?

2. *Pathway:* What is the flow along the value stream? Who (or what team) is responsible for performing what steps in what sequence? How do you know that each step was done successfully?

3. *Connections:* How do people (teams) know exactly what their immediate customers need and when they need it? How do people (teams) send a signal to an immediate supplier that they need something, what exactly they need, and when they need it? How do people (teams) know if they are ahead or behind in supplying their immediate customers and in getting what they need from their immediate suppliers?

4. *Methods:* How do people know how to actually do their work? How do they know they are successful? How do they get help when they are not?

We have dealt quite extensively with the fourth level, that is, the *methods* used inside cross-functional development teams, in previous chapters. But the biggest opportunity for game-changing improvement is usually found at team and organizational boundaries, where handovers occur. So let's take a look at the first three levels.

Output

The first level, *output*, starts and ends with the final customers—those who pay for, use, support, or derive value from the work. Making it clear who the final customers are and what they need from us is important because boundary-spanning problems are resolved by *focusing on the customer*. People who are doing work should understand the purpose of their work, *and* they need to be alerted when the system fails in any way to achieve its purpose.

Pathway

Teams should know specifically where their work comes from and where it goes. They should have a very direct knowledge of their *immediate supplier* and *immediate customer* (see Figure 4-1). In addition, they should know what other steps the work goes through before it arrives in their area and what steps it takes for the work to get to the final customers.

Connections

It is the supplier's job to determine exactly what the immediate customer wants and needs are, and the immediate customers' job to specify exactly what they need and when they need it. Consider, for example, those running a system test on our code. Do we know exactly what "system-testable" code is? Do we push code into system test or do they pull it? Do we have ways for people running

Figure 4-1   *Test-driven handovers*

system tests to signal us if there are problems? Do we respond to each problem aggressively and try to keep it from ever happening again?

After system test, do we know exactly what the next customer (i.e., the downstream operations department) needs from us? Do we understand what their definition of quality is? What they consider adequately tested software? What kind of installation scripts they require? How do we know they are ready for our software? What do they need to get ready? How do we know when they find escaped defects? How long does it take us to find out?

On the upstream side, do we have clear criteria for what kind of information we need to do our job? Do we accept work that is not "ready to code" and then struggle to figure out what to do with it, or do we have clear criteria for what we need in order to complete our part of the work? Do our suppliers know how many stories they need to make ready and when? Are they alerted immediately when we have problems?

With every handover, it is important to clarify the immediate customer's needs, timing, signaling when a problem is found, and so on. It is often appropriate to do this with a simple checklist. But in addition, it is essential that when something goes wrong with the handover, the failure is immediately apparent. The ability to be precise about handovers must be coupled with the ability to *know immediately when they fail.*

Test-Driven Handovers

Think about test-driven development. The idea is to use tests to *design* how the system should work and *fail immediately* whenever the design is violated. This is the exact same idea applied to the way work is done, aimed directly at handovers. In software development, the best teams fix every broken test immediately, and suddenly problems are easier to find, the code base becomes robust, and both quality and productivity improve substantially. This is a very reliable pattern.

Inside a development team practicing collective code ownership, an additional dynamic occurs. With collective code ownership, any member of the team may make changes to a particular piece of code; changes are not limited to an "owner" of a section of code. In order for the design to be handed off to the next developer successfully, the code must be accompanied by tests that will signal any failures caused by the next set of changes.

What we are proposing is that the same technique should be used for boundary-spanning handovers. The expectations of downstream customers should be defined with a test. When a test fails, the cause (some ambiguity in the handover) should be discovered immediately, the problem contained, and as soon as possible the handover details should be clarified—by the people doing the work.

Designing the Work of Software Development

If we describe the work of creating software in terms of Spear's four design steps, we have to first ask, "What is the output?" Eventually, the output is a working program. The test of working is that all the acceptance criteria are satisfied. Second, we need to identify a path, a collection of steps that will generate the output. Third, we need to define the connections and dependencies among the steps. Fourth, we need to choose the best way to carry out each step.

But, looking deeper, we see that the process is fractal. Software is created to solve a problem for someone, so the first level is to understand the problem. This is not easy! Someone has to go and see the actual situation, the task being done, the people doing the task, the issues they encounter, and formulate a collection of hypotheses that might address the problem as they see it. Each hypothesis needs to be verifiable at a number of levels. At the first level, the people whose problem is being addressed must concur that the proposal would work for them. At the second level, it needs to be ascertained that the proposal can plausibly be implemented technically. The creativity comes in designing the path and the connections and selection of methods. Whom will you talk to, what materials will you study, whose perspectives need to be considered, how do the myriad apparent constraints fit together, what methods will you use to figure these things out? Every problem is unique in some way and is best addressed by a different combination of methods connected in different ways and executed in a different order. Yet there will be patterns, and the deeper your domain and technical expertise, the quicker you will be able to create or adapt a work process that will create the needed outputs.

Developing software is not about writing code or drawing pictures. At its core, it is about developing and refining a nested collection of work processes, each of which produces a result that is verifiable by a test or test suite. Each result is a hypothesis about a part of the solution to the full problem. The execution of each work process certainly involves writing code and perhaps drawing pictures, but this is not the core.

The agile approach to problem analysis eventually produces stories, each of which describes an output. Spear observes that in high-velocity organizations, each output must be defined by tests to verify that the output is correct so that any deviation can be addressed and corrected immediately. The task of those implementing each story is to identify a path that will generate the desired outputs—that is, first, to identify a combination of connected behaviors that, when combined, will pass all the tests, and second, to select or devise methods that will produce each behavior and connection. Interspersed with all this design activity is the actual work of writing code. From this perspective, continuous integration and test-driven development are techniques that Spear would expect to generate high-velocity results.

Tom Poppendieck

Process Standards

Any discussion of work design inevitably brings up the controversial issue of process standards. In an article titled "The Coming Commoditization of Processes,"[14] Thomas Davenport writes that the purpose of process standards is to enable clear communication and clear handoffs across the business; as a result, it is possible to create comparative performance measures and outsource work more easily. Davenport claims that in particular, CMMI has had an enormous impact on improving the quality of software as well as facilitating the outsourcing of software development. Framing process standards in this manner carries the implicit assumption that once processes are sufficiently commoditized (de-skilled), anyone should be able to do any job—so people become fungible resources. This framing of process standards tends to be accompanied by the belief that it is important to roll out the same processes to all parts of a company.

We believe that this is an unfortunate distortion of the purpose of effective process standards. We have seen little evidence that pushing a centrally devised development process across all locations in a company is particularly effective, or that de-skilling development work leads to better systems. On the contrary, we observe that some of the best systems around—the Internet, the Google Search Engine, the Amazon Cloud—are the result of empowering local teams to act with courage and creativity to meet challenges and to independently devise and improve their own processes.

---

14. Davenport, "The Coming Commoditization of Processes," 2005.

Process standards had their origins in the scientific management movement of the early 1900s and rested on the theory that process experts and supervisors were the best qualified to design and control the work of individual workers in the pursuit of the most efficient output. A half century later, when Japanese products started outperforming their competitors in both price and quality, process standards were revitalized. It was observed that top Japanese companies followed detailed process standards, so efforts to copy this practice spread. Assessment approaches such as ISO 9000 and CMM/CMMI focused on assuring that companies had formal standards in place that were explicit and rigorously followed. But this framing of process standards led many companies to miss the real reason for standards: *The purpose of process standards is to act as a baseline for continuous improvement.* It is the overhead incurred to enable auditability that induces the waste, not the standards themselves.

In the book *Workplace Management*, Taiichi Ohno laid out his thinking on process standards:[15]

There is something called standard work, but standards should be changing constantly. Instead, if you think of the standard as the best you can do, it's all over. The standard is only a baseline for doing further kaizen. It is kai-aku [change for the worse] if things get worse than now, and it is kaizen if things get better than now. Standards are set arbitrarily by humans, so how can they not change?

When creating standard work, it will be difficult to establish a standard if you are trying to achieve "the best way." This is a big mistake. Document exactly what you are doing now. If you make it better than now it is kaizen. If not, and you establish the best possible way, the motivation for kaizen will be gone.

That is why one way of motivating people to do kaizen is to create a poor standard. But don't make it too bad. Without some standard, you can't say "We made it better" because there is nothing to compare it to, so you must create a standard for comparison. Take that standard and if the work is not easy to perform, give many suggestions and do kaizen.

We need to use the words "you made" as in "follow the decisions you made." When we say "that were made" people feel like it was forced upon them. When a decision is made, we need to ask who made the decision. Since you also have the authority to decide, if you decide, you must at least follow your decision, and then this will not be a decision forced upon you at all.

But in the beginning you must perform the standard work, and as you do, you should find things you don't like, and you will think of one kaizen idea after another. Then you should implement these ideas right away, and make them the new standard.

Years ago, I made them hang the standard work documents on the shop floor. After a year I said to a team leader, "The color of the paper has changed, which

15. Ohno, *Workplace Management*, 2007, p. 124. Used with permission.

means you have been doing it the same way, so you have been a salary thief for the last year." I said, "What do you come to work to do each day? If you are observing every day you ought to be finding things you don't like, and rewriting the standard immediately. Even if the document hanging there is from last month, this is wrong."

At Toyota in the beginning we had the team leaders write down the dates on the standard work when they hung them. This gave me a good reason to scold the team leaders, saying "Have you been goofing off all month?" If it takes two months to create these documents, this is nonsense. You should not create these away from the job. See what is happening on the gemba [in the workplace] and write it down.

In the book *What Is Total Quality Control? The Japanese Way*, Kaoru Ishikawa writes: "Standards and regulations are imperfect. They must be reviewed and revised constantly." "If newly established standards and regulations are not revised in six months, it is proof that no one is seriously using them." "Detailed standards and regulations are useless if they are established by headquarters staff and engineer-specialists who do not know or do not try to know the workplace and who ignore the wishes of the people who have to use them."[16]

If process standards are rules telling people what to do, improvement will be suppressed. If they are a baseline that workers are expected to improve, people will discover better ways to do their work than a central organization could ever imagine.

Frame 15: Expose Problems

I always want bad news first. Good news takes care of itself.

—*Barack Obama*[17]

Steven Spear started out studying Toyota, then moved to the heavy process industry and Alcoa, to the U.S. Navy Nuclear Propulsion group, and finally he worked with hospitals. His theory works in all these areas, so he speaks with some authority when he tells us what keeps these organizations ahead of the pack. High-velocity companies share goals among all departments along the value stream. They don't tolerate random workflow or stopgap measures. Not only do they specify how every handover is supposed to work, but they also create a test or checklist so everyone knows immediately when it doesn't. But the most important thing is that when the test fails, *people stop and swarm the*

---

16. Ishikawa, *What Is Total Quality Control? The Japanese Way*, 1985, pp. 62 and 56.
17. From an interview by Nina Easton, "Barack Obama on the Economy," *Fortune*, June 9, 2008.

problem close in time, place, and person to its occurrence.[18] They fix the problem once and for all and then share their new knowledge across the organization.

We know that this technique works for software development. We create automated test suites, and then when a test fails, we stop and fix the problem immediately. It's a tough discipline, but when it's done well, the results are amazing; we no longer have to spend half (or more) of our time debugging code, and we get higher quality as a side benefit. The same thing happens in work processes. We need to create an environment where problems are not ignored, but rather are exposed and dealt with immediately. But this is not as easy as it sounds, especially in cultures where people are expected to focus on the positive aspects of every situation.

Bad News First

On our study tour of Japan in 2009, we frequently heard the phrase "bad news first." What does "bad news first" mean? It means that you first look at everything you are doing from the point of view of what is wrong with it, not what is right about it. Instead of accentuating the positive, you constantly look for what needs to improve.

"Bad news first" reminds me of an Olympic athlete who has just completed an amazing performance and then talks to her coach. No matter how good the performance was, the first thing they discuss is what went wrong with the performance and needs to be improved, and only then do they discuss what went right.

I grew up in a culture where the operative frame is "good news first." We do not spend much time looking for what was wrong with what we just did and how it might be improved; we focus on the good aspects and use these positive points to gain approval from our peers and managers.

One of the most pervasive feelings I got on the study tour of Japan is that the people we met are much more diligent about looking for what is wrong and reflecting on how to improve than we tend to be.

Mary Poppendieck

One former Toyota manager we met in Japan said that when Toyota went to the United States to start the NUMMI plant, they had a lot of difficulty getting Americans to accept the concept of "bad news first." American employees were

---

18. Spear, "How Toyota Turns Workers into Problem Solvers," 2001.

trained not to bother their bosses with problems, so of course they routinely told their new Japanese managers there were "no problems" in their area. The Japanese managers would respond, "'No problem' is a problem." Still, it took a long time for workers to accept the practice of bringing problems to the surface so that they could be addressed.

> James Wiseman remembers the moment he realized that Toyota wasn't just another workplace but a different way of thinking about work. He joined Toyota's still-new Georgetown plant in October 1989 as manager of community relations. In Wiseman's early days, Georgetown was run by Fujio Cho [who eventually became the president of Toyota worldwide]. Every Friday, there was a senior staff meeting. "I started out going in there and reporting some of my little successes," says Wiseman. "One Friday, I gave a report of an activity we'd been doing . . . and I spoke very positively about it, I bragged a little. After two or three minutes, I sat down.
>
> "And Mr. Cho kind of looked at me. I could see he was puzzled. He said, 'Jim-san. We all know you are a good manager, otherwise we would not have hired you. But please talk to us about your problems so we can all work on them together.'"
>
> Wiseman says it was like a lightning bolt. "Even with projects that had been a general success, we would ask, 'What didn't go well so we can make it better?'" At Toyota, Wiseman says, "I have come to understand what they mean when I hear the phrase, 'Problems first.'"[19]

People who study catastrophes—from airplane crashes to nuclear power plant failures—have found that there is almost never a single cause for the disaster. In most cases, all of the things that went wrong leading to the catastrophe had gone wrong many times in the past without serious consequences. This situation led to complacency; small problems were ignored, so they became noise. But over time, several of these small failures lined up in exactly the wrong way and produced a disaster. It was just a matter of time.

You can view each failure that raises a small alarm as an opportunity to discover a better way to do work, or you can brush it off as bothersome noise that gets in the way of your "real" work. We believe that to get really good at your "real" work, you need to consider each small failure as a signal that you do not understand how work works, take it seriously, and learn from it. The purpose of problem solving is not so much to fix a problem as it is to really understand more about the complex system of work flowing through your organization and learn how to make things work better.

The most important thing in a continuous improvement environment is to expose problems, look for them, learn how to see them, and welcome them. Do not ignore problems or think of them as background noise. Problems are simply

---

19. From Fishman, "No Satisfaction," 2006.

the work process telling you that you don't understand it well enough, so pay attention and learn. Problems should never—ever—carry blame, because then they will just be suppressed and the opportunity to learn will be extinguished. Ignore problems and, like Gloria, you will get to work around the same problem every day, year upon year. Expose and welcome problems and you will have the opportunity to resolve them once and for all.

Go to the Workplace

Jeff Bezos, CEO of Amazon.com, sees great opportunity in exposing problems. "Everywhere we look (and we all look), we find what experienced Japanese manufacturers would call 'muda' or waste. I find this incredibly energizing. I see it as potential—years and years of variable and fixed productivity gains and more efficient, higher velocity, more flexible capital expenditures."[20]

Bezos was not speaking rhetorically when he wrote that he looks everywhere in the company for waste. He notes, "Every new employee, no matter how senior or junior, has to go spend time in our fulfillment centers within the first year of employment. Every two years they do two days of customer service. Everyone has to be able to work in a call center. Even me."[21]

And Bezos practices what he preaches. In March 2009, he spent a week at the Lexington, Kentucky, fulfillment center working alongside hourly employees to see what they do and hear their comments about their work. The local newspaper heard about the CEO's visit and asked for an interview, but it was turned down because "He's there to work."[22] Bezos's April letter to shareholders contained a hint about what he learned: "At a fulfillment center recently, one of our Kaizen experts asked me, 'I'm in favor of a clean fulfillment center, but why are you cleaning? Why don't you eliminate the source of dirt?' I felt like the Karate Kid."[23]

Do you know as much about your development processes as Jeff Bezos knows about packing boxes? Improving your work process is not about hiring consultants and having them deliver their wisdom to development teams. It's about everyone in the organization cultivating a firsthand awareness of the details of how things really work and a keen appreciation of how they can be improved.

---

20. Bezos, "Annual Letter to Shareholders," 2009.
21. Bezos, "The Institutional Yes," 2007.
22. Reported in the *Lexington Herald-Leader*.
23. Bezos, "Annual Letter to Shareholders," 2009.

Frame 16: Learn to Improve

At regular intervals, the team reflects on how to become more effective, then tunes and adjusts its behavior accordingly.

—Principle behind the Agile Manifesto[24]

Agile teams are encouraged to reflect on how they might become more effective, and many of them do this very well. However, a good number of agile teams lack the tools, capability, or time to adjust their processes continuously. End-of-iteration reflections—often called "retrospectives"—don't always progress beyond identifying problems, and problems don't get solved just because they have been identified. Problem solving takes time, so it must be an essential part of the work being done, not a peripheral activity that takes place when there's some leftover time.

Let's face it; there is never going to be enough time. People and teams need to learn to stop when something goes wrong, find out what caused it, and make time to fix it. They already know from system development that work goes much faster if they don't tolerate defects. The same philosophy holds true for work processes: First design a test-driven workflow, and when a test fails, take the time to find and fix the cause of the problem.

The Goal Is Learning

Say you have a problem that you want to solve once and for all. Just how do you do that? The *wrong* way to solve a problem is to try various things until the problem goes away and then consider it solved. Why? Think of a sick patient in a hospital. To cure the patient, someone must *diagnose* the cause of the sickness so that the known treatment for that cause can be prescribed. Problems for which a diagnosis is achievable can usually be rapidly and efficiently treated. Randomly giving patients medication until they get better would not even be considered. And yet, we randomly give our work processes medicine, adding on more and more "best practices," until the processes seem to get better. To make matters worse, we often keep the medicine in place out of superstition, adding more treatments on top of it to chase away other problems, until the work-arounds overwhelm us.

If you have not diagnosed why a problem occurred and do not have a good theory for why a particular countermeasure should work, adopting it as a solution is unlikely to address the root cause of the problem. This is not what problem

---

24. See http://agilemanifesto.org/principles.html.

solving is all about. It is important to start from the premise that *the purpose of problem solving is not just to get rid of the problem. The primary goal of problem solving is to learn about the way things work*, become better able to diagnose problems, become competent at prescribing countermeasures, and become experienced at monitoring countermeasures and adjusting them to achieve the best results.

"How Am I Going to Compete?"

We know of a manager who used to hold a high position at a Toyota plant, but he was offered a position he couldn't refuse: the job of general manager of a nearby competing automotive plant. After a few months on his new job, he confided to a close friend: "When I was a manager at the Toyota plant, I had 2000 problem solvers working in the plant. Now I have 10. How am I going to compete against 2000 problem solvers?"

Not very well, we speculate.

Mary and Tom Poppendieck

Problem/Countermeasure Board

One good tool for exposing and resolving problems that are local to a team is a problem/countermeasure board, one similar to the example in Table 4-1. An agile team might put such a board next to its iteration or kanban tracking board.[25]

Table 4-1   *Problem/Countermeasure Board*

Problem	Containment	Countermeasure	Owner	Status	Date
Escaped DB exceptions	Add catch statements		Marie	Plan	10/14
Browser Display inconsistencies	Fix inconsistencies	Test each feature for all supported browsers each iteration	Ashok	Act	10/01
Excess validation waste	Remove validation code from sections that could not be invalid	Clearly define trusted zones to establish where validation is reqd.	Bill W.	Check	10/16
Order Status too complex	Refactor current implementation	Establish arch guidelines for status	DGP	Do	10/05
Persistence of maiden name	Add to missing instances		ARG	Plan	9/28

---

25. Thanks to Jason Yip for introducing us to problem/countermeasure boards. See http://jchyip.blogspot.com/2009/05/problem-countermeasure-board.html.

Whenever someone spots a problem, that person writes it on the board, along with the containment or work-around that is being used if the problem cannot be resolved immediately. People who put problems on the board also add their name as the owner, unless someone else volunteers to be responsible for developing a permanent countermeasure. The status of each problem is either P (plan), D (do), C (check), or A (act). When a countermeasure is being worked on, it is entered in the "Countermeasure" column. The problem/countermeasure board is reviewed regularly, perhaps even daily, to recognize progress and encourage everyone to take the time to solve problems with the way things work.

Suggestion Systems

Suggestion systems are difficult to do well. All too often a suggestion box is put in a central location, people put in suggestions, and nothing happens. That's not much motivation for suggesting something else. We knew this when we started a suggestion system at our plant, and we were determined not to let our suggestion system languish from inattention to the ideas submitted.

We tried. We formed review committees, had deadlines for responses, got back to everyone, made valiant attempts to act on each suggestion. But it was too hard. There were no criteria for a good suggestion, so a huge number of the submissions were simply not actionable. And there were not enough people in the plant to act on even the good ideas. So for most of the suggestions, nothing happened.

When I read that Toyota implements a million ideas a year, one per employee per month,[26] I wondered one more time how this could possibly work. Then suddenly I realized what was wrong with our system: It was a *suggestion system*! We were asking people to turn their ideas over to someone else to implement. What we should have done was provide each person who had a suggestion with a mentor, to help guide him or her in clarifying and ultimately implementing the suggestion. Instead we took ideas away from people who could become passionate about them and turned them over to busy people who were usually far away from the problem that prompted the suggestion.

When people show up for work, invariably they are annoyed by some aspect of their job. It happens to me, it happens to you, it happens to the people in your organization. So ask yourself, "Are those people supposed to just grin and bear it, or do they have a way to fix the annoyance—permanently?" The change in Gloria's hospital came when she decided that she would no longer be annoyed, she would—personally—take the annoyances one at a time and

---

26. May, *The Elegant Solution: Toyota's Formula for Mastering Innovation,* 2007.

fix each one. No one gave her permission; she got her authority from developing a consensus among everyone necessary to institute each change.

Forget suggestion systems where people abandon their annoyances to a box and become increasingly cynical when no one notices how inane their work process is. Instead, provide mentors for everyone who is annoyed, someone who will guide them through the steps it takes to get rid of the annoyance once and for all. You will find that complaining clock punchers turn into passionate problem solvers when they are the ones responsible for fixing the things that make their job difficult.

Mary Poppendieck

A3 Thinking

No matter how cross-functional a team may be, there are always boundaries on either side, and as we noted before, the most intractable problems are likely to show up across those boundaries. So while a team can usually solve its internal problems, it also has to learn how to solve problems with the suppliers and customers of its work, and with the tools and methods it uses that span multiple teams. It may seem attractive to send a leader off to "remove impediments," but it is better for team members to learn how to solve the boundary-spanning problems themselves, with guidance from a leader.

A good tool to facilitate this process is the A3 problem-solving report.[27] An A3 report captures not just the problem-solving process, but also its rationale. It provides a mechanism for establishing responsibility, soliciting collaboration, and providing mentoring for solving boundary-spanning problems. A3 is a paper size: 297×420 mm, or roughly 11×17 inches. Figure 4-2 shows a template for an A3 problem-solving report, which is confined to one side of an A3 sheet and is typically handwritten.

The left side of the template has four planning steps to diagnose the real source of the problem, to ensure that the treatments make the situation sustainably better. The first step is to write a background statement, one that will catch the attention of anyone glancing at the report. Think of it this way: A lot of busy people will probably look at this report to contribute their perspectives

---

27. Shook, *Managing to Learn: Using the A3 Management Process to Solve Problems, Gain Agreement, Mentor, and Lead*, 2008, is an excellent book about how leaders can use the A3 process to mentor people in problem solving and gaining agreement. Sobek and Smalley, *Understanding A3 Thinking: A Critical Component of Toyota's PDCA Management System*, 2008, is a good summary of A3 thinking, including problem-solving techniques, proposal A3s, and status A3 reports. See also Poppendieck, *Implementing Lean Software Development: From Concept to Cash*, 2006, pp. 168–72, for an example of problem solving by a software development team.

Title: *What is this about?*

Owner: *Author of report*
Mentor: *Person guiding/assessing the process*
Date: *Current report version date*

Background:
1) *Why is this problem important?*
2) *What is the consequence of the problem?*
3) *Why should the reader care about it and contribute to improving?*

P

Current Condition:
1) *Show concisely how things work today. Tables, Graphs, Process Maps, Baseline Metrics, etc.*
2) *Exactly where is the problem?*

P

Goal / Target Condition:
1) *How much ought we be able to improve?*
2) *What improvements in metrics are likely?*

P

Root Cause Analysis:
1) *Build a Cause-Effect model to ensure you really understand the root causes of the problem. Use a sufficient problem analysis approach such as five whys, fishbone diagrams, or a cause/effect network to understand where changes can be made to address the problem under investigation.*
2) *Your hypothesis about how things work.*

P

Countermeasures (Experiments):
1) *Propose countermeasure to address each hypothesized root cause.*
2) *Predict quantitative improvement expected from each countermeasure.*
   If you do not have a basis for predicting the impact of a countermeasure, you do not understand your problem well enough. Do more analysis!
3) *Do quick experiments to prove or disprove your root cause analysis.*

D

Confirmation (Results):
1) *Actual Results - how the system responds to each countermeasure attempted.*
2) *Do the countermeasure impacts prove or disprove the hypothesis from your root cause analysis?*

C

Follow-up (Actions):
1) *What have we learned?*
2) *What should we do differently based on the results?*
3) *How should we change our standard way of working?*
4) *What do we need to do next to extend our understanding?*

A

Figure 4-2   *A3 problem-solving report template*

and ideas. You may have ten seconds to convince them to look at the rest of the report. The purpose of the "Background" section is to catch people's attention so they are intrigued enough to read the rest of the report.

In the "Current Condition" section, careful consideration is necessary to frame the situation well, so that people will collaborate with the owner to uncover the root cause, articulate credible theories, and devise and try counter-measures. When we ask teams in our classes to fill out this template, we often get a current condition statement such as "Customers can't make up their minds." This kind of statement needs to be clarified, so we might ask, "How do you find out what customers want?" or "Exactly what problem do you have because customers can't make up their minds?" It is often a good idea to sketch a simple value stream map of how things work today and then come up with a specific problem statement, for example, "The work coming into the planning meeting is often not ready to code." This section establishes both a baseline that characterizes the impact of the problem on the organization and a measure of whether steps taken actually make things better.

The "Goal/Target Condition" section makes it clear to everyone who reads the report what the ideal situation would be—what perfection looks like. This lays out the challenge; it tells people where the owner would like to be in the future.

The most important—and the most difficult—part of the planning side of the template is the "Root Cause Analysis"; it can be very difficult for a team without problem-solving experience to identify the root cause of a problem. A simple and often adequate way to find a root cause is to ask "Why?" five times; however, even this exercise can easily go astray. When those doing the analysis lack a holistic perspective on the cause-and-effect relationships in the environment, finding the root cause can be difficult.

Five *Whys*

When we use the A3 problem-solving template in our classes, one of the most common problems teams tackle is this: *Stories are not done at the end of iterations.*

Here is a typical "five *whys*" analysis of this problem:

1. Why aren't stories always done at the end of iterations?
   Because we underestimate how long they will take.

2. Why do we underestimate?
   Because the stories are too big.

3. Why are the stories bigger than we thought?
   Because José [or Maria, or whoever] doesn't break them down enough for us to fully understand them.

4. Why not?
   Because José/Maria doesn't know what we need—or because it is too hard.

5. Why don't they know what to do/Why can't they do it?
   We don't have ready-to-code criteria/the criteria are too difficult to meet or understand/the developers do not work with José/Maria to break down the stories sufficiently.

Thus the "five *whys*" help to bring us closer to the root cause of the problem, which in this case appears to be an ambiguous process for a handover from a supplier.

Mary Poppendieck

Sometimes there are many paths you can go down to find contributing root causes, in which case a fishbone diagram can be useful (see Figure 4-3). Note that in this figure, each branch may need further investigation (a few more *why*s) to get to the root cause or causes.

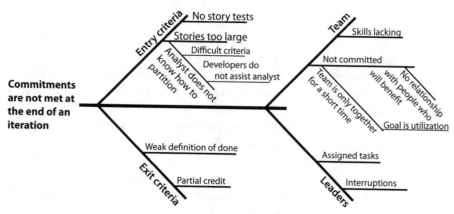

Figure 4-3 *Fishbone diagram*

Once the root cause or causes have been identified, list possible experiments to address each root cause. The experiments should be as rapid and inexpensive as possible, and as a general rule it is a good idea to predict the result of each experiment before doing it. If you create a theory of how the system will work with a countermeasure, you will always learn something from the experiment, whether the countermeasure succeeds or fails. The goal is to prove or disprove your diagnosis, check whether your proposed countermeasure resolves the problem, and thus learn more about the system.

After carrying out several quick experiments, some of which don't work and some of which do, you have increased your understanding of the system. Perhaps you know enough to recommend which countermeasures to make permanent. A summary of how the system works with these countermeasures should be included in the A3 report, along with an action plan to make the countermeasures permanent and spread the learning.

The criterion for a good A3 report is this: Someone familiar with the topic should be able to glance at an A3 report and understand it in ten minutes or less. This means that the report should use carefully constructed graphs, diagrams, tables, and a few short sentences.

Effective problem solving, with good analysis, experiments, and recommendations, is not a skill that most people bring to the job; it has to be learned. Therefore, it is important for individuals and teams to have a mentor to guide them in finding a good description of the current situation, doing an effective analysis, arriving at appropriate root causes, gaining cross-functional involvement, and trying out and implementing countermeasures.

Pull-Based Authority

In the upper right corner of the A3 problem-solving template, there is a place for its owner's name. Complex problems that span boundaries take time to resolve, and they should belong to someone who takes on the job of gaining the consensus necessary to solve the problem. The best person to lead the effort to resolve a problem is often the person who is most annoyed by the problem, or the person who was bold enough to raise the problem, or the person who was interested enough to suggest a solution. Below the owner's name is the name of a mentor, the person responsible for guiding the problem-solving process.

In the book *Managing to Learn*, John Shook shows how to use an A3 problem-solving report as a tool for the owner of a problem to *pull* the authority necessary to solve the problem. Let's walk through Shook's description of how lean companies solve boundary-spanning problems.

When a boundary-spanning problem and its "owner" are identified, the owner creates an initial A3 and signs it. The owner fills in as much as possible about the current condition and brings the A3 to a mentor, who reviews it and asks questions aimed at improving the description of the current condition. These questions will likely lead the owner to contact other involved parties and get their perspective, using the A3 as a quick way to present the problem to various people as they are drawn into the discussion.

Once the mentor sees a good assessment of the current condition, the owner of the A3 will work with team members and affected parties to come up with a root cause analysis. Under guidance from the mentor and with further collaboration with interested parties, the owner will be able to make the root cause analysis more insightful. Once the mentor agrees that credible root causes have been identified, the owner solicits ideas for countermeasures and their expected consequences, going to team meetings and talking with individuals, using the continually refined A3. It now becomes a summary sheet to track proposed experiments and their results. The affected groups *do* the countermeasure experiments and *check* the impact of each.

Finally, the A3 owner summarizes all of the findings in the "Confirmation" section and convenes a meeting where everyone will reflect on the findings and the resulting data. There are no surprises at this meeting, because the owner, with help from the mentor, has made sure that everyone involved understands the issues and agrees with the proposals ahead of time. After the reflection (check), the group agrees to move forward with the proposed action as the new way they will work. Since all affected parties have been involved and are in agreement, action will take place without delay.

Responsibility ≠ Authority

"Lean managers focus on responsibility and ownership, which means keying on 'doing the right thing,' as opposed to authority, which deals with who has the *right* to make certain decisions," says John Shook in *Managing to Learn*. "As a result, decisions are made by a fundamentally different approach. The authority to make decisions is not established by hierarchy or titles. Rather, the owner of the A3, through the process of producing a dialog, takes responsibility to *get decisions made*."

"Another counterintuitive aspect of A3 learning is that the process of coaxing agreement from key stakeholders becomes the means of gaining the authority needed for any plan or action. . . . Agreement in a lean organization emerges from the inclusive process, which in turn produces authority. Essentially, authority is created by framing the issue properly and gaining agreement."[28]

Share the Knowledge

"High velocity organizations multiply the power of their new knowledge by making it available, not only to those who discovered it, but also throughout the organization. They do this by sharing not only the solutions that are discovered, but the processes by which they were discovered—what was learned and how it was learned," Steven Spear writes.[29] We saw this in the pharmacy exper-

---

28. From Shook, *Managing to Learn: Using the A3 Management Process to Solve Problems, Gain Agreement, Mentor, and Lead*, 2008, p. 81. Italics in the original.
29. Spear, *Chasing the Rabbit*, 2009, p. 27.

iment at the beginning of this chapter. One hospital ran a simulation and found what kept the pharmacy from filling orders in three minutes, and the pharmacists implemented many simple measures to solve the problems. Another hospital tried to copy the measures, but that did little good. Only when the second hospital ran its own simulation did its pharmacy make headway in improving its processes. What that hospital needed to learn was how to run the simulation, not how to organize the medicine storage area.

There are many well-known mechanisms for sharing knowledge inside a company, including central information-sharing groups and publications, internal conferences that include a site tour, online specialty forums, speaker programs, job rotations, visiting senior specialists, strong encouragement for attending external courses or conferences and publishing in industry journals, and so on. Competency leaders or communities of practice are often used to collect and disseminate knowledge that relates to a specialized technical area.

Disincentives for Knowledge Sharing

Many compensation systems, especially in America, rank individuals against each other for the purpose of determining pay raises. Under such a system, the best way to earn more money is to know as much as possible while being compared against others who know as little as possible. This creates the best incentive we have ever seen for knowledge hoarding rather than knowledge sharing.

In his book *Reward Systems,* Steven Kerr, former chief learning officer, General Electric and Goldman Sachs, points out that incentive systems that rank people against each other are inappropriate when teamwork is essential to success. He uses a sports analogy:

> If you tell a golfer, "I'll give you $500 for each stroke below 85," he is likely to practice harder and take the next stroke more seriously.
>
> If you tell a basketball player, "I'll give you $500 for every point you score," he's likely to engage in self-serving behaviors that hurt the team.
>
> The problem is that, by offering individual rewards where teamwork is essential, you're rewarding the wrong things.[30]

Tom and Mary Poppendieck, with quote from Steve Kerr

Spear finds that the single common characteristic of leading companies in every industry he has studied is their ability to capitalize on the intelligence of

---

30. Kerr, *Reward Systems: Does Yours Measure Up?*, 2009, pp. 116–17.

every person and have each person's learning contribute to the advancement of the whole company. This has a multiplier effect—high-velocity companies keep on getting better faster than their competitors.

Portrait: Manager as Mentor

"Managers in high-velocity organizations make sure that a regular part of their work is both the delivery of products and services and also the continual improvement of the processes by which those products and services are delivered. They teach people how to make continual improvement part of their jobs and provide them with enough time and resources to do so," says Steven Spear. "High velocity managers are not in place to command, control, berate, intimidate, or evaluate through a contrived set of metrics, but to ensure that their organizations become ever more self-diagnosing and self-improving, skilled at detecting problems, solving them and multiplying the effect by making the solutions available throughout the organization."[31]

In Frame 16: Learn to Improve, we noted times where the A3 report was reviewed by a mentor who was teaching problem-solving skills, often by asking questions. The mentor might ask, "Is this really a complete picture of the current condition? Have you thought of everything that might cause the situation? Are there other people you should talk with to get their perspective on this? What quick experiments might you do to prove that theory?"

Who is this mentor? It is often the first- or second-line manager, the person who has challenges to meet and knows that the only way to meet them is to help the people doing the work to see problems and solve them. Mentors need to understand the work being done—in detail—in order to be effective. And managers have to believe that the only way to achieve their goals is to leverage the intelligence and dedication of the people who do the work and engage all of those smart, capable people in meeting the challenge. You probably know this. The question is, How do you actually do it?

Answering this question is the focus of *Managing to Learn* by John Shook. This book walks the reader through a challenging problem-solving exercise from the dual perspective of a problem solver tackling a difficult, boundary-spanning problem and a manager who needs the problem solved to meet critical organizational goals. Shook frames the approach in the introduction:[32]

---

31. Spear, *Chasing the Rabbit*, 2009, p. 26.
32. Shook, *Managing to Learn: Using the A3 Management Process to Solve Problems, Gain Agreement, Mentor, and Lead*, 2008, pp. 2–3.

The Toyota leader will strive whenever possible to eschew simple command in favor of leading by being knowledgeable, fact-based, and strong-willed, yet flexible; in other words, by being a true leader. The manager's job is to see problems. . . . . It is assumed that there will be problems, and that nothing will go according to plan.

The Toyota leader engages in the messy details of the work being done in order to learn and become thoroughly knowledgeable about the process at hand. Questioning, coaching, and teaching take precedence over commanding and controlling. . . . Where the laissez-faire, hands-off manager will content himself to set targets and delegate everything, essentially saying, "I don't care how you do it, as long as you get the results," the Toyota manager desperately wants to know how you'll do it, saying, "I want to hear everything about your thinking, tell me about your plans." Only then can the manager mentor the problem solver.

It all boils down to the way the job of a manager is framed. There is the frame that says any manager can manage any job; it is not necessary for a manager to understand the job he or she manages. In this frame the manager sets targets and the workers are expected to meet the targets. But in any complex system there will be problems; what happens then? In this frame, problems are not welcome because they get in the way of meeting the goals. Ambiguities and unwelcome problems spawn work-arounds. The work system becomes dysfunctional.

At this point, an antidote is usually sought. For example, in agile environments *self-organizing teams* are often thought of as an antidote to directive management. But as Peter Scholtes says in *The Leader's Handbook*, "All of the empowered, motivated, teamed-up, self-directed, incentivized, accountable, reengineered, and reinvented people you can muster cannot compensate for a dysfunctional system."[33] When the work system is the problem and the manager has little understanding of how it works or why it is not working, self-organizing teams may help, but only if they have the skills to see and solve the problems in the work system. This may happen with mature teams, but certainly not with every team.

Our frame provides another approach. In this frame, line managers have a good knowledge of the work they manage and are deeply involved in understanding how work gets done. True, they may not know all of the latest technology, but they have a keen sense of the important issues and are willing to delve into the details. In this frame, managers *do not focus on achieving goals*, and they *do not tell people what to do*. They focus on improving the system whereby the organization's work gets done. They know that alone they are not able to improve the system; this requires the best efforts of all of the smart people they lead. So they make the organization's challenges clear and work to help everyone learn how to see problems, solve problems, and spread the knowl-

---

33. Scholtes, *The Leader's Handbook: A Guide to Inspiring Your People and Managing the Daily Workflow*, 1988, p. 17.

edge. They know that if they develop good problem solvers, the hundreds of problems, large and small, that are getting in the way of good performance will be uncovered one by one, and their organization's chances of success will be greatly improved.

Your Shot

1. Pick a date five years in the future. Assume you are still in the same organization and it has been quite successful over the last five years. What does that success look like? How big is your customer base? Your code base? How many employees does the organization have? What does your competitive environment look like? What is your organization's culture like? What does your system architecture look like?

   Looking backward from five years out, what were the major steps you took to get to this successful position? What did you do to rise to the top (or remain at the top) of your market niche? How did you keep your code base clean and easy to extend and support? How did you increase the productivity of your development organization to support the growth that led to success? How did you evolve your architecture to support the growth?

   What problems do you still struggle with in this five-years-from-now scenario—from a technical perspective? From a people perspective? From a process perspective? What kinds of support issues still plague you? What do you wish you had done better over the five years?

   Given all of this, what three challenges might you formulate that would prepare your organization to be successful five years in the future?

2. Using Figure 4-1 as a guide, have your team create a sketch of its immediate suppliers and immediate customers.

   a. List the job of each customer and the output you supply for the customer to do that job. List the feedback mechanism in place to assure that you always meet the customers' needs. Discuss what happens if you should fail to meet their needs: How would you know? What would you do about it? What would you do to be sure such a failure never occurs again? Create a checklist for each handover.

   b. List the job of each supplier and how it supports your job. List what you need from that supplier to do your job well and do it better/faster in the future. List how you let your suppliers know if they have not met your needs: How would they know? What would they do about it? Would they act to be sure such a failure never occurs again? Create a checklist for each handover.

3. Is your culture one of "bad news first" or "good news first"? If it is the second, how do you make sure that problems are exposed and confronted early, often, and honestly?

Is honesty about mistakes likely to be rewarded, ignored, or punished in your organizational culture? What is the impact of this culture on exposing problems?

4. We know of one company that runs retail stores and has a "Walk a Mile in Their Shoes" program. In this program, every employee must spend time working in a retail store and at a customer service call center at least once a year. Does your organization have such a program? Are members of development teams expected to participate?

   Consider establishing a job rotation system with your immediate supplier and your immediate customer. Would it work in your organization? If so, what would it take to make it successful?

5. Put up a problem/countermeasure board in your team area and teach everyone how to use it. What will it take to have this board live up to its potential of driving continuous problem solving?

6. Choose a boundary-spanning problem and have your team fill out the first part of an A3 problem-solving report. Use the form to discuss the problem with affected parties, and continue filling it out. When you get to the root cause analysis, find a mentor to check your conclusion and give you advice. List some experiments. Try them. See how the process works.

7. Do teams have time set aside for problem solving in your organization? How much? How regularly? Is it used? Is it enough time to foster a climate of continuous improvement?

Chapter 5

Great People

Snapshot

"The first time I came to North America, I was surprised to see that Japan is on the far right side of the map," wrote Namiko Abe. "It felt very strange. Japan is always located at the center of the map that I grew up with."[1] The experiences of childhood have a huge influence on the way people frame their world—what is at the center and what is peripheral. We are unlikely to change the cultural frame that we grew up with, but we can become sensitive to cultural differences and learn to understand and respect other cultures. It turns out that there is no one way to motivate people, no best way to organize teams, and no universal rule governing interactions. In addition to cultural differences, each individual has unique strengths, styles of learning, and values.

Some things are more universal than others. Take reciprocity: *If you treat me well, I'll treat you well, but if you treat me poorly, I will do the same to you.* Reciprocity formed the basis of exchange in societies prior to the use of money, and it remains a powerful basis of exchange today. Closely associated with reciprocity is mutual respect, which goes a long way toward creating trust-based relationships. And no matter what culture they grow up in, people thrive when they are proud of their work, proud of the way they do their work, and proud of the contribution their work makes to a larger purpose.

The leaders who really must understand these things are front-line leaders, because they have by far the greatest influence on the dedication, creativity, and even the skill of the people doing the work.

1. Abe, "Japan and the World Map," 2008.

Cultural Assumptions

Geert Hofstede was born in Haarlem, the Netherlands, in 1928. He was 18 months older than Edsger Dijkstra, who grew up 70 km away in Rotterdam; both were young teens during World War II. After the war, Hofstede took his first trip out of the country—as a ship's engineer—and ended up in Indonesia, where he experienced quite a cultural shock. Shortly after returning home, Hofstede took a trip to England, which gave him an even greater culture shock. He wondered what could make the English culture, only 200 km from home, so very different from his own.[2]

After a decade as an engineer, Hofstede joined IBM and got the opportunity to pursue this question. As a psychologist in the training department, he surveyed over 100,000 IBM-ers throughout Europe and the Middle East, looking for cultural differences that might be of interest during training. On a sabbatical from IBM, he started asking the same questions of people outside the company. Hofstede was surprised to discover great similarities in the way that people from the same country tended to answer the questions. Hofstede urged IBM to analyze the large database he had gathered, but instead the data was given to a university. Hofstede followed the data and became deeply engaged in analyzing it for correlations. Six years passed before he published a book on his results, and it took even more time for his work to be appreciated. But over time Hofstede's work on cultural dimensions has been corroborated and expanded. Today, cultural dimensions are one of the most widely used framing tools in cross-cultural psychology.[3]

Hofstede found four dimensions in which national cultures instill in children deeply held assumptions about how to live: power distance, individualism, masculinity, and uncertainty avoidance. Later Hofstede realized that he had brought a Western bias to this work, so he collaborated with Asian researchers on a survey focused on Confucian values, and based on the results, he added a fifth dimension to his cultural perspective: long-term orientation. Figure 5-1 shows the relative cultural dimensions of a few countries.[4]

2. See Hofstede, "Culture Does Not Exist," 2006, for much of the information in this section.
3. See, for example, Gladwell, *Outliers: The Story of Success*, 2008, pp. 202–23.
4. Data and descriptions of dimensions from Hofstede and Hofstede, *Cultures and Organizations: Software of the Mind*, 2005. Country data from many more countries may be found at www.geert-hofstede.com/hofstede_dimensions.php.

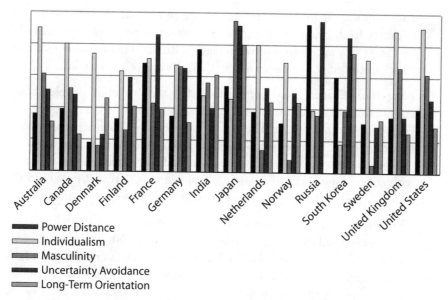

Power Distance
Individualism
Masculinity
Uncertainty Avoidance
Long-Term Orientation

Figure 5-1   *Geert Hofstede's cultural dimensions for several countries*

A brief explanation of each dimension follows:

- *Power Distance:* All cultures have an unequal power distribution among people, but in some cultures this is considered appropriate, while in others it is not. The extent to which the *less powerful members of a country accept unequal power* is the country's power difference index (PDI). Russia, India, and France are examples of countries with high power distances.

- *Individualism:* Some cultures (all of them Western, with the United Sates at the top) emphasize individual achievement, while others (for example, South Korea, Russia, Japan, India) emphasize collective achievement and cohesive groups of people looking after one another. The extent to which the individual is emphasized over the group is the individualism index (IDV).

- *Masculinity:* Masculinity is the degree to which the culture accepts gender roles, expecting men to be assertive, tough, and focused on material success and women to be modest, tender, and concerned with the quality of life. Japan has the highest masculinity index (MAS), and Sweden, Norway, the Netherlands, and Denmark have the lowest indices.

- *Uncertainty Avoidance:* Some cultures have a much more difficult time dealing with unpredictable situations than others. In cultures with high uncertainty avoidance you are likely to see an emphasis on rules and a low tolerance for the new, the different, the foreign. Surprisingly, you may also find more risk taking to resolve ambiguity. Russia, Japan, and France have a high uncertainty avoidance index (UAI); Denmark's is very low.

- *Long-Term Orientation:* Confucius taught that virtuous people should acquire skills and education, work hard, spend no more than necessary, and be patient and preserving. This means taking a long-term view of work—for example, making decisions based on profits ten years from now instead of next quarter. Japan, South Korea, and India are examples of countries with strong long-term orientation (LTO). Canada, Great Britain, and the United States are among the countries with a very short-term orientation.

As children grow up, they learn what behavior is acceptable and what is not, how they are expected to act in the presence of elders, whether patience is a virtue, how much they are expected to look out for themselves and others. Adults instinctively understand the cultural norms they learned as small children, whether they agree with them or not. The cultural dimensions of a country are not the way individual people act; they are the way the culture *expects* individuals to act. These expectations are passed from one generation to the next during childhood; they are part of who we are and how we think.

"That's the Way Managers Are Around Here"

Our friend took us to dinner in Oslo. As we were eating, she commented, "You know the kind of manager you talk about, the one who delegates work and doesn't tell people what to do? Well, that's the way *all* managers are here in Norway. It's very Norwegian."

Later we were biking in Sweden, and our host at a bed-and-breakfast turned out to be an engineer and lean consultant who took summers off when work was slow. We talked about lean, which he knew well, and about the Swedish culture. "You have to understand that in Sweden, everyone wants to grow up to be an engineer," he said. "A friend of mine went to Cambridge, and he complained that most of his classmates were getting engineering degrees so they could become managers after working a few years as engineers. Here in Sweden, children do not grow up dreaming about becoming managers; they want to be engineers."

So we asked a friend in Copenhagen, "Is this true? Is it common for managers to understand the work they manage and expect the workers to make decisions?"

"Well," he said, "if anything, Danish managers can be too laissez-faire. But they certainly don't tell people what to do. However, managers come here to Copenhagen from other countries, and they can be a problem. They just don't understand the Danes."

I got to thinking about the management culture in which I had spent 20 years and where I learned to be a manager. I realized that 3M is a Minnesota company, founded in 1906 when Minnesota was a predominantly Scandinavian area. Its corporate culture no doubt had deep Scandinavian roots. No wonder Scandinavian management attitudes feel so natural!

Mary Poppendieck

The Cultural Heritage of Management Practices

When Hofstede was a young engineer, a manager from the United States interviewed him for a job. He brought an understated résumé and waited for the interviewer to ask about his past experience. But after an unsatisfying interview on both sides, he headed for the long train ride home without the job. Only when Hofstede became a manager and started interviewing both American and Dutch applicants did he discover what he had done wrong. He found out that Americans boasted in their résumés and in their interviews, something considered inappropriate in the Dutch culture. Clearly the American manager had expected him to sell himself aggressively, which never occurred to him. When cultural frames get misaligned in business, a lot of potential can be lost.

"Most management theories have been developed in the United States by Americans," according to Nancy Adler, whose book *International Dimensions of Organizational Behavior* is in its fifth edition. "Rather than being applicable worldwide, many traditional models effectively guide thinking and action only within the American context within which they were developed."[5] This is particularly true of theories of motivation. Adler writes:[6]

Most motivation theories in use today were developed in the United States by Americans and about Americans. Of those that were not, many have been strongly influenced by American theories. . . .

Unfortunately, many American as well as non-American managers have treated American theories as the best or only way to understand motivation. They are neither. American motivation theories—too often assumed to reflect universal values— have failed to provide consistently useful explanations for behavior outside the

---

5. Adler, *International Dimensions of Organizational Behavior*, 2002, p. 195. Adler grew up in California and is a professor at McGill University in Montreal.
6. Ibid., p. 182.

United States. Managers must therefore guard against imposing domestic American management theories on their global business practices.

Agile software development practices were principally conceived of in an American cultural setting, whereas lean thinking had its origins in a Japanese cultural setting. So it is appropriate to ask, "To what extent are agile and lean software development approaches constrained by their cultural heritage?"

Agile Software Development

Consider the principles behind the Agile Manifesto:[7]

1. Our highest priority is to satisfy the customer through early and continuous delivery of valuable software.
2. Welcome changing requirements, even late in development. Agile processes harness change for the customer's competitive advantage.
3. Deliver working software frequently, from a couple of weeks to a couple of months, with a preference to the shorter timescale.
4. Business people and developers must work together daily throughout the project.
5. Build projects around motivated individuals. Give them the environment and support they need, and trust them to get the job done.
6. The most efficient and effective method of conveying information to and within a development team is face-to-face conversation.
7. Working software is the primary measure of progress.
8. Agile processes promote sustainable development. The sponsors, developers, and users should be able to maintain a constant pace indefinitely.
9. Continuous attention to technical excellence and good design enhances agility.
10. Simplicity—the art of maximizing the amount of work not done—is essential.
11. The best architectures, requirements, and designs emerge from self-organizing teams.
12. At regular intervals, the team reflects on how to become more effective, then tunes and adjusts its behavior accordingly.

To American ears, all of these principles probably sound like good ideas. But in a culture with high uncertainty avoidance, several of the principles might create dissonance, especially ones that appear to discount the deep-felt need for predictability. Hofstede notes: "The need for rules in a society with a strong uncertainty avoidance culture is emotional. People . . . have been programmed since their early childhood to feel comfortable in structured environments. Matters that can be structured should not be left to chance. . . . Countries with weak uncertainty avoidance can show the opposite, an emotional horror of for-

---

7. http://agilemanifesto.org/principles.html.

mal rules."[8] Thus welcoming change (principle 2) and a bias toward oral communication (principle 6) may feel quite appropriate in countries that are comfortable with uncertainty, but countries with high uncertainty avoidance may find them less than satisfactory.

Self-organizing teams (principle 11) may seem like an obviously good idea, but Hofstede points out, "When power distances are large, dependence on more powerful people is a basic need that can be a real motivator."[9] So in countries with high power distances, teams are likely to feel more comfortable with more direction. On the other hand, when those countries also favor collective achievement over individualism, teamwork is likely to feel very natural. In countries that value individualism, teamwork may be more of a challenge; even the reward structures are likely to be incompatible with teamwork.

Countries with strong long-term orientation may not be quite as interested in early and frequent delivery of software (principles 1 and 3). In these countries it can be more important to create a consensus before implementing a system, and developing the capability to build high-quality software may be a higher priority than frequent delivery.

Lean Software Development

The way we discuss lean software development is similar to and supportive of the principles of agile software development, and it certainly has an American bias. But lean thinking has a Japanese heritage, and it is this heritage that makes lean concepts counterintuitive to Westerners. Consider the principles:

1. Eliminate Waste

2. Build Quality In

3. Create Knowledge

4. Defer Commitment

5. Deliver Fast

6. Respect People

7. Optimize the Whole

Probably the most challenging of these from a Western perspective are principle 4, "Defer Commitment," and principle 7, "Optimize the Whole." To countries with a long-term orientation, these are natural ideas. Delivering fast

---

8. Hofstede and Hofstede, *Cultures and Organizations: Software of the Mind*, 2005, p. 182.

9. Ibid., p. 272.

seems like a good idea to Western ears, until it becomes apparent that speed requires abandoning deeply held beliefs such as maximizing utilization. Creating knowledge also seems like a good idea, until the discipline of plan-do-check-act appears to slow everything down and people begin to wonder, "What happened to *fast?*"

What Happened to Fast?

Our study tour group was being given a lesson in cultural differences at the Danish embassy in Japan. Masayuki Yamaguchi projected a picture of how decision making in Japan differs from decision making in the West (see Figure 5-2). In Japan, decisions take time, but once agreement is achieved, execution is very fast. In the West, decisions are made quickly—so quickly that later rethinking and reevaluation are considered essential. Viewed from an overall perspective, the Japanese model delivers results more quickly.

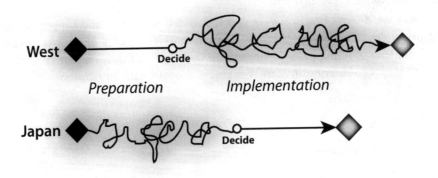

Figure 5-2 *Who gets done faster?*

Tom and Mary Poppendieck

Lean principles—whether in manufacturing, logistics, or development—seem counterintuitive and internally inconsistent in cultures with a short-term orientation. They tend to create dissonance in places where a focus on short-term results feels like the only rational approach. This is probably why lean initiatives have been so difficult to implement in a sustainable manner in Western cultures.

Company Culture

Perhaps one of the most remarkable examples of moving management styles across cultures is the growth of Toyota factories outside of Japan. In 1984 Toyota began its move to the United States, and the company focused the efforts of top executives for many years on moving the culture of Toyota—called the Toyota Way—to its plants in other countries.

> The Toyota Way is very rooted in Eastern culture. The challenge then becomes how can Toyota possibly bring the Toyota Way to Western countries when its basic cultural assumptions are in some cases antithetical to the local culture? The answer to the question is that Toyota has brought key aspects of the culture to the West with remarkable success through a process of experimenting, reflecting, and learning.
>
> [Toyota] leaders established the goal that they must transfer the essence of the Toyota Way to America, regardless of culture. Of course the first question was: what is the essence? Even that was not obvious as the Toyota Way was simply the way they did things. Through discussion, debate, and experimentation, and with the help of the Americans, they began to figure what elements of the culture needed to be transferred.[10]

Toyota recognized that its success in transferring the Toyota Way was all about people. The company carefully selected the right kind of leaders, trained them—usually in Japan—and then provided mentors who remained in the background, reinforcing the values, in decreasing numbers over the years. This is actually the essence of the Toyota Way anyway, so using it to move manufacturing outside of Japan was very natural. It required the persistence and patience that only a long-term orientation allows. Toyota president Katsuaki Watanabe said in an interview published in the *Harvard Business Review*[11]:

> The Toyota Way has been and will continue to be the standard for everyone who works for Toyota all over the world. Our guiding principles define Toyota's mission and values, but the Toyota Way defines how we work. To me, it's like the air we breathe. The Toyota Way has two main pillars: continuous improvement and respect for people. Respect is necessary to work with people. By "people" we mean employees, supply partners, and customers. "Customer first" is one of the company's core tenets. We don't mean just the end customer; on the assembly line the person at the next workstation is also your customer. That leads to teamwork. If you adopt that principle, you'll also keep analyzing what you do in order to see if you're doing things perfectly, so you're not troubling your customer. That nurtures your ability to identify problems, and if you closely observe things, it will lead to *kaizen*: continuous improvement. The root of the Toyota Way is to be dissatisfied with the status quo; you have to ask constantly, "Why are we doing this?" People can apply these concepts throughout the world, not just in Japan. The question is how long it takes to train people to develop the Toyota mind-set.

---

10. Liker and Hoseus, *Toyota Culture: The Heart and Soul of the Toyota Way*, 2008, p. 26.
11. Watanabe, "Lessons from Toyota's Long Drive," 2007.

While they were exporting their culture, Toyota leaders took the opportunity to learn from other cultures and adopt values that would broaden their company culture. Slowly at first, and then over time with increasing speed, Toyota has expanded its global design and manufacturing presence along with its capability to create effective global teams. Toyota leaders truly understand: *It's all about people.*

Frame 17: Knowledge Workers

Give me a fish and I'll eat for a day. Teach me to fish and I'll eat for life.

Peter Drucker, sometimes called "the man who invented management,"[12] grew up in Vienna in the 1920s, moved to the United States in 1937, and wrote his most famous book, *The Practice of Management*, in 1954. Drucker coined the term *knowledge worker* in 1959 to emphasize the fact that knowledge workers were becoming an increasingly large portion of the labor force. By "knowledge workers" Drucker meant people who create value through mental rather than manual effort. Clearly, software systems are developed by knowledge workers.

Knowledge Worker Productivity

In his 1999 book, *Management Challenges for the 21st Century*, Drucker says:[13]

Six major factors determine knowledge worker productivity:
1. Knowledge worker productivity demands that we ask the question: *"What is the task?" not "How should the work be done?"*
2. It demands that we impose the responsibility for their productivity on the individual knowledge workers themselves. Knowledge workers *have* to manage themselves. They have to have *autonomy*.
3. Continuing innovation has to be part of the work, the task, and the responsibility of knowledge workers.
4. Knowledge work requires continuous learning on the part of the knowledge worker, but equally continuous teaching on the part of the knowledge worker. [Share the knowledge.]
5. Productivity of the knowledge worker is not—at least not primarily—a matter of the *quantity* of output. *Quality* is at least as important. Measure the

---

12. Byrne, "The Man Who Invented Management: Why Peter Drucker's Ideas Still Matter," 2005.
13. Drucker, *Management Challenges for the 21st Century*, 1999. From the list on p. 142, some with added explanations from the same section. Italics in the original.

"results" for a given enterprise and a given activity. [Don't measure number of drawings or lines of code.]

6. Finally, knowledge worker productivity requires that the knowledge worker is both seen and treated as an "asset" rather than a "cost." It requires that knowledge workers want to work for the organization in preference to all other opportunities.

Each of these requirements—except perhaps the last one—is almost the exact opposite of what is needed to increase the productivity of the manual worker.

If you reflect on these points, it should be blindingly obvious why we struggle when trying to apply management practices developed for manual labor to knowledge work. Most of these practices—concepts such as high utilization and low variation, identical processes and fungible resources—are the *exact opposite* of what is needed to increase the productivity of knowledge workers, as Drucker points out.

Peter Drucker believed that increasing knowledge worker productivity is the most important management challenge of the twenty-first century. According to Drucker, "Productivity of the knowledge worker will almost always require that the *work itself* be restructured and be made part of a *system*."[14] He insisted that the only way to measure knowledge worker productivity was to measure the outcomes of the system in which they work. Counting the quantity of the "things" knowledge workers produce—for example, how many stories were completed—is sort of like measuring how many students a teacher has in a class. This is not the way to measure productivity. What's important is how well a teacher educates students, or how much value stories deliver to customers.

Drucker insisted that knowledge workers must improve their own productivity. "Work on knowledge worker productivity begins with asking the knowledge worker themselves:

What is your task? What should it be? What should you be expected to contribute? What hampers you in doing your task and should be eliminated?[15]

Build on Strength

When I was a new manager, I bought the book *People and Performance: The Best of Peter Drucker on Management*.[16] I learned one lesson from this book that had a profound influence on the way I managed people. Drucker said that

---

14. Ibid., p. 154. Italics in the original.
15. Ibid., p. 143. Italics in the original.
16. Drucker, *People and Performance: The Best of Drucker on Management*, 1977.

the important thing in assigning work—and in choosing what work to do your-self—is to make sure that everyone is working on things that they are good at. People should work to their strengths; don't waste time trying to improve on their weaknesses.

Every time I took over a new department or had someone new reporting to me, the first thing I would ask each person was "What are you good at? What do you like working on? What aren't you good at? What would you rather not work on?" Then I would try to organize the work so that everyone was work-ing on things they were good at, or at least not particularly bad at. I also tried to find someone in each department who was good at the things I did poorly and have that person cover for my weaknesses.

I learned that when everyone (myself included) worked on things they liked doing and were good at—the two seemed to be about the same—they enjoyed coming to work in the morning. They also tended to finish up what they were doing before they went home at night, rather than flying out the door when the clock said their time was up. It turned out that one of my greatest strengths was the ability to turn quiet people who used to "just do what they were told" into great contributors and leaders. It was mostly a matter of unlock-ing the potential that people had within themselves by building on their strengths.

I often wonder how companies can expect superior performance from knowl-edge workers when there is no one whose job it is to uncover the strengths of each person and match the job to the individual. I wonder how people will reach their full potential if their work does not build on their strengths and pro-vide opportunities for growth. And I wonder how companies can expect to retain knowledge workers if they do not provide leaders who understand what it means to treat people as an asset rather than a cost.

Mary Poppendieck

Results Are Not the Point

In knowledge work, success comes entirely from people and the system within which they work. Results are not the point. Developing the people and the sys-tem so that together they are capable of achieving successful results is the point.

"Fine," you say, "but I have software to deliver, budgets to stay within, schedules to meet." Indeed you do. But here's the thing: Either your system is capable of delivering those results or it is not. Recall that in Frame 2: System Capability we recommended that you start by creating a time series chart of your current process capability. It will tell you what results your system is capa-ble of. Trying to force results beyond what your development system is capable of might achieve results in the short term, but it will invariably make things worse over the long term.

You are not going to improve your system by stressing it to achieve aggressive targets. Systems don't work that way. You may get a local or temporary optimization, but you will not get a system capable of delivering high-quality software reliably, repeatedly on time.

"It's hard for Americans to understand the idea that a business organization cannot improve its long term financial results by working to improve its financial results. But the only way to ensure satisfactory and stable long term financial results is to work on improving the system from which those results emerge," says H. Thomas Johnson, winner of the Deming Medal. He notes that the Deming approach and the Toyota Way *"nurture the system and people who produce the results*, rather than trying to force the system to meet targets beyond its current capability—a strategy pursued by virtually all large companies in the US today."[17]

This is a very difficult concept to grasp, even for lean consultants. For example, a typical kaizen event at many companies might proceed like this: A group is gathered together to improve a specific operation. A facilitator, perhaps a consultant, guides the group in analyzing the operation and coming up with improvements. At the end of the week, the group reports to the management team and the improvement is either implemented or approved, depending on how long it takes to make the change. The savings are added to the list of savings that kaizen events have generated, to help justify continued kaizen events. Then everyone goes back to their real jobs, having done their part to improve the operation.

This may sound like a good approach, but it stands in sharp contrast to similar events at Toyota. In that company groups also gather for improvement exercises, but they are not called kaizen (which happens at one's own workplace); they are called *jishuken*, or "voluntary self-study." There is a *sensei*, or "teacher," who gives the group a challenge, just as in the kaizen event described in the last paragraph. But that's where the similarities end. At Toyota, the *sensei* gives the team no direct help and little guidance. When team members come for assistance, the *sensei* is likely to insist that they explain their thinking so far and then challenge the group further, asking tough questions. Individuals are expected to be motivated to improve themselves and their thinking, with the *sensei* as their mentor. In the end, the team will come up with ideas, run experiments, collect data, and implement effective countermeasures. The results are not tallied to justify the event, because what matters is the *learning* of the participants,

---

17. See Johnson, "Manage a Living System, Not a Ledger," 2007. Italics added.

not the results of their work. Team members expect to return to their jobs with improved problem-solving skills.[18]

It is extremely difficult for Westerners to understand that *solving the problem* is not what matters most; developing the problem-solving skills in people is what really matters. Think about training in a military organization. The outcome of the training is not important; it is the *learning* that matters. A *jishuken* is a training exercise, not a problem-solving exercise. People learn how to solve problems by solving a real problem, it is true, but the solution to the problem is not what solving problems is all about. People learn by solving problems so that they can get better and better at solving problems. Then they return to their workstation and use their problem-solving skills to improve the way they work.

So how do you get results? You start by making sure that work is structured so that it is a system—one that gives knowledge workers visibility into the needs and expectations of your customers. Then you focus on developing the technical capability of the system and of the people developing your products. You structure your delivery system so that workflows are steady and predictable. Finally, you develop workers who accept the challenge to continuously improve their system so that it delivers increasingly better customer outcomes. Nothing is going to get you very far if you do not grow and protect the people who understand customers, decide what tests to run, write the code, keep up the cadence, deploy the software, provide support, and constantly improve the system so it delivers more value to customers.

Frame 18: The Norm of Reciprocity

Treat other people the way you would like them to treat you, and they probably will.[19]

—James Parker

In Frame 7: Evolutionary Development we recommended that you try ethnography—closely observing what customers actually do—to gain a real understanding of what kinds of problems they struggle with every day. Ethnography was more or less invented by Bronislaw Malinowski, a Polish physicist and anthropologist, in the early twentieth century. This was a time of colonization,

---

18. From Liker and Hoseus, *Toyota Culture: The Heart and Soul of the Toyota Way*, 2008, p. 23. *Kaizen* means "change for the better."
19. Parker, *Do the Right Thing: How Dedicated Employees Create Loyal Customers and Large Profits*, 2008, p. 251.

and the attitude of his contemporaries toward so-called primitive people struck Malinowski as condescending. His signature work was a study of the everyday life of Trobriand Islanders in New Guinea; he learned their language and observed the day-to-day behaviors underlying ownership, trade, and rituals. He was not surprised to find that the people were every bit as intelligent and creative as people in so-called civilized societies; they had developed a sophisticated culture that was well suited to their particular environment.

The people of the Trobriand Islands did not use the concept of money. Instead they used a system of mutual obligations to govern work and trade interactions. Malinowski showed that reciprocity—the inner symmetry of social transactions—was the mechanism that governed both work and trade. Food was obtained and distributed through "a well-assessed give and take, always mentally ticked off and in the long run balanced." Enlightened self-interest governed life; people were generous in giving to others because they knew that in time they would receive more or less equal generosity from the recipient. When people did not live up to their obligations, the slighted parties reciprocated by not living up to theirs.

Malinowski wrote that without reciprocity, communities could not exist; reciprocity is the economic mechanism that makes communities work and the enforcement method that keeps exchanges fair.[20] When you think about it, reciprocity facilitates the interactions of most non-market communities to this day, including open-source software. And it mediates most market exchanges that are built on trust-based relationships.

Reciprocity is a social norm, or expectation, that people will try to keep their interactions with others more or less in balance. People, in other words, want to live in a world they perceive to be fair. The norm of reciprocity means that you can expect favors to be returned, but you should also expect self-serving behavior to generate a self-serving response.

Remuneration or Reciprocity?

There are two kinds of companies in this world: remuneration companies and reciprocity companies. People who work in a remuneration company have this agreement with their company: "I will show up for work and you will pay me for my time. If you want more than that, pay me more. I return effort for remuneration." On the other hand, people who work in a reciprocity company have this agreement: "I will treat you the way you treat me. I expect fair compensation, but if you want care and commitment on my part, then you agree that you

20. See Malinowski, *Crime and Custom in Savage Society*, 1926.

will demonstrate care and commitment toward me, and you will help me develop my potential to its fullest extent."[21]

Southwest Airlines is a reciprocity company. It has the highest productivity and the lowest turnover in the industry, and the way it achieves this is by treating employees as an asset rather than a cost. Former CEO James Parker says that the secret of Southwest's success is its people; they are committed to the company because the company is committed to them. Southwest employees treat customers well because their managers treat them well. He says that there is no way to copy the Southwest model without copying its commitment to its employees—and he doesn't mind revealing this secret because he doesn't think that most other executives will really hear what he is saying.[22]

The norm of reciprocity suggests that when employers provide wages, benefits, and training that are perceived to be generous, employees are likely to reciprocate with increased discretionary effort. And if companies cut back on things employees have come to expect, employees are likely to cut back on their effort and loyalty to maintain a fair balance.[23]

In the United States, long-term commitment to employees has gone out of style these days. After all, the thinking goes, people will move from one company to another, so there's no sense investing too much in them. But we think this is a vicious circle. The moment employees sense that a company cares more about its bottom line than its employees, the norm of reciprocity comes into play. Employees will withhold dedication from a company that is not dedicated to them.

▼ ——————————————————————————— ▼

Layoffs

Our CEO at 3M used to have meetings where technical people could gather after lunch in a cafeteria and ask impromptu questions. The meetings were very popular and many interesting questions were asked. I remember that one day someone asked, "Why do you control headcount so tightly and make it so difficult for us to hire people?"

21. See de Geus, *The Living Company*, 2002, p. 118. De Geus calls the reciprocity company a "river" company and the remuneration company an "economic" company. De Geus's research indicates that reciprocity companies tend to live for very long times whereas remuneration companies, even very large ones, tend to disappear within 30 to 60 years.

22. Parker, *Do the Right Thing: How Dedicated Employees Create Loyal Customers and Large Profits*, 2008.

23. Pfeffer, *What Were They Thinking?*, 2007, pp. 8–9.

"Which would you rather have," he answered, "headcount constraints or big layoffs? I've been frequently criticized by Wall Street for not laying off people. Most big companies [he named names] have bragged about how many people they have laid off. To me, this is not something to be proud of. It means that they have not controlled their hiring so they have to have layoffs. I think our approach is much better, even though it forces you to get more done with fewer people."

As the American auto industry experienced serious financial hardships in 2009, financial reporters spoke highly of companies that laid off large fractions of their workforce and closed multiple plants. They were quick to criticize companies they didn't think were aggressive enough in releasing workers. The message: Good companies lay off workers.

Toyota and Southwest—the giants in their respective industries—try to avoid layoffs. They prefer to take care of their people and develop their skills in down times, so that when the economy picks up, they will have skilled people ready to take advantage of new opportunities. Occasionally financial analysts criticize these companies for refusing to dismiss workers, even as they praise them for their superior financial results. Somehow the analysts fail to see the connection between treating people well and excellent financial performance. So I suppose it's no wonder that this connection is so difficult for managers to see—at least in our U.S. culture.

Mary Poppendieck

Frame 19: Mutual Respect

The Toyota Way pillar of Respect for People continues to provide the framework for our company's growth.[24]

One of the most important and yet the easiest way to practice reciprocity is to be generous with respect for other people. Since respect is free and returns are enormous, this is an investment with just about the best ROI in business. It's amazing that more people don't take advantage of it.

- *Respect your organization's customers*—those who pay for, use, support, or derive value from the systems you create. Don't waste their time. Don't make promises you can't keep. Don't deliver systems with defects. Don't fail to get their feedback, early and often. Don't fail to provide what they really need. Don't waste their money on things they don't value.

---

24. From www2.toyota.co.jp/en/vision/traditions/may_jun_06.html.

- *Respect your organization's suppliers*—the companies your organization contracts with for goods and services. Mutual respect between you and your suppliers can replace a lot of contract language and make trust-based contracts possible.

- *Respect your immediate customers*—the next team down the value stream. Find out exactly what they need and when, and be sure they get it.

- *Respect your immediate suppliers*—the next team up the value stream. Be sure they know exactly what you want and when, and be sure they have rapid, respectful feedback.

- *Respect your subordinates*—respect their time; do not ask them to do wasteful activities or work they cannot be proud of.

- *Respect your teammates*—be generous with your contributions and help teammates out so the whole team can meet its goals.

- *Respect your managers*—understand their concerns and help them be successful. If you think that managers are not treating you well, ask yourself how well you treat them. Managers are people, too.

Cross-Cultural Teams

The nature of developing software allows much of the work to move around the world in seconds, so it is increasingly common for development teams to have members in different countries, different time zones, and, most important, with different cultural contexts. Hofstede tells this cautionary story:[25]

> In the early 1990s two European car manufacturers, Renault of France and Volvo of Sweden created a joint venture. In the IBM studies, France scored high on UAI and MAS [uncertainty avoidance and masculinity], Sweden quite low. A mixed team of engineers and technicians from both nations worked on the design of a new model. After a few years the venture was dissolved. French and Swedish social scientists interviewed the actors to find out what went wrong and possibly learn from the experience. D'Iribarne [who is French] described what they found:
>
> "In the joint team, the French rather than the Swedes produced the more innovative designs. French team members did not hesitate to try out new ideas and to defend them aggressively. The Swedes, on the other hand, were constantly seeking consensus. The need for consensus limited what ideas they could present, even what ideas they could conceive of. To the Swedes the expression of ideas was subject to the need for agreement between people; to the French it was only subject to the search for technical truth. The French were primarily concerned with the qual-

---

25. Hofstede and Hofstede, *Cultures and Organizations: Software of the Mind*, 2005, pp. 184–85.

ity of decisions; the Swedes with the legitimacy of the decision process. In the negotiations within the team, the French usually won. They had the support of their superiors who were involved all along, while the Swedish superiors had delegated the responsibility to the team members and were nowhere to be seen."

It's easy to detect that D'Iribarne wrote this from the French perspective. Hofstede concludes that even "the results of social research are not independent of the nationality of the researcher."

Ignoring its bias, this story highlights the serious problems that can easily arise when teams work across countries with different cultures. Beyond language issues, economic differences, and technical backgrounds, there is a good chance that the team members will misunderstand each other's basic approach to work. Culturally unassertive members can easily be bullied by the culturally aggressive members. Those who are uncomfortable with uncertainty may have little patience with those who want to examine multiple alternatives. Those who prefer having a leader who takes charge will not be comfortable with leaders who have a hands-off style. Those who are highly motivated by individual achievement will be frustrated by teams that place higher value on harmony and consensus—and vice versa.

The Value of Diversity

Just because working across cultures is challenging doesn't mean it should be avoided. On the contrary, the best decisions are most likely to come from a team with people from many different backgrounds who enrich the deliberations with different experiences.

The thesis behind James Surowiecki's book *The Wisdom of Crowds*[26] is that a group of people can make better decisions than any individual, even the most expert in the field. But this occurs only under certain circumstances. First, the group has to have a diversity of opinions. If everyone thinks alike, the answer will be biased by the group's bias. If people in the group have lots of different opinions, there will be far more perspectives and options to choose from. Variety and diversity give the highest probability that the best option will at least be considered.

Second, the people in the group have to be able to come to conclusions independent of each other. Without independence, you get the well-known *groupthink* phenomenon where the strength of opinions of individuals in the group or the predominance of opinion favoring a certain course of action sways those who hold different opinions. Research has shown time and again that people are strongly influenced by apparent choices of others around them. Thus not only

---

26. Surowiecki, *The Wisdom of Crowds*, 2004.

should people make decisions independently, but decentralization is important, because it assures that individuals can draw on different experiences.

Finally, there must be a way to pool the private judgments of the group into a collective decision, without compromising independence of judgment based on diverse local knowledge. This may seem like a challenge, but it is much more easily done with software than with other endeavors. Open-source software, for example, creates an environment where Surowiecki's criteria of diversity of opinions, decentralization of experience, and independence are all in place. The genius of open source is that private judgments are pooled into a collective decision through a combination of committer review and community comment.

If you want to capitalize on the value of diversity, you need to find a way to allow independent thinking while effectively pooling different ideas into an effective solution. You do not want everyone to be absorbed into a single homogeneous team, nor do you want segregated subteams. You want teams where people from different backgrounds develop a deep mutual respect for each other, while maintaining an appreciation for their own particular perspective.

Make sure that everyone truly understands that their particular outlook on life is not the only one in the world. While this may seem obvious, it is amazing how often it is not. People around the world think that their experience is the universal experience until they discover that it is not. Provide opportunities for these discoveries to be made by every member of the team. As team members learn to see beyond their own cultural frame, it is easier for a deep mutual respect to develop among all team members.

Self-Organizing Teams?

A typical orchestra has perhaps 100 musicians in different instrument groups, with a generally accepted hierarchy in each group. The orchestra is led by a conductor, and often the lead violinist is second in command. A chamber orchestra is smaller, with fewer than 50 musicians, and may call its leader a music director. But it is rare that you find an orchestra that operates like the Orpheus Chamber Orchestra in New York City:[27]

> A self-governing organization, Orpheus was founded in 1972 by cellist Julian Fifer and a group of fellow musicians, who aspired to perform diverse orchestral repertoire using chamber music ensemble techniques. Today, Orpheus continues this philosophy, performing without a conductor and rotating musical leadership roles for each work, literally changing the way the world thinks about musicians, conductors, and orchestras. The orchestra strives to empower its musicians by integrating them into virtually every facet of the organization.

---

27. This quote is from www.orpheusnyc.com/. See also Pfeffer, *What Were They Thinking?*, 2007, Chapter 6.

The New York Orpheus Chamber Orchestra is excellent, and its self-governing model works extremely well. Of course it is small (30 members), and members self-select based on their interest in the egalitarian model. But just because self-management works extremely well for the Orpheus Chamber Orchestra doesn't mean that all orchestras should fire their conductors and rotate chairs.

We have seen many highly successful self-organizing software development teams, but we have also seen many relatively unsuccessful self-organizing software development teams. We have seen many very successful teams with deeply involved leaders, and we have seen many managers who suppress the initiative of team members. In short, we are quite sure that success does not lie in the model of team organization; it lies in striking the right balance between respect for people and excellent execution.

John Shook, senior adviser at the Lean Enterprise Institute and the first American hired by Toyota, considers a lean enterprise to be a socio-technical system—one that depends on both people and process for its ultimate success. He says:[28]

> I like to refer to the Toyota Way as a socio-technical system on steroids. You have to work BOTH the social side and the process side to be successful with it. It has to be an integrated, balanced, total system . . . the two—process and people—must be in balance. And I must say that I find that companies never get this right. They may err in either direction, on the social side or on the technical side, but they always err to one side to the detriment of the other.
>
> In my view, when "continuous improvement" started, the initial emphasis was heavy on the social side. Teams, teamwork, empowerment, and all that. Sounded and felt good. But a lot of those companies never DID anything. And companies wondered why they didn't get results. Then we had the imbalance in the opposite direction. Companies slammed the tools and processes in place, worker involvement and employee understanding be damned.
>
> It's the balance that makes the difference. The integrated balance. . . . And it's the role of management to balance the two.

"There Is No Such Thing as Good Management"

"There is no such thing as good management." My friend was very adamant. "Managers just mess things up. They have to get out of the way."

"No," I said. "*Some* managers in *some* companies are bad. Certainly I worked with a lot of great managers at 3M."

"That doesn't count. It's an exception," he said.

"But I know a lot of companies with good managers," I replied.

---

28. Shook, "Purpose, Process, People," 2009.

"You work with a really small minority, then, or you just don't see the problems," he insisted. "Managers never understand developers and they make
life miserable."

I knew I wasn't going to change his mind; I had heard this same refrain too
many times before. When people have almost no experience with good leadership, it's hard to convince them that such a thing exists.

Mary Poppendieck

Unfortunately, we often find that the rationale for self-organizing teams
stems from a belief that managers routinely interfere with development, so self-
organizing teams seem like a good way to keep managers out of the way. In this
case the term *self-organization* is taken to mean that managers are not supposed to influence the team, since that influence is presumed to be bad. Managers are supposed to get out of the way and leave the team alone.

The problem with this point of view is its obvious lack of mutual respect
between developers and managers. We observe that a failure to understand and
respect the other party—whether the other party is a manager or a developer—
is the root cause of many problems in system development. But keeping the parties apart is not going to solve the underlying problem; it is far better to focus
on creating mutual respect between developers and managers than to try to find
ways to keep them apart.

Leadership Needs to Be Gently Refactored into Agile

I have done a lot of committee work, both profit and nonprofit, where everyone on the project has equal rank. If everyone carefully avoids seeming too
bossy, and tries to give everyone a chance to contribute to the goals, objectives, and strategies, I find that the committee trudges on politely with slow
progress. The constant social "dancing" and the slow progress can make the
whole activity depressing.

But on my favorite projects, both profit and nonprofit, there is a totally energized, inspirational leader with a dream. These leaders share their dreams,
teach new skills, and use their political power to nudge people past conflicts.
It is really fun working on these projects, and when they are over, you feel like
you are more capable. You want to repeat the experience again and again. I
think great leaders teach and inspire more people to become great leaders.

Sometimes the leader is the boss. Sometimes it is the founder of the organization in a non-hierarchical role. Sometimes it is a junior member of the team
who is so organized that everyone follows them. Sometimes I get to be the
inspirational leader, but often I am following someone else.

The agile paradigm emphasizes treating team members as people, collecting many ideas, and empowering people to take control of their own work. I will gladly salute to that. But there does not seem to be much in there about leadership. I think it is missing and needs to be gently refactored into the methodology.

Once, long ago before agile had a name, I was trying to measure productivity. I was disappointed to see how few lines of code per day anybody at my company was writing. At least, after all the redesign and debugging were done, it seems like the productivity was a tiny fraction of the little projects I was hacking out at home. But then I found a friend who had founded a company and told me that they had 100 times more productivity, and he offered to show me. It was true! They were actually using some of the agile techniques, but one of the founders was in a non-management role as the system architect. He had godlike powers over the design of the system, but social structure was strong, and everyone followed him. The team loved their jobs, loved the company, and they had amazing productivity.

As I read some of the agile philosophy, I think they would find my friend too authoritarian and recommend that he should stand back so that the team could be more democratic. I don't think that would, necessarily, lead to better software or happier teams. I think we need to think more about how to combine the best of self-directed teams with the best of inspirational leadership.

Posted by Tomo Lennox on the *leandevelopment*
Yahoo discussion group, message #3900; used with permission

Frame 20: Pride of Workmanship

Remove Barriers to Pride of Workmanship.

—*W. Edwards Deming*

W. Edwards Deming used an interesting technique to create respect between workers and their supervisors. He used to start out a consulting engagement by meeting with workers without supervisors present, but with a tape recorder. Then he would ask the workers to describe their frustrations at not being able to do their jobs the way they would like to do them. Usually the managers were shocked when they heard the tapes. They heard their workers say they knew their jobs depended on productivity and quality, understood what it took to do their jobs well, and yet were allowed neither to do a good job nor to fix the problems that kept them from doing work they could be proud of.[29] So began the education of supervisors about how to respect their subordinates by removing barriers to pride of workmanship.

---

29. Walton, *The Deming Management Method*, 1986, p. 81.

This would be of passing interest if it were a phenomenon confined to production workers in factories. But imagine Deming arriving at your office tomorrow and holding the same kind of meeting; what do you think would be said? Recognize that such a meeting can't occur unless and until the person holding the meeting has a deep respect for the people attending the meeting and the people trust that they can speak freely without recrimination. With those conditions, imagine what might be said if the people you are responsible for were asked to describe things about their work that they find frustrating.

Enabling pride of workmanship is one reason why the relentless improvement we discussed in Chapter 4 is so important. It is also why we recommend that people learn how to solve their own problems. Teams should be given the time and mentoring necessary to investigate their biggest frustration, find the root cause, experiment with countermeasures, and implement the best one. And then do it again and again and again. When team members personally create an environment in which they can be proud of their work and work processes, you have made a good start.

Purpose-Passion-Persistence-Pride

We find that if people are proud of their work, proud of the way they do their work, and proud of the contribution their work makes to a larger purpose, they are motivated to do a good job, they persevere in their efforts despite obstacles, and over time they are successful. Pride comes easily when you have a personal connection with the people who benefit from your work, so understanding the purpose of work is important. Our recipe for an energized workforce is this: Make sure everyone understands the overall purpose of their work, generate passion around meaningful goals, recognize that hard work and persistence are necessary to be successful, and give everyone the opportunity to be proud of the way they work and the result of their efforts.

An Extraordinary Tour

Olve took us to the conference room to show us his company's products. "See this display?" he said, pointing to one of the huge displays on the wall. "People use it to communicate. Everything we do in this company is done to make it easy for people to communicate using this screen." He showed off how the Tandberg system worked. We were impressed.

The next person to greet us was a vice president. "See these displays?" he began. "People use them to communicate around the world. Everything we do in this company is done to make it easy for people to communicate using these displays." And he proceeded to discuss the competitive position of the company and the overwhelming amount of work that the company had to do to maintain this position.

We went on a plant tour and ended up in an electrical lab. An engineer was doing some work on a new camera. "Everything we do in this company is done to make it easy for people to communicate visually," she explained to us. "We need cameras to capture the pictures for our displays. We buy them on the market when we can, but for this new system, we decided that the quality of the cameras we could buy at the price point our customers could afford was not good enough. So we are developing our own camera; its resolution is xxx, its speed is yyy, its cost will be zzz. What I'm doing here is . . ."

We met with project teams who described their projects. A typical description started off: "Our displays are located around the world; any customer who uses our system will need two or three different languages the first time they use the system. In order to communicate easily, our customers need simple menus in their own language. We have people on this team who speak seven different languages, so our menus are naturally multilingual. It gives us a big advantage because our products are ready to ship anywhere in the world the minute the software is done."

"This is a great company," Olve said. "I'm just a C++ programmer, and I had the idea of inviting you here. I got full support from my managers. That's because in our company we think about engineers and salespeople as being the most important and respected positions; the 'others,' like the VP you met, all think of themselves—and express loudly—that they are in a supporting role. As one of the founders often says, 'In this company we focus on two things: We make spectacular stuff and we sell it.'"

Everywhere we went, we met people who knew exactly why they were doing what they were doing, and they were obviously proud of their product and their work. I could see that people felt the deep respect their managers had for them, and they in turn respected their managers. I think of this company as the gold standard when it comes to people who know the purpose of their work, are passionate about it, are persistent when meeting challenges, and are immensely proud of their accomplishments.[30]

Mary Poppendieck, with Olve Maudal,
Software/System Developer, Tandberg, Oslo

30. See http://olvemaudal.wordpress.com/2009/03/26/advanced-feedback-driven-development and follow the link on that blog to www.pvv.org/~oma/Software DevelopmentAtTandberg_March2009.pdf for further discussion and another example.

Portrait: Front-Line Leaders

Great leadership is most important at the front line levels of any organization because this is where a business most directly touches its employees and customers.[31]

—*James Parker*

There was a time when generals could direct a battle from atop a nearby vantage point, or personally lead a cavalry charge to exploit an enemy weakness. But with the improvement of small-arms capabilities in the 1800s, battlefields grew much larger at the same time that the pace of battle increased. Available communication devices were inadequate, and it became almost impossible for generals to keep track of what was going on, let alone exploit opportunities. But this did not keep them from trying. Tactics used in the American Civil War were hopelessly obsolete, and yet the generals on either side had no better ideas.

Meanwhile in Europe, the evolving weapons technology generated new thinking on battlefield tactics. It had always been clear that the army that could most rapidly exploit opportunities during battle would win. The question was, How could decisions be made faster? The biggest delay was in the time it took for information to go up the chain of command and commands to come back down. What if that delay were eliminated? What would it take for front-line commanders to be able to make decisions themselves?

Helmuth von Moltke (1800–1891) was appointed Chief of the Prussian (later German) General Staff in 1857. One of the important concepts he promulgated was *Auftragstaktik* (literally, "mission tactics"); a command method stressing decentralized initiative within an overall strategic design. Moltke understood that, as war progressed, its uncertainties diminished the value of any detailed planning that might have been done beforehand. He believed that, beyond calculating the initial mobilization and concentration of forces, ". . . no plan of operations extends with any degree of certainty beyond the first encounter with the main enemy force." He believed that, throughout a campaign, commanders had to make decisions based on a fluid, constantly evolving situation.

Auftragstaktik encouraged commanders to be flexible and react immediately to changes in the situation as they developed. It replaced detailed planning with delegation of decision-making authority to subordinate commanders within the context of the higher commander's intent. Moltke realized that tactical decisions had to be made on the spot; therefore, great care was taken to encourage initiative by commanders at all levels. For Moltke, "The advantage which a commander thinks he can attain through continued personal intervention is largely illusory. By engag-

31. Parker, *Do the Right Thing: How Dedicated Employees Create Loyal Customers and Large Profits*, 2008, p. 91.

ing in it he assumes a task that really belongs to others, whose effectiveness he thus destroys. He also multiplies his own tasks to a point where he can no longer fulfill the whole of them." Moltke's thought, summarized in these statements, lies at the heart of mission command.[32]

Excerpts from the German army field manual, from 1933/1934 *Truppenführung* (Unit Command), demonstrate how the implementation of *Auftragstaktik* evolved after the first World War:[33]

Section 4: Lessons in the art of war cannot be exhaustively compiled in the form of regulations. The principles must be applied in accordance with the situation. Simple actions, logically carried out, will lead most surely to the objective.

Section 6: The command of an army and its subordinate units requires leaders capable of judgment, with clear vision and foresight, and the ability to make independent and decisive decisions.

Section 7: An officer is in every sense a teacher and a leader.

Section 10: The decisive factor, despite technology and weaponry, is the value of the individual soldier. The battlefield requires soldiers who can think and act independently, who can make calculated, decisive and daring use of every situation and who understand that victory depends on each individual.

When Success Is a Matter of Life and Death

I learned as a young shave-tail (second lieutenant) that the most effective (successful) fighting force is the one where small unit leaders make local decisions. They are closest to the fighting and therefore need the flexibility to make on-the-spot decisions based on the circumstances. This model works at all levels of command. This command and control approach has been proven time and time again throughout history to be successful. This doesn't mean that senior leadership leaves it all to the small unit commanders. Their job is to set the objectives, remove obstacles, and very importantly lead by example. Let the leaders on the ground figure out how to best execute. A small sidebar here: When opinions are asked, the tradition in the military is to let the junior person (rank in this case) speak first. This approach gets ideas on the table without having the senior set the direction at the outset.

Posted by Tom Stephen on the *leanagile* Yahoo discussion group, message #1477; used with permission

---

32. U.S. Department of the Army, *Mission Command: Command and Control of Army Forces,* field manual, 2003, pp. 1-15–1-16.

33. German Army, *On the German Art of War: Truppenführung,* field manual, 2001.

Military organizations are interesting because they can teach us the principles behind effective small units, and certainly we would like effective small teams in our companies. Figure 5-3 summarizes the difference in thinking between mission command—the delegation of local decisions to local unit leaders—and detailed command—the kind of military command that usually comes to mind when we say *command and control*. Amazingly, we see that mission command, on the left side, lines up very well with agile values, whereas on the right side we see that detailed command rests on quite the opposite perspective. However, both mission command and detailed command are approaches to command and control. It just happens that military organizations have found that mission command works much better.

Mission Command		Detailed Command
Probabilistic Unpredictable	**Assumes War is**	Deterministic Predictable
Disorder Uncertainty	**Accepts**	Order Certainty
Decentralization Spontaneity Informality Loose rein Self-discipline Initiative Cooperation Acceptable decisions faster Ability at all echelons Higher tempo	**Tends to lead to**	Centralization Coercion Formality Tight rein Imposed discipline Obedience Compliance Optimal decisions but later Ability focused at the top
Implicit Vertical and horizontal Interactive	**Communication types used**	Explicit Vertical Linear
Organic Ad hoc	**Organization types fostered**	Hierarchical Bureaucratic
Delegating Transformational	**Leadership styles encouraged**	Directing Transactional

Figure 5-3 *Two approaches to command and control (U.S. Department of the Army,* Mission Command: Command and Control of Army Forces, *field manual, 2003, p. 1-15.)*

Leaders who use mission command assume that the world is unpredictable; they accept uncertainty and even disorder. This tends to lead to loose reins, self-discipline, initiative, and cooperation. They look for acceptable decisions sooner rather than optimal decisions later. Ability is developed at all levels of the organization rather than at the top. Rather than sending detailed directives through a hierarchy, mission command communicates command intent. Because responsibility for the details is delegated to front-line leaders, operations can proceed at a much higher tempo.

And a higher tempo is important. John Boyd was a U.S. fighter pilot who has had a significant impact on both military and business strategy. He observed that decisions are made in cycles of Observe-Orient-Decide-Act, a cycle that is often called the OODA loop. Boyd theorized that organizations that can complete this decision loop faster than their competitors will inevitably beat those competitors. Note that Boyd's loop is not[34]

$$O\text{-}O\text{-}O\text{-}O\text{-}O\text{-}O\text{-}O\text{-}O \rightarrow O\text{-}O\text{-}O\text{-}O\text{-}O\text{-}O\text{-}O\text{-}O \rightarrow D\text{-}D\text{-}D\text{-}D\text{-}D\text{-}D\text{-}D\text{-}D \rightarrow A\text{-}A\text{-}A\text{-}A\text{-}A\text{-}A\text{-}A$$

It is

$$O\text{-}O\text{-}D\text{-}A \rightarrow O\text{-}O\text{-}D\text{-}A \rightarrow O\text{-}O\text{-}D\text{-}A \rightarrow O\text{-}O\text{-}D\text{-}A \rightarrow O\text{-}O\text{-}D\text{-}A \rightarrow O\text{-}O\text{-}D\text{-}A \rightarrow O\text{-}O\text{-}D\text{-}A \rightarrow O\text{-}O\text{-}D\text{-}A$$

In the introduction of this book we asked, "What do Svenska Handelsbanken, Nucor Steel, SAS Institute, W. L. Gore, Southwest Airlines, Semco, and Toyota have in common?" Each of these companies has developed a *culture of high involvement*, each thrives in *an industry of high change*, and each has sustained *best-in-industry performance* over time. The leaders at these and similar great companies realize that their world is moving too fast for information to go up the chain of command and instructions to come back down. In order to compete effectively, they have shortened their response loop. They do this the same way military organizations around the world have learned to respond quickly to uncertainty and discontinuous change: They focus their attention, training, and organizational energy on making sure that they have great front-line leaders.

"Excellence throughout an organization requires consistent performance at all levels by employees who understand their company's mission, who understand their role in achieving it, and who are dedicated to accomplishing that mission," James Parker wrote. "Their information, knowledge, and inspiration will come, to a great extent, from the immediate manager or supervisor who most directly touches them and affects their lives."[35] This is the secret of Southwest

---

34. Thanks to our friend Arun Batchu for this idea.
35. Parker, *Do the Right Thing: How Dedicated Employees Create Loyal Customers and Large Profits*, 2008, p. 90.

Airlines that was missed by those who tried to copy its success. And it is the secret of every great organization we have encountered.

Your Shot

1. If you have cross-cultural teams:
   a. Have everyone look up the Hofstede indices of the culture of their childhood.[36]
   b. Ask each person to give a short presentation of these indices and discuss whether they seem to be a good representation of their home culture (not them personally).

2. Are all members of your development team considered "knowledge workers"? Are they treated as an "asset" or a "cost"? Would everyone on the team agree with your answers?

3. Make time for a discussion with everyone whose work assignments you influence:
   a. What are you good at?
   b. What do you like working on?
   c. What aren't you good at?
   d. What would you rather not work on?
   e. What is your job?
   f. What should it be?
   g. What should you be expected to contribute?
   h. What hampers you in doing your job and should be eliminated?

4. Have your team list as many communities as they can where the norm of reciprocity governs member contributions and interactions. Then list as many organizations as possible where contributions are governed mostly based on remuneration. Which organizations work better?

5. List which human resources practices in your company are focused on managing behavior through remuneration, and which are more focused on managing behavior through the norm of reciprocity. Which approach are you more comfortable with? Which seems to work better? Why?

6. Do people on your team respect their managers? Do they know what their managers' goals are? Do they try to help their managers meet their goals?

7. Let's say I am a developer or tester in your organization. Could I answer these questions:
   a. Who knows me and looks out for my welfare?
   b. Who decides what team(s) I work on?

---

36. See www.geert-hofstede.com/hofstede_dimensions.php.

c. Who guides my work?

d. Who helps me when I have problems?

e. Who cares if my work gets done—well?

f. Who provides feedback on how well I am doing?

g. Who makes sure that I have the necessary training, information, and tools?

h. Who lets me know the purpose of my work and inspires me to work for that purpose?

i. Who takes care that my assignments provide opportunities to learn and advance?

j. Who keeps me informed about what is going on in the company?

k. Who decides on my compensation?

l. Who cares about my career?

Chapter 6

Aligned Leaders

Snapshot

There's a lot to be learned by following a real agile transformation in a very large company: IBM. We look at what went right, what went wrong, how problems were overcome, what lessons were learned. We see how the definition of agile development—*short, stable iterations with customer feedback every iteration*—helped to align everyone in the organization, from development teams to executives.

Next we investigate how to bring about change in an organization. As it turns out, the biggest problem with changing the way things are done is often the existing governance system, typically a planning system in which performance targets are agreed upon in advance and financial rewards are dispensed accordingly. Another challenge is aligning the perspective of the leadership team on issues of cause and effect—if we do *this*, do we all agree that *that* is the likely result? Finally, there is the matter of sustainability: How do lean principles become simply *the way things are done*?

Leaders make the people around them better. Great leaders make the people around them great. And great companies have great leaders at every level.

Agile@IBM

At IBM, agile software development is a product, not a prescription.

Consider the magnitude of cultural change required to transform an organization as large as IBM's Software Group from traditional methods to agile: More than 25,000 engineers develop over 500 commercial software products, and roughly half of the engineering team now in place joined the company by way of acquisition. Several of IBM's commercial software projects are larger (in size and revenue) than almost any project ever observed doing software development with lean and agile methods that we have found publicly reported. How would you bring about dramatic change in such a venue?

The Transformation

Even in 2006, IBM had seen enough evidence that agile approaches to development could bear substantial fruit: shorter delivery cycles with high quality were being realized in projects as diverse as small XP projects in its San Jose labs, to IBM's front-door Web site at www.ibm.com, to the IBM Websphere Service Registry and Repository (more on this project later).[1] The trouble was, the take-up rate for additional agile projects within IBM could have been impeded by myriad factors: organizational barriers, comfort with established approaches, process inflexibility, and a lack of broad expertise with lean and agile methods, to name a few.

We received several phone calls about a possible engagement with IBM late in 2006, and our initial impulse was to say, "Thanks, but no thanks." Our concern was that any involvement with an organization as big as IBM could easily consume us. One aspect of IBM's approach persuaded us that this might be different from what we expected, however: In these initial discussions we were dealing with two IBM vice presidents, but two leading engineers were also actively engaged; it appeared to be a true top-down and bottom-up approach. The proposed plan was simple: "Help us teach three or four sessions, and we'll take it from there." We decided to take them at their word and taught several classes early in 2007 in which we found the participants to be consistently energetic and engaged.

---

1. A Gartner Case Study on the IBM Websphere Service Registry and Repository project was published on January 15, 2009; www.gartner.com/DisplayDocument?ref=g_search&id=857414. See Norton, *Case Study: IBM Uses Agile Methods to Develop WebSphere Service Registry and Repository,* 2009.

After learning as much as they could about agile and lean concepts, the members of the transformation team distilled their insights into a simple product, which they branded Agile@IBM and sold inside the company. They created a Web site, newsletters, and videos. They tried a wide range of different approaches; some persisted and others were abandoned. "Two key characteristics of the IBM approach are *collaborative leadership* and *experimentation*,"[2] said transformation team vice president Sue McKinney. "In addition, there is a distinct emphasis in the lean and agile approach employed, which we call *stakeholder involvement*."

While McKinney made the case for agile development at the executive level, two of the team members, Ted Rivera and Paul Gibson, helped develop courses to get teams started. The basic two-day "Disciplined Agile" course was an instant hit, so the duo traveled around the world, teaching developers and creating local trainers at the same time. IBM's Quality Software Engineering teams were early converts and helped develop and spread the message further to software engineers across the IBM corporation. They encouraged business units to supply their own coaches, who received training and support from the transformation team, with additional support from a small but effective Agile Center of Competency.

"This was the most successful development initiative rollout I have ever seen at IBM," Paul Gibson commented, and he has seen a lot of rollouts. "Agile@IBM has been embraced, while most new processes seem to encounter resistance," someone else commented. We think we know why. First, although Agile@IBM is based on the same approach and measurements across the company, it is being pulled by development teams rather than pushed at them. Second, the teams are in direct contact with their real stakeholders,[3] are able to do what stakeholders really want and nothing more, and are given regular feedback from stakeholders who really care about what they are doing. That makes it fun to come to work every day. And finally, the disciplined approach to developing high-quality code that is essential for successful iterative development means that developers are proud of the software they produce.

---

2. IBM has leveraged some of the ideas of collaborative leadership espoused by Pollyanna Pixton and others. See http://collaborativeleadership.com/ for further perspective.

3. *Stakeholders* in this section means "the people who will ultimately engage with and benefit from the product" (Kessler and Sweitzer, *Outside-in Software Development: A Practical Approach to Building Successful Stakeholder-Based Products*, 2008, p. 2). We use the term *customers* to refer the same people throughout the rest of this book.

Stakeholder Involvement

Carl Kessler and John Sweitzer have long expressed a consistent concern: Software must be consumable;[4] that is, software must be increasingly easy to deploy and use, so that it is easy for customers to get the kind of return on their investment that would keep them buying more software. This is especially important when you consider the proportion of business that typically comes from existing or returning customers. Kessler and Sweitzer challenged IBM's Software Group to make software increasingly consumable in part by writing the book *Outside-in Software Development.*[5]

In a nutshell, the book says that the way to improve consumability is to get stakeholder feedback early and often during development, and to act on that feedback. But some traditional development organizations are not naturally designed to do this. You can get all the feedback you want, but in practice, managers may have to commit to deliverables at the beginning of what can be a very long development cycle. So there can be a potential disconnect between outside-in development and some traditional software development approaches.

But when developers have direct feedback from stakeholders after every iteration, good things happen. So the transition team made this a requirement and let teams find creative ways to get that immediate stakeholder feedback. Some teams used early access programs with forums linking customers and developers. Others leveraged concepts such as transplant testing, residencies, and reverse residencies to make feedback routine.[6] The aim of the outside-in approach thus seeks to move from speculation to meaningful engagement that improves software.

And this kind of feedback drove good behavior, including changes in the development process itself. First of all, the software really had to be done at the end of an iteration, because customers and other stakeholders were going to see it. That meant each iteration had to deliver a coherent set of features, reasonably well documented, and without defects—at least no serious defects. Second, developers had to listen to their stakeholders and act on what they heard. This meant developers had to match their mental models directly with customers' models. Third, marketing ideas that did not hold up in practice lost their priority and were replaced by features that customers really wanted. When changing priorities lead to immediate sales on the first day of release, everyone is happy, including customers who get highly consumable software.

---

4. Carl Kessler's title within IBM Software Group's Information Management brand is Vice President, Worldwide Development, Content Management. John Sweitzer's role is that of IBM Distinguished Engineer and Chief Architect, Outside-In Driven Consumability and Integration, and he is also a part of IBM's Software Group.
5. Kessler and Sweitzer, *Outside-in Software Development: A Practical Approach to Building Successful Stakeholder-Based Products*, 2008.
6. Ibid., pp. 135–37.

An Early Experiment

The WebSphere Service Registry and Repository team, early pioneers, needed to develop its product in a ten-month window and was leveraging an agile approach. The development team knew that without real stakeholder input throughout development, there would be little chance of getting the details right. Thus the first hurdle was to find a way to obtain stakeholder feedback. The answer was to post interim releases on a Web site every month through an early access program. Interested customers could sign a confidentiality agreement and download the software as it was being developed, post their comments on a forum, and thus engage in direct interaction with the product's developers. There was a lot of interest; more than 90 customers participated in the early access program.

The discussion forum created an interesting dynamic between developers and their customers, as well as between customers with varying needs. Customers tended to keep each other from pursuing one-off requests, but when the customers spoke with one voice, the development team listened intently. Thus partway through development it became clear that a feature slated for a future release had to be included in the first release, and that some of the first-release features weren't really that important. So the team changed course, and by the time the product was released at the end of the ten months, the product was one that the customers loved. In fact, sales on the first day of release were phenomenal, because most of the early access customers were ready with a purchase order. The overall revenue targets—which had been set very aggressively—were achieved.

But even more interesting, the support team members who sat ready to take the calls that inevitably swamped them right after a release stared at nearly silent phones. How could this be? "Support calls are caused by a difference in the mental model of the developer and the customer," Paul Gibson told us. "But since the developers continually discussed the software on a forum with real stakeholders, everyone had the same mental model. Thus, far fewer support calls were necessary." Saving the cost of all those support tickets was huge, but saving the cost of defects was even larger; customers had found most of them during the early access program.

Lessons Learned

While the journey continues, and many challenges remain even two full years into the transformation, "there is compelling evidence that employing agile methodologies are consistently allowing us to reap a positive return," says Sue McKinney. We concur, because we have observed that when a company creates a process that encourages workers to focus their intelligence and their efforts directly on delighting stakeholders, the end result tends to be—no surprise here—delighted stakeholders.

It is probably more educational to understand what problems IBM encountered, rather than just to hear the success stories, so we asked managers to share with us what they learned along the way. "If you are going to take into account stakeholder feedback, you cannot commit ahead of time to 100% of what you are going to do. You can only commit to 50% or occasionally 70% of what will be delivered in a release," one line manager told us emphatically. "This requires trust on the part of your management, and in turn, you have to trust the team."

A key problem was the static business process, a governance process that required detailed approval of content prior to development. The transformation team often heard from students in its classes that this process was simply incompatible with agile, and yet it was not going to disappear. So the transformation team worked to change the business process in two ways. First, the features committed to during the approval process would now be high-level descriptions, with details to be determined during development. And second, each approval list had to have both mandatory and "run-at"[7] features; that is, there had to be space for stakeholder feedback to change the plan. Other corporate groups also had to change to accommodate agile development. The legal department had to figure out how to support the early access program. Testing, HR, globalization, translation, and other business processes had to be adapted. The transformation team worked to help these groups and others understand how their policies might inhibit agile development.

The other big lesson was that line managers really need to understand agile in order to guide their teams to success. Trust is not enough if teams and their leaders do not understand how to go about successful agile development. Starting agile development without the necessary technical discipline and tools in place is dangerous, and no manner of goodwill and trust can save a bad implementation of agile.

Per Kroll, also a part of the transformation team, provided these observations: "It's true that the Agile Manifesto rightly emphasizes individuals and interactions over processes and tools. But what some people miss is that this doesn't mean you need no processes or tools. On the contrary, tools need to be in place, and consistent practices need to be leveraged to do what we call 'Agility at Scale.' And finally, how do you know if you're doing the right thing? We have found that meaningful metrics are also essential." In sum, for IBM, a simultaneous top-down and bottom-up approach to organizational transformation—with extensive ongoing and varied stakeholder feedback—was ultimately

---

7. Features the team will take a "run at" but will not guarantee to finish.

key. No one-size-fits-all strategy would work. Experimentation, constant learning, feedback, and collaboration were hallmarks of the approach.

Helen's Story[8]

"It's not wise to jump into agile before you've invested the time to truly learn about agile, from the engineers to the organization's leaders," Helen said. As the director of a worldwide team of 500 people working on well over a dozen significant projects, Helen had not learned much about the details of agile practices when one of her managers volunteered to give it a try. "The potential problem with first-time agile adoption is that there is a tendency to pick up on the elements that appear attractive, build assumptions around them, but without the right understanding of the discipline, fail to see the elements that are required to be successful."

Helen told us three stories. "Carlos was an excellent first-line manager with consistent success in delivering his projects as committed, and I had seen good success in trusting him with new projects. So when he recommended taking an agile approach to his next project, I gave him the green light. But he didn't have the concept of pulling together the whole team in a manner that would deliver working software by the end of an iteration. He didn't understand the discipline; he hadn't learned what it really meant. Developers were writing code, but testers were not engaged, and with agile, you don't need to worry about documentation, right? When testing started to engage—late—they didn't have a good understanding of what the capabilities were that they needed to verify.

"As a leader of the organization, I could see that things were starting to fall apart and didn't have the right training myself to ask the right questions. My goal was to enable us, as a team, to have a good understanding of how we were going to deliver what we had committed to the business, with quality. We had a good track record of having done that before. I wanted to support the team through this transition but found myself asking the team 'waterfall-style' questions, which the team of course could not answer in this new world they'd ventured into.

"*Lesson one:* Ensure that your team is trained, and ensure that the leaders of the organization understand how to look at agile projects differently.

"We started mapping content onto iterations and, as we delivered those iterations, worked with a variety of stakeholders to review what we'd done to date. The stakeholder review process was one of the most valuable things we did with this release. However, we then discovered that we didn't have enough

8. Names have been changed.

room to address the feedback we were getting. The team asked for another month. I challenged them, but they had truly done their homework. They demonstrated that they really understood what our stakeholders needed and why, and they convinced me. So I backed them up, but given our rocky start, we had some selling to do to the organization.

"Lesson two: Allow enough time in the overall project plan to accommodate that critical stakeholder feedback, and ensure that the leadership team understands the necessity and value of building this flexibility into the plans from the beginning.

"The bumps in the road that we encountered in this first agile project were painful for all of us. This team is scaling back on which agile practices they will take on in their next project but continues to focus on those practices that brought the most value, active and iterative stakeholder involvement being top of that list.

"A few months later we tried again with another project, after we did more homework. Rene was a great people manager and pulled in the broader team for a more successful whole-team approach, but we started seeing technical debt accumulate. The burn-down charts were not looking good and tests were not successful often enough. This should have been a red flag, but we had old assumptions still in place that we could simply address this later, in the 'hardening' iterations. Our criteria for 'done' were not defined well enough. Technical debt was growing badly. We pulled in the agile champion for our area and he nailed the real problems and suggested remedies.

"Lessons three and four: Be sure your team understands the meaning of 'done' and how to appropriately address technical debt. We also discovered firsthand that continuous integration is *soooo* important.

"Despite these challenges and resulting lessons learned, the team delivered a product that they were proud of: They delivered new capabilities that were very much influenced by stakeholder feedback throughout the release, something that would not have been achieved using our more traditional development approach. This team is now fully on board with agile.

"Our first two experiences with agile resulted in delays to our initially planned delivery dates due to midcourse adjustments to address the challenges we encountered. But everyone still believed that this was the right direction because we were delivering more of the right content. We saw firsthand the benefits of stakeholder feedback and cross-discipline teams. So we tried again, adjusting based on lessons learned, and this time the results were awesome!

"A third team started a new agile project a few months after the first two, led by Charlie. Charlie had studied agile and he made sure the team's leaders and members were trained. He planned extensively before he started, and the team even built an automated system which continuously integrates and tests the code. The product is in its seventh iteration, and the quality and stability are amazing. It's been tremendously exciting to be seeing new capabilities, based on working code, just weeks into the new project.

"I would advise a peer leader who is new to agile to get better acquainted with the stuff—know how to ask the right questions, and give people the flexibility to deliver the best possible solution, recognizing that we won't know at the beginning exactly what that will look like! Giving your teams the right support means giving them the freedom to innovate and take on new practices, but also giving them the tools and training they need to be successful."

Helen

Charlie's Story

"I went to your class and we had lunch together," Charlie said. "And after that lunch I said to myself: 'Are they serious? Iterations of one month would never happen here.' But you know, now our iterations are three weeks long. We started out with a month but determined that was too long, so we went to three weeks.

"A few months ago I found myself about to lead an agile team. So I picked Jeff to be the tech lead, and we formed a planning team—test lead, tech lead, and architect. We were doing interim work, so we had three months to try things out. We held daily meetings and spent our time getting the TDD and automation strategy in place. We were lucky that we had the time to get everything in place and get the team trained. It would have been very difficult otherwise.

"We knew test automation was key to our success. We figured out what was wrong with the old strategy—it had many technical issues including data setup and tear-down. Jeff and the team developed a test strategy and set of tools that allow us to run over 1500 test cases every night on ten environments, something that used to take days. By morning every bit of code that was written the day before has run against all possible databases and operating systems. So you can write something to run in DB2, and by morning you will know if it works in Oracle, SQL Server, and so on. We never found out this stuff until the end of development before.

"We wrote separate functional test suites. You can run any test suite quickly with no interdependence between suites. We wrote plug-ins for the development environment so tests can be run from any sandbox. We now build every two hours. We wanted automated unit test cases to be treated with just as much priority as product code; therefore, we run all unit tests as part of the nightly build, and a unit test case failure is considered a build break.

"It's not perfect; we are running most of our functional test cases with test data and not real data. We're looking into ways to populate our databases with real data or calibrated manufactured data. And I wish I had done scale and performance testing earlier; I definitely will the next time."

Charlie

Frame 21: From Theory to Practice

In theory, there is no difference between theory and practice,
but in practice there is.

Competitive advantage does not come from good theories; it comes from good theories that are well implemented. Implementation is hard. The Agile@IBM case study provides a lot of lessons in moving from theory to practice.

Focus on Customer Outcomes

One lesson from the case study stands out above all of the rest: Early and frequent feedback from stakeholders (customers) directly to those who are developing the system—*without intermediaries*—fosters pervasive alignment by focusing everyone on customer outcomes. Here are just a few examples:

1. Helen's teams struggled to learn how to do agile development, and initial results were not promising. So why did she continue to support it? *"We were delivering more of the right content."*

2. The WebSphere Service Registry and Repository team changed the priorities originally set by marketing to match customer feedback, but the marketing people were happy with the change. Why? *Sales on the first day of release were phenomenal.*

3. Support calls were dramatically lower than expected when the WebSphere Service Registry and Repository was released. Why? *"Support calls are caused by a difference in the mental model of the developer and the customer."*

4. The existing process did not support agile development, and it certainly did not go away, but it did get changed. How did this happen? Executives realized, *"If you are going to take into account stakeholder feedback, you cannot commit ahead of time to 100% of what you are going to do."*

5. It was not necessary to force agile software development upon teams; they were eager to try it. Why? *Developers are given regular feedback from stakeholders who really care about what they are doing. That makes it fun to come to work every day.*

Change the System

The Agile@IBM case study gives us an additional insight into systems thinking. When software is released, a company should know how many support calls to staff for, based on previous experience. This data is a reflection of the *current system capability*; the number of support calls generated by a typical release is a function of development practices, release size, number of customers, customer deployment practices, and so on. If none of the processes have changed, support call volume should be predictable within a range.

Conceivably, executives could insist that the number of support calls be reduced and set a target—for example, cut support calls in half. However, setting a target does not do much to change the number of support calls; the only way to reduce the support calls is to change the system: Change one or several of the processes used in developing the software that generates a lot of support calls. You can make the software package easier to deploy, easier to use, less likely to crash, and so on. To figure out what to do to reduce support calls, you have to come to a deep understanding of why support tickets are being raised in the first place.

The insight in this case was that the root cause of support calls was a mismatch between the mental models of developers and users. To address this root cause, IBM set out to improve consumability through stakeholder feedback. One technique to obtain stakeholder feedback was to create an early access program coupled with a developer-user forum. These steps were not driven by a target for reducing support calls; they were put in place to address the root cause of consumability problems: unaligned mental models. Frequent stakeholder feedback changed the development process in many ways, and the new process resulted in much better alignment of developer and user mental models. This alignment reduced support calls by a huge amount. Focusing on reducing the number of support calls would not have had the same effect as changing the development process to address their root cause.

Create a Sense of Urgency

A successful pattern for turning theory into practice was outlined by John Kotter in his book *A Sense of Urgency*,[9] and the Agile@IBM case study is a good example of how to follow this pattern:

1. **Create a sense of urgency.**

   A sense of urgency was created at IBM by senior executive Carl Kessler, who challenged IBM's Software Group to adopt "Outside-In" development.

2. **Pull together a guiding coalition.**

   A small but powerful transformation team was formed at IBM, with dedicated vice presidents and lead engineers.

---

9. From Kotter, *A Sense of Urgency*, 2008, pp. 14–15.

3. **Develop a change vision and strategy.**

   The transformation team adopted the strategy of selling agile to business units, rather than imposing it on them, in line with agile principles. To implement this strategy they developed a brand, support materials, Web site, coaches, and training approach.

4. **Communicate for understanding and buy-in.**

   The transformation team focused on demonstrating the value of the new approach. A two-day class was delivered around the world by a single pair, who taught local teachers and coaches how to replicate the class at their local sites.

5. **Empower all others to act.**

   The transformation team actively looked for obstacles to implementation and focused on changing organizational policies that got in the way of the new approach.

6. **Produce short-term wins.**

   The WebSphere Service Registry and Repository provided an early win that was widely publicized.

7. **Don't let up.**

   Staff support for agile development is expanding as its benefits are seen.

8. **Make sure change sticks.**

   An organizational focus on consumability and the availability of tools such as the powerful test harness described in the case study have helped make agile development a method of choice.

There are several things that the IBM transformation team did *not* do. They did not hire a large number of consultants or greatly increase central staffing. They did not set targets for the number of agile teams the organization was supposed to have; they let the program sell itself based on results. Although they set standards (for example, stakeholder feedback every iteration), they did not tell teams how to meet the standards; they let the teams figure it out for themselves. Finally, they did not dramatically change their governance process; they just modified it appropriately.

Frame 22: Governance

In preparing for battle I have always found that plans are useless, but planning is indispensable.

—Dwight D. Eisenhower

One of the biggest obstacles that had to be dealt with when implementing agile development at IBM was the governance process that required detailed approval of product content prior to development. This is likely to be one of the biggest obstacles to any large-scale implementation of lean development, because the governance process for system development in most large organizations is based on creating detailed project plans and measuring performance against those plans. This is true whether the systems are developed under contract between firms or development is done completely within a vertically integrated organization. The governance process in many companies boils down to the equivalent of negotiating a contract for development and measuring performance against that contract. As long as this governance process remains in place without modification—whether inside of or between firms—the full potential of lean development processes will not be realized.

Beyond Budgeting

The problem with plans and contracts may be best understood by looking at an even more pervasive governance process found in most organizations: the annual budgeting process. What's wrong with budgets? In the book *Implementing Beyond Budgeting*, Bjarte Bogsnes counts the ways:[10]

1. *The Trust Problem:* Most performance measurements that are based on detailed budgets and plans telegraph a deep lack of trust and need for control. While we preach democracy in politics, people have to check their democratic beliefs at the door of most companies. The control systems are in place to keep the few untrustworthy people in the company in line, yet they signal a lack of trust of everyone, telling them they aren't expected to act in a trustworthy manner. Bogsnes wrote:[11]

   The skeptics asked us again and again: what will prevent people from uncontrolled spending if we drop budgets? Can we really trust these guys to manage their own costs? It was their concern number one, two, and three. But what kind of people are we actually talking about? It was the people we trusted with building and working on million- and billion-dollar machines. It was people we trusted with trading crude oil or handling currency exposures for millions every single day. But manage their own travel costs? Are you kidding?

2. *The Cost Management Problem:* One problem with cost budgets is that they are viewed as entitlements, so they act as a floor as well as a ceiling on spending. Similarly, the problem with plans is that Parkinson's Law holds: Work expands to fit the time (budget) allotted. Costs and time are better managed if there is ongoing incentive to question every investment

---

10. Bogsnes, *Implementing Beyond Budgeting: Unlocking the Performance Potential*, 2009. These points are summarized in pp. 8–52 of this book.

11. Ibid., p. 11.

of time or money, rather than assuming that if something is in the plan it is necessarily valuable.

3. *The Target-Setting and Evaluation Problem:* Budget targets, as well as project plans, are usually laid out in great detail, and the variance between plan and actual is measured at the same detailed level. The amazing thing is the assumption that it is possible to guess, at such a detailed level, long in advance, exactly what the right thing to do will be. But people are not evaluated on whether or not they made the best, most effective, most value-generating decision at the time; they are evaluated on whether or not they followed—in detail—the long-outdated guesses from the past.

4. *The Bonus Problem:* Individual bonus systems are very common in the United States and are expanding in Europe. One of the biggest objections to abandoning budgets is that there would then be no basis for incentive bonuses. Similarly, plans often serve as the basis for incentive bonuses in system development. Bogsnes says he has lost all belief in individual bonuses, because both research and experience have shown him that they do much more harm than good. In particular, when targets form the basis of bonuses, unethical behavior—not motivation—is most likely the ultimate consequence.[12] Profit sharing across a broad group makes more sense; individual bonuses should be avoided.

5. *The Timing Problem:* Annual budgets mean we take a look at our business and the competitive situation once a year. That is not enough in a changing world. Similarly, detailed plans frozen far in advance do not allow for feedback. IBM, for instance, found that product feature descriptions should be limited to high-level statements and a portion of the available time should be left free to allow time and space for customer feedback.

6. *The Quality Problem:* Budgets and plans have three purposes: (1) Set goals, (2) make forecasts, and (3) allocate resources. It would seem efficient to use a single plan to accomplish all three purposes, but in fact, combining the purposes compromises all of them. Goals should be challenges with an element of stretch and ambition, but without the evaluation problem mentioned above. Forecasts should be brutally honest and not involve any wishful thinking, so we can act on gaps as soon as they are evident. These two purposes are diametrically opposed to each other, so we end up with a compromise that does not serve either purpose well. And finally, resource allocation should be a dynamic process, done as late as possible when we have the best information.

---

12. For much more on the Bonus Problem, see ibid., pp.28–41.

7. *The Efficiency Problem:* The last and probably the least problem with budgets and plans is the enormous waste of time and effort spent in their preparation, and then in measuring and explaining variances. It might be different if this work added value, but for the most part it does not. Planning can be very useful. The plans themselves rarely are.

In the introduction of this book we told the story of Svenska Handelsbanken and its visionary leader, Jan Wallander. In 1972 he organized the bank around local branches and instituted a governance system that compared the profitability and productivity of the branches. With branch managers making local decisions and minimum central control, Handelsbanken became one of the top banks in Europe and was well positioned to weather the financial storms of the 1990s and 2008–9.

Since he was an economist, Wallander was well aware that financial markets are subject to periodic cycles of economic slowdown, and one of his responsibilities was to create an organization that could survive the inevitable downturns. He observed that discontinuous changes are never predictable, even though they might seem obvious in hindsight. So he gave up trying to predict such change; he decided that the safest approach for a bank was to be in a position to adjust rapidly to changing situations as they occurred. He felt that developing and following an annual plan (in the form of a budget) was the antithesis of rapid response, saying, "A budget will either prove roughly right, and then it will be trite, or it will be disastrously wrong, in which [case] it will be dangerous. My conclusion is thus: Scrap it!"[13]

Many companies use the budgeting system as a primary governance mechanism, and scrapping this system is usually beyond contemplation, even when its shortcomings are obvious to all. Similarly, most companies use a combination of portfolio management, project planning, and earned value monitoring as a primary governance mechanism for system development, and these governance systems are not going to go away. But they can be modified; for example, IBM changed its governance system so that high-level descriptions replaced detailed descriptions, and space had to be reserved for responding to feedback.

12 Principles

In 1997, Jeremy Hope and Robin Fraser formed the Beyond Budgeting Round Table (BBRT) to look for governance options beyond budgets and to help companies be more responsive to change. Their book *Beyond Budgeting*[14] documents

---

13. Wallander, "Budgeting—An Unnecessary Evil," 1999.
14. Hope and Fraser, *Beyond Budgeting: How Managers Can Break Free from the Annual Performance Trap*, 2003.

the results of their work. Over time they came to realize that the issue they were struggling with was larger than budgets and could not be solved with processes or tools. They came to the conclusion that a coherent leadership model is required to provide guidance in changing the governance system of a company—a leadership model that moves decision making to local teams and gives those teams the autonomy and responsibility to focus on customer outcomes and respond to market changes.

The BBRT leadership model is as relevant for system development governance as it is for corporate governance; since it was designed for senior executives, it is a model that can be effective at all levels of the organization. The BBRT leadership model has 12 principles:[15]

Leadership Principles:

1. *Customers:* Focus everyone on customers, *not on hierarchical relationships.*

2. *Organization:* Organize as a lean network of accountable teams, *not centralized functions.*

3. *Responsibility:* Enable everyone to act and think like a leader, *not merely follow the plan.*

4. *Autonomy:* Give teams the freedom and capability to act; *do not micromanage them.*

5. *Transparency:* Promote open information for self-management; *do not restrict it hierarchically.*

6. *Governance:* Adopt a few clear values, goals, and boundaries, *not fixed targets.*

Process Principles:

1. *Goals:* Set relative goals for continuous improvement; *do not negotiate fixed contracts.*

2. *Rewards:* Reward shared success based on relative performance, *not fixed targets.*

3. *Planning:* Make planning a continuous and inclusive process, *not a top-down annual event.*

4. *Controls:* Base controls on relative indicators and trends, *not variances against a plan.*

---

15. Bogsnes, *Implementing Beyond Budgeting: Unlocking the Performance Potential,* 2009, p. 55.

5. **Resources:** Make resources available as needed, *not through annual budget allocations.*

6. **Coordination:** Coordinate interactions dynamically, *not through annual planning cycles.*

What Is Productivity?

Among the 12 BBRT principles is a focus on relative, rather than absolute, performance measurements. As we noted in Frame 2: System Capability, relative goals—goals that measure performance relative to competitors, relative to peers, or relative to past performance—are better than fixed targets. This is because the definition of "good" performance is constantly adjusted based on reality; it is not forecast long in advance. However, ranking performance against peers can create destructive internal competition that must be counteracted by basing rewards on shared performance. There is also a case to be made that absolute goals have their place when measuring competencies; for example, the criteria for earning a black belt in karate are fixed. The bottom line is that adopting "a few clear goals" that challenge people without motivating them to game the system is a difficult, context-specific task.

The most widely used relative goal in software development is productivity, but a good definition of software development productivity remains elusive. The problem is that software development in and of itself is rarely the goal of the system that it supports. Therefore, true productivity has to be measured relative to the outcomes of the overall system, not just the software. Just producing a lot of lines of code or function points is irrelevant; the real question is, How much improvement in customer outcomes has the development team generated?

This is what makes software development governance so difficult; it seems that most people desperately want to divorce development performance measurements from system outcome measurements and consider software as a separate entity. But we observe that this separation is a big source of dysfunction in a software development organization. Measuring and trying to maximize subsystem performance is a well-known way to sub-optimize overall performance, yet most software development governance systems do exactly that. It doesn't matter if we are measuring lines of code or function points or variance from plan; none of these measurements focuses the development team on what really matters: customer outcomes.

Consider an advertising campaign. We expect the advertising agency to bring us several options to consider; we don't say, "Be productive; develop only one option." We do not measure the agency's performance based on how few resources they used in developing the campaign or how quickly it is finished; we measure performance based on increased sales of the advertised product. We wouldn't consider any other approach—unless the advertising involves developing a Web site.

Software development governance should not be based on internal measures; it should be based on customer outcomes, whatever that means in your world. Software is part of a system, the system produces value, and the thing you need to know is how much value the *system* produces per developer, and how the value/cost ratio of your development organization compares with that of your competitors.

Frame 23: Alignment

The secret of success is not to foresee the future, but to build an organization that is able to prosper in any of the unforeseeable futures.

—*Michael Hammer*

Changing a governance system is hard; changing a leadership model is very difficult; but these changes have been successfully made by some organizations, often triggered by duress such as serious competition or a dramatic change in market conditions. On the other hand, many attempts to change organizations are unsuccessful. So the question is, What is the difference? What conditions are necessary to make organizational change work?

Cause and Effect

Clayton Christensen has been studying this topic for years. He coined the term *disruptive technology* and pointed out that most organizations are unable to detect the importance of a disruptive technology until it's too late, and they are unable to change to deal with the new reality. This matches Jan Wallander's observation that discontinuous changes are never predictable ahead of time, even though they might seem obvious in hindsight. Both men observed that the only way to survive discontinuous change is to establish the capability to detect the early warning signs of disruptive change and rapidly adapt to it.

So what does it take to change an organization to make it more perceptive and responsive? Clayton Christenson and coauthors wrote:[16]

> Over our many years observing management successes and failures up close, we've found that the first step in any change initiative must be to assess the level of

---

16. Christensen, Marx, and Stevenson, "The Tools of Cooperation and Change," 2006. Italics in the original.

agreement in the organization along two critical dimensions. The first is the extent to which people agree on *what they want:* the results they seek from their participation in the enterprise; their values and priorities; and which trade-offs they are willing to make in order to achieve those results.

The second dimension is the extent to which people agree on *cause and effect:* which actions will lead to the desired outcome. When people have a shared understanding of cause and effect, they will probably agree about which processes to adopt.

It is the second dimension—*agreement on cause and effect*—that is especially critical for a leadership team about to head down the path of change in system development. The lean frame is counterintuitive. It is based on long-range thinking and a systems perspective that feels uncomfortable to many people. It challenges the conventional wisdom of many organizations. Thus, even when it is easy for members of the leadership team to agree on *what they want*, it is often very difficult for them to agree on *cause and effect*. Worse, the lack of agreement is often not obvious. Leaders often assume that their colleagues think the same way they do, when in fact their views may be quite different.

If you are considering a lean initiative, your leadership team would do well to discuss the members' individual beliefs about cause and effect: *If we do **this**, we can expect **that** result.* Before you start down the path of change, make sure that the members of the leadership team are in substantial agreement on cause and effect.

We have developed a set of six questions that we often ask leadership teams to discuss—questions that help the team discover if everyone agrees on cause and effect. These questions are presented in Tables 6-1 to 6-6. Each table starts with a question across the top. On the left side of the table you will find a very common answer to the question, along with the thinking that supports that answer. On the right side of the table, you will find our preferred answer to the question, along with the reasons why we think this is a better answer.

The first question, in Table 6-1, concerns the best way to control costs. We find that members of a leadership team often have different opinions on how to go about cost control. On the left side we list the approach taken by most companies: Have each department drive down its costs. This is rather easy and usually delivers quick results. But it rarely results in the lowest total cost, because in reality, optimizing subsystems sub-optimizes the whole system. Thus achieving the lowest total cost often means that some departments have to *raise* their costs. On the right side of Table 6-1, we show that our preferred approach for cost control is to eliminate the costs between departments, because we believe that this is where the biggest opportunity lies. Have your leadership team discuss this table and find out if everyone has a similar view of what it takes to optimize the whole system.

Table 6-1   *Cost Cutting*

The current economic conditions require steep cost cutting. What is the best approach to reducing cost?	
Drive the costs out of each department.	**Eliminate costs between departments.**
Total cost is the sum of individual department costs.	Driving down costs in each department will usually drive *up* overall costs.
Cutting costs across the board is the easiest, fastest way to drive down total cost.	The best opportunity for cost reduction is found *between* departments.
Department heads should be responsible for costs they can control.	Department heads should be responsible for costs they can *influence*.

Does everyone on your leadership team agree on the likely outcomes of each choice?

Members of a leadership team frequently hold different opinions about the nature of plans and planning, as can be seen in Table 6-2. There is a reason why many leaders consider a plan to be a commitment; their governance systems are based on this premise, so they have little choice. But let's face it; plans made back when we had the least information are not right by definition. In fact, they invariably have to change, and then we have to change requirements and explain variances. If people could walk away from their governance system and

Table 6-2   *Conformance to Plan*

What is your point of view about committing to a plan and meeting the commitment?	
A plan is a commitment.	**Planning is indispensable, but plans are useless.**
Predictability comes from conformance to plan.	The most predictable performance comes from maintaining options until we have the most information.
The plan is always right.	Plans are scenarios for what might occur and are useful to help us respond quickly as events unfold.
Variance against plan indicates a failure to execute and should be explained.	Variance against plan is welcomed as a learning opportunity, a way to discover more about the complexities of the work.

Does everyone on your leadership team have the same philosophy and perspective?

really do the right thing, would they stay on the left side of the table? We believe that the only safe approach for long-term survival is to be able to respond to change rather than predict it, so we are solidly on the right side. What do the members of your leadership team think of conformance to plan? Is everyone on the same side of the table?

One of the biggest differences of perspectives among members of a leadership team comes from opinions about what is involved in effective resource allocation, as summarized in Table 6-3. From our perspective on the right side of this table, it's impossible to underestimate the damage that has been done in development organizations in the pursuit of efficiency and high utilization. We observe that most attempts at full utilization actually decrease utilization while at the same time telegraphing the message that people are fungible "resources." But when efficiency is valued above effectiveness and adaptability, when short-term results are valued over long-term survival, the left side of the table will prevail. Does everyone on your leadership team have the same perspective on this issue?

Table 6-3 *Utilization*

What is your point of view about having everyone with a full load of work at all times?	
We need full utilization of expensive resources.	It is impossible to move rapidly without slack.
The best way to increase productivity is to keep everyone 100% assigned.	100% utilization leads to thrashing and decreases overall productivity.
Large queues of work allow managers to make better priority decisions and help keep everyone busy.	Batch and queue mentality is the biggest detriment to system-wide performance.
Does everyone on your leadership team have the same philosophy and perspective?	

A common way of characterizing organizations is to classify some as more "mature" than others. Maturity is taken to mean being disciplined and repeatable, although we would argue that maturity means being disciplined and adaptable. With that in mind, the original purpose of work standards is depicted on the right side of Table 6-4. We wonder how their purpose ever got morphed into the interpretation on the left side of the table. What do the members of your leadership team think about the purpose of work standards? Does everyone have the same opinion?

Table 6-4   *Work Standards*

What do you believe is the purpose of work standards?	
The purpose of standards is to make it possible for anyone to do any job.	**The purpose of standards is to provide a baseline for improvement.**
Standards are initiated by process groups.	If standards are not changed frequently, improvement efforts have stalled.
Written standards are to be followed, not changed.	When someone is annoyed by his or her job, help the person find a better way.
One or a few standard approaches are sufficient across the entire organization.	Work standards embed the best knowledge the team has about how to do its own current task.
Does everyone on your leadership team have the same philosophy and perspective?	

There are two ways of thinking about finances: balance sheet thinking and cash flow thinking. When a leadership team has people with both perspectives, they will see the world very differently, as shown in Table 6-5. As a pioneer in the just-in-time manufacturing movement, coauthor Mary found that calling inventory an *asset*, as balance sheet accounting does, means that driving down inventory is bad. A whole generation of accountants had to retire before manufacturing thinking shifted to the right side of the table. It's time for the rest of the world to discover what manufacturers found out long ago: Cash flow thinking leads to better decisions, higher quality, and more responsiveness to the market. Does your leadership team make cash flow or balance sheet decisions?

Table 6-5   *Finances*

What kind of financial thinking drives day-to-day decisions?	
Balance sheet thinking: What is the breakup value of the company?	**Cash flow thinking: How long does it take to convert capital into cash?**
Delay doesn't matter.	Delay creates waste.
Just-in-case is wise.	Just-in-time is wiser.
Work-in-process has value.	Work-in-process is waste.
Queues support better decisions and full utilization.	Queues gum up the works and slow things down.
Does everyone on your leadership team have the same philosophy and perspective?	

Members of leadership teams often have strong differences of opinion on how to achieve the best results, as shown in Table 6-6. We are solidly on the right side of this table; we are convinced that results are a second-order effect. If you improve the capability of the system and people to deliver results, you will do far better than if you set targets that are mere guesses about what is possible. It's not that you don't collect data—you certainly do—but the data is used in an evidence-based improvement process. This is a very counterintuitive concept; is your leadership team aligned on what success means and how to achieve it?

These are not the only areas where a leadership team needs to agree on cause and effect, but they are some of the more likely areas where differences of opinion might arise. There is considerable evidence that the beliefs in the left column do not lead to sustained superior results, while those in the right column frequently do. Alignment of the perspective of the leadership team members on these fundamental questions is one of the most critical success factors for an organization when it sets out to change the way its systems are developed.

Table 6-6   *Performance Measurements*

What is the best way to achieve important company goals?	
Set targets.	Improve the capability of the system and the people.
If you want to improve the performance of anything, the obvious way to proceed is to find the right measures and use them as levers to improve the results.	"If you have a stable system, then there is no use to specify a goal. You will get whatever the system will deliver. A goal beyond the capability of the system will not be reached."[a]
Set targets to clearly communicate what management considers important.	Meeting targets without changing the system generates wide oscillations in performance and makes things worse.
Data is used as metrics.	Data is used for process improvement.
Individual performance appraisals and bonuses motivate improved individual performance.	Individual bonuses discourage effective collaboration and motivate unethical behavior.
Does everyone on your leadership team agree on the likely outcomes of each choice?	

a. Deming, *Out of the Crisis*, 2000, p. 76.

Frame 24: Sustainability

Create constancy of purpose toward improvement of product and service, with the aim to become competitive and stay in business, and to provide jobs.
                                                        —W. Edwards Deming

Leadership alignment is two-dimensional: First, the members of the current leadership team must align their perspectives; and second, the leadership perspective has to be maintained over time, and not just a short time—over decades of time. It's pretty obvious that this is not easy. No matter what name or initials a change initiative has—TQM, CMMI, Lean, Six Sigma—the tendency of these initiatives to plateau after harvesting the low-hanging fruits is well documented, and the rate of relapse is high. So what is the difference between the majority of companies that do not sustain change initiatives and the few that sustain top performance over time? We think the difference lies in the very idea of having a change initiative in the first place.

Consider the companies listed in the introduction: Svenska Handelsbanken, Nucor Steel, Semco, SAS Institute, W. L. Gore, Southwest Airlines, Toyota. The first three changed from average companies to great companies under the guidance of a visionary leader, and the last four started out with visionary leaders. All of these companies have sustained top performance over time, but *none* of these companies attributes its stellar performance to an "initiative," lean or otherwise. They attribute their superior performance to their underlying culture, a culture that pervades the way everyone thinks and acts. There is the Toyota Way, the Southwest Airlines Way, the Semco Way, and so on. Typically these companies provide secure employment, promote from within, and focus more on customer satisfaction than financial results. They could be called reciprocity companies—they treat their employees well and employees treat the company well in return.

Great companies look at the world through a different frame. They do not have initiatives they are trying to sustain; they have *companies* they are trying to sustain. And the way they do this is consistent: They do not focus first of all on efficiency; they focus first of all on adaptability. Being adaptable is not necessarily the most efficient approach in the short run, but it always seems to win out in the long run.

John Shook, a senior adviser at the Lean Enterprise Institute who worked for Toyota for more than a decade, wrote:[17]

---

17. Shook, "Survive to Make Money or Make Money to Survive?," 2008.

The real secrets to Toyota's success aren't to be found in successful implementation of tools and techniques, systems or even "principles". It really gets into basic thinking. . . .

Toyota wants to make money as much as the next company, and they do it extremely well. However, the company's real aim is something much deeper, and is the thing that has driven the company to be so successful for so long: the will to survive. Everything else—tools, systems, even principles—follows from that. A highly developed instinct for survival will take you a long, long way. . . .

Yes, GM wants to survive. . . .Yet had GM been seeking long-term survival a la Toyota, it would have made different decisions all along. GM wants to survive, all right, it wants to survive so it can continue to make money. Toyota on the other hand, wants to make money to survive. . . .

Those contrasting senses of purpose will take you down very different paths.

Shook goes on to list technique after technique that Toyota uses to remain adaptable, and he points out that every single one of these techniques would be considered "inefficient" on the surface. Techniques that appear to be inefficient on the surface will never survive a change in leadership that changes the organization's focus from survival to efficiency.

Shook also notes that Toyota's techniques depend upon a shift in leadership style—from telling people what to do, to engaging the creativity and curiosity of people doing the work. This is also a survival technique; the company wants all of its people to be on the alert to detect a change in their environment and to know that they are expected to adapt to that change.

So bottom line, sustainability is not about sustaining change. It's about sustaining the company itself by creating a deep-seated ability to adapt to change. If you are measuring the results of agile or lean on a financial scale, you are measuring the wrong thing. You should be measuring the ability of the company to create satisfied customers, to quickly adapt to change, and to develop its people so that whatever the future brings, the company will be in a position to adapt and thrive, long after the current leadership team has turned over the company to the next generation.

In the end, sustainability is dependent on developing leaders, especially new leaders. Senior leaders must believe that the ultimate measure of their success is the quality of the first-line leaders, the team leads, the technical leaders, the product champions, and the mentors who guide relentless improvement. Consider whether the leaders you need are in place, are well trained, and have mentors to guide them. Consider whether leaders at all levels of the organization understand that it is their job to *be* mentors and guide those who look to them for leadership.

Portrait: Leaders at All Levels

Great organizations have great leaders at every level.[18]

—James Parker

We have plenty of portraits of senior leaders at the top of great organizations. But as James Parker points out,[19] great companies have great leaders at all levels of the organization, or they wouldn't be great. So we close with a portrait of the kind of leaders who are found at all levels of a great company.

Leaders Provide Purpose

People want to be part of something meaningful; they want to be part of a team where they can feel proud, feel a sense of fulfillment, and know that they are making a contribution. They want to understand how their jobs matter and how they fit into the overall picture. People will be committed to the success of their organizations only if they understand what *success* means and how their jobs contribute to it. When people feel valued and respected, they will value and respect their company and its customers.

Leaders define and communicate the purpose of an organization and provide guidance on how the purpose might be achieved. They solve problems, give feedback, arrange for learning. Leaders make sure people have the ability and resources to be successful and provide mentoring to help ensure success.

Leaders Set the Tone and Tempo

Different types of organizations, different levels in an organization, and different-sized groups need different approaches to leadership. Sometimes leaders are appointed and sometimes they emerge. But in all cases, when groups and organizations are successful on a sustained basis, you will always find good leaders setting the tone and the pace.

Consider the jazz band. Whenever the band performs, there is always a leader. If the band has just a few musicians, the leadership rotates. At the beginning of each piece, the musicians glance at each other and then one of them takes the lead, sets the tempo, and signals the start. In a big band—around 18 musicians—there is usually a conductor who leads the band. The conductor sets the tempo and volume, signals when various sections start, and occasionally

---

18. Parker, *Do the Right Thing: How Dedicated Employees Create Loyal Customers and Large Profits*, 2008, pp. 83, 89.
19. This section paraphrases various writings in ibid. See especially pp. 145 and 222.

turns the floor over to a soloist. A soloist's skill and competence make that person the best suited to lead this section of the performance, so the conductor steps back while the soloist takes the lead during the solo.

Similarly, in small development efforts where few people are involved, leaders can emerge from the team. But in larger, more complex efforts, leaders with deep experience, good relationships, and well-honed instincts are invaluable. In both cases, it is important to frame the role of leadership correctly: Leaders create an atmosphere, set the cadence, coordinate efforts, provide guidance, and help people solve problems.

Leaders Make People Better

James Parker, former CEO of Southwest Airlines, says that the only way to systematically ensure that you have great people at every level is to ensure that you have great leaders at every level—leaders who make the people around them better:[20]

Great leaders:
1. Have a passion for the mission they are leading.
2. Recognize that the success of their mission, and their personal success, ultimately depends on the performance of others.
3. Care deeply about the well-being and success of the people they are leading.
4. Show respect for each person and the role performed by that person.
5. Are always fair and honest in dealing with other people.
6. Possess the patience to coach and teach others.
7. Recognize talent and have a knack for putting people in the right position to utilize that talent.
8. Have the strength of character to accept responsibility and to not look for scapegoats in the face of failure.
9. Have the judgment and humility to share credit in the face of success.
10. Act naturally, without pretense, taking advantage of their natural talents and personality.

Trust and mutual respect are ultimately the keys to successful leadership.

Leaders Create Space for Others to Succeed

William McKnight joined 3M in 1907 as an assistant bookkeeper, and he rose rapidly in the small, struggling company, effectively taking over day-to-day operations by 1916. He was president of the company from 1929 to 1949, chairman of the board until 1966, and honorary chairman until 1972. In his long tenure as 3M's leader, McKnight created a corporate culture that nurtured

---

20. Ibid., pp. 94–95.

employee initiative and innovation. In 1948, McKnight summed up his philoso-phy this way:[21]

> As our business grows, it becomes increasingly necessary to delegate responsibility and to encourage men and women to exercise their initiative. This requires consid-erable tolerance. Those men and women, to whom we delegate authority and responsibility, if they are good people, are going to want to do their jobs in their own way.
>
> Mistakes will be made. But if a person is essentially right, the mistakes he or she makes are not as serious in the long run as the mistakes management will make if it undertakes to tell those in authority exactly how they must do their jobs.
>
> Management that is destructively critical when mistakes are made kills initiative. And it's essential that we have many people with initiative if we are to continue to grow.

When the time is right, leaders get out of the way and give people the space and support to be creative and make their own success.

Gary Convis, who succeeded Fujio Cho as president of Toyota Motor Manu-facturing Kentucky, wrote: "I'll never forget the wise advice given me by a man I grew to respect and admire very deeply, Mr. Kan Higashi, who was our second president at NUMMI. When he promoted me to vice president, he said my greatest challenge would be 'to lead the organization as if I had no power.' In other words, shape the organization not through the power of will or dictate, but rather through example, through coaching and through understanding and helping others to achieve their goals. This, I truly believe, is the role of manage-ment in a healthy, thriving, work environment."[22]

21. http://solutions.3m.com/wps/portal/3M/en_US/our/company/information/history/ McKnight-principles/.
22. Convis, "Role of Management in a Lean Manufacturing Environment." 2001. See www.sae.org/manufacturing/lean/column/leanjul01.htm.

Bibliography

"100k Lives—Getting Started Kit: Prevent Central Line Infections." Institute for Health Care Improvement, n.d. www.ihi.org/NR/rdonlyres/ BF4CC102-C564-4436-AC3A-0C57B1202872/0/ CentralLinesHowtoGuideFINAL720.pdf.

Abe, Namiko. "Japan and the World Map." Namiko's Japanese Language Blog, March 5, 2008. http://japanese.about.com/b/2008/03/05/sekai-chizu-no-naka-no-nihon.htm.

Adler, Nancy. *International Dimensions of Organizational Behavior, Fourth Edition*. Cincinnati: South-Western, 2002.

Anonymous. "Skyscrapers: The Paper Spires." *Fortune*, September 1930.

Baker, F. T. "System Quality Through Structured Programming." *AFIPS Conference Proceedings*, 1972, pp. 339–43.

Ballé, Michael, Godefroy Beauvallet, Art Smalley, and Durward K. Sobek. "The Thinking Production System." *Reflections: The SoL Journal* 7, no. 2 (May 2006), pp. 1–12.

Bazerman, Max, interview by Sean Silverthorne. "When Goal Setting Goes Bad." Harvard Business School Working Knowledge, March 2009.

Beck, Kent. "Simple Smalltalk Testing." *Smalltalk Report*, October 1994.

Bezos, Jeff. "Annual Letter to Shareholders," April 17, 2009.

———, interview by Julia Kirby and Thomas A. Stewart. "The Institutional Yes." *Harvard Business Review*, October 2007.

Boehm, Barry W. "An Early Application Generator and Other Recollections." In *In the Beginning: Personal Recollections of Software Pioneers*, by Robert L. Glass, pp. 67–97. New York: Wiley/IEEE Computer Society, 1997.

———. "Software Engineering." *IEEE Transactions on Computers*, December 1976, pp. 1226–41.

Bogsnes, Bjarte. *Implementing Beyond Budgeting: Unlocking the Performance Potential*. New York: Wiley, 2009.

Brooks, Fred. "No Silver Bullet: Essence and Accidents of Software Engineering." *Information Processing 1986, Proceedings of the IFIP Tenth World Computing Conference*, edited by H. J. Kugler, pp. 1069–76. Amsterdam: Elsevier Science B.V., 1986.

Brown, Tim. "Design Thinking." *Harvard Business Review*, June 2008, pp. 84–92.

———. "Strategy by Design." *Fast Company*, December 2007.

———. "The Deans of Design." *U.S. News & World Report*, October 2, 2006.

Byrne, John A. "The Man Who Invented Management: Why Peter Drucker's Ideas Still Matter." *Business Week*, November 28, 2005.

Charette, Robert. "Why Software Fails." *IEEE Spectrum*, September 2005, pp. 42–49.

Christensen, Clayton, Matt Marx, and Howard Stevenson. "The Tools of Cooperation and Change." *Harvard Business Review*, October 2006, pp. 72–80.

Colvin, Geoff. *Talent Is Overrated: What Really Separates World-Class Performers from Everybody Else.* New York: Portfolio, 2008.

Converse, Donald. "Thank You Herb!" *Fast Company*, June 2008.

Convis, Gary. "Role of Management in a Lean Manufacturing Environment." *Learning to Think Lean.* SAE International, July 2001. www.sae.org/manufacturing/lean/column/leanjul01.htm.

Conway, Melvin E. "How Do Committees Invent?" *Datamation*, April 1968.

Crispin, Lisa, and Janet Gregory. *Agile Testing: A Practical Guide for Testers and Agile Teams.* Boston: Addison-Wesley, 2009.

Cunnningham, Ward. "The WyCash Portfolio Management System." OOPSLA '92 Experience Report, 1992.

———. "Wiki Inventor Ward Cunningham with John Gage." Computer History Museum, 2006. Video at www.youtube.com/watch?v=bx6nNqSASGo.

Dahl, O.-J., E. W. Dijkstra, and C. A. R. Hoare. *Structured Programming: A.P.I.C. Studies in Data Processing No. 8.* New York: Academic Press, 1972.

Davenport, Thomas H. "The Coming Commoditization of Processes." *Harvard Business Review*, June 2005, pp. 100–8.

de Geus, Arie. *The Living Company.* Boston: Harvard Business School Press, 2002.

Deming, W. Edwards. *Out of the Crisis.* Cambridge, MA: MIT Press, 2000. First published in 1982 by MIT Center for Advanced Educational Services.

Denne, Mark, and Jane Cleland-Huang. *Software by Numbers.* Upper Saddle River, NJ: Prentice Hall, 2004.

Denning, Peter J., Chris Gunderson, and Rick Hayes-Roth. "Evolutionary System Development." *Communications of the ACM*, December 2008, pp. 29–31.

Dijkstra, Edsger W. "A Constructive Approach to the Problem of Program Correctness." *BIT Numerical Mathematics* 8, no. 3 (September 1968), pp. 174–86.

————. "Complexity Controlled by Hierarchical Ordering of Function and Variability." *Software Engineering: Report on a Conference Sponsored by the NATO Science Committee*, edited by Peter Naur and Brian Randell. Garmisch, Germany, October 7–11, 1968. http://homepages.cs.ncl.ac.uk/brian.randell/NATO/index.html.

————. "On the Role of Scientific Thought." In *Selected Writings on Computing: A Personal Perspective*, pp. 60–66. New York: Springer-Verlag, 1982.

————. "Structured Programming." *Report on a Conference Sponsored by the NATO Science Committee*, Rome, 1969. Reprinted in *Classics in Software Engineering*, edited by Edward Nash Yourdon, pp. 43–48. Yourdon Press, 1979.

————. "The Humble Programmer." *Communications of the ACM* 15, no. 10 (1972), pp. 859–66.

————. "Two Views of Programming." 1975. www.cs.utexas.edu/users/EWD/.

Drucker, Peter. *Management Challenges for the 21st Century*. New York: Harper Business, 1999.

————. *People and Performance: The Best of Drucker on Management*. New York: Harper & Row, 1977.

Ericsson, K. Anders, Neil Charness, Paul Feltovich, and Robert Hoffman. *The Cambridge Handbook of Expertise and Expert Performance*. Cambridge: Cambridge University Press, 2006.

Evans, Eric. *Domain-Driven Design: Tackling Complexity in the Heart of Software*. Boston: Addison-Wesley, 2003.

Fagan, Michael E. "Design and Code Inspections to Reduce Errors in Program Development." *IBM Systems Journal* 15, no. 3 (1976), pp. 182–211.

Feathers, Michael. *Working Effectively with Legacy Code*. Upper Saddle River, NJ: Prentice Hall, 2004.

Fishman, Charles. "No Satisfaction." *Fast Company*, December 2006.

Fowler, Martin. *Patterns of Enterprise Application Architecture*. Boston: Addison-Wesley, 2003.

Freeman, Peter. *Software Systems Principles: A Survey*. Chicago: Science Research Associates, 1975.

Freiberg, Kevin, and Jackie Freiberg. *Nuts: Southwest Airlines' Crazy Recipe for Business and Personal Success*. New York: Broadway Books, 1998.

Gawande, Atul. "The Checklist." *New Yorker*, December 10, 2007.

German Army. *On the German Art of War: Truppenführung*, field manual, edited by Bruce Condell and David T. Zabecki. Boulder, CO: Lynne Rienner Publishers, Inc., 2001. Originally published 1933–34.

Gilb, Tom. "Evolutionary Development." *ACM SIGSOFT Software Engineering Notes*, April 1981, p. 17.

———. "Multidimensional Quantified Goals Should Direct Software Design Processes." *ACM SIGSOFT Software Engineering Notes*, July 1978, pp. 26–28.

———. "Using Design by Objectives Tools (DBO)." *ACM SIGSOFT Software Engineering Notes*, April 1984, pp. 104–13.

Gladwell, Malcolm. *Outliers: The Story of Success*. New York: Little, Brown and Company, 2008.

Grittell, Jody Hoffer. *The Southwest Way*. New York: McGraw-Hill, 2003.

Hackman, Richard. "Why Teams Don't Work." *Harvard Business Review*, May 2009, pp. 99–105.

Hiranabe, Kenji. "Kanban Applied to Software Development: From Agile to Lean." January 2008. www.infoq.com/articles/hiranabe-lean-agile-kanban.

———. "New Car Development at Toyota." Agile 2008, Toronto, August 2008.

Hofstede, Geert. "Culture Does Not Exist." *InterCultures Magazine* 2, no. 3 (October 2006).

——— and Gert Jan Hofstede. *Cultures and Organizations: Software of the Mind*. New York: McGraw-Hill, 2005.

Hope, Jeremy, and Robin Fraser. *Beyond Budgeting: How Managers Can Break Free from the Annual Performance Trap*. Boston: Harvard Business School Press, 2003.

Immelt, Jeff, and Thomas Stewart. "Growth as a Process." *Harvard Business Review*, June 2006, pp. 60–70.

Ishikawa, Kaoru. *What Is Total Quality Control? The Japanese Way*. Englewood Cliffs, NJ: Prentice Hall, 1985.

Jakobsen, Carsten, and Jeff Sutherland. "Scrum and CMMI—Going from Good to Great: Are You Ready-Ready to be Done-Done." *Agile 2009 Proceedings,* IEEE, 2009.

Johnson, H. Thomas. "Manage a Living System, Not a Ledger." *Lean Manufacturing 2007,* Society of Manufacturing Engineers, 2007, pp. 89–93.

Jones, Bassett. "The Empire State Building. VIII. Elevators." *Architectural Forum,* January 1931.

Kelley, Tom, with Jonathan Littman. *The Art of Innovation.* New York: Doubleday, 2001.

———. *The Ten Faces of Innovation.* New York: Doubleday, 2005.

Kerr, Steve. *Reward Systems: Does Yours Measure Up?* Boston: Harvard Business School Press, 2009.

Kessler, Carl, and John Sweitzer. *Outside-in Software Development: A Practical Approach to Building Successful Stakeholder-Based Products.* Indianapolis: IBM Press, 2008.

Kniberg, Henrik. "Kanban vs Scrum." April 2009. www.crisp.se/henrik.kniberg/ Kanban-vs-Scrum.pdf.

Kotter, John. *A Sense of Urgency.* Boston: Harvard Business School Press, 2008.

Kroner, Niels. *Svenska Handelsbanken: A Blueprint for Better Banking.* Hampshire, UK: Harriman House, 2009.

Ladas, Corey. *Scrumban: Essays on Kanban Systems for Lean Software Development.* Seattle: Modus Cooperandi Press, 2008.

Larman, Craig, and Bas Vodde. *Scaling Lean & Agile Development: Thinking and Organizational Tools for Large-Scale Scrum.* Boston: Addison-Wesley, 2009.

Leiner, Barry, et al. "The Past and Future History of the Internet." *Communications of the ACM,* February 1997, pp. 102–8.

Levine, Michael K. *A Tale of Two Systems: Lean and Agile Software Development for Business Leaders.* New York: CRC Press/Taylor and Francis Group, 2009.

Liker, Jeffrey, and Michael Hoseus. *Toyota Culture: The Heart and Soul of the Toyota Way.* New York: McGraw-Hill, 2008.

Malinowski, Bronislaw. *Crime and Custom in Savage Society.* 1926.

Martin, Robert C. *Clean Code: A Handbook of Agile Software Craftsmanship.* Upper Saddle River, NJ: Prentice Hall, 2009.

May, Matthew E. *The Elegant Solution: Toyota's Formula for Mastering Innovation.* New York: Free Press, 2007.

McCracken, Daniel D., and Michael A. Jackson. "Life Cycle Concept Considered Harmful." *ACM SIGSOFT Software Engineering Notes* 7, no. 2 (April 1982), pp. 29–32.

McGirt, Ellen. "How Chris Hughes Helped Launch Facebook and the Barack Obama Campaign." *Fast Company,* March 2009.

Mills, Harlan. *Software Productivity.* New York: Dorset House, 1988.

———. "Top Down Programming in Large Systems." In *Debugging Techniques in Large Systems,* edited by R. Rustin, pp. 41–55. Englewood Cliffs, NJ: Prentice Hall, 1971.

Naur, Peter, and Brian Randell, eds. *Software Engineering: Report on a Conference Sponsored by the NATO Science Committee.* Garmisch, Germany, October 7–11, 1968.

Norton, David. *Case Study: IBM Uses Agile Methods to Develop WebSphere Service Registry and Repository.* Gartner, January 2009.

Nygard, Michael. *Release It! Design and Deploy Production-Ready Software.* Raleigh and Dallas: Pragmatic Bookshelf, 2007.

Ohno, Taiichi. *Workplace Management,* translated by Jon Miller. Mukiltco, WA: Gemba Press, 2007.

Ordóñez, Lisa, Maurice Schweitzer, Adam Galinsky, and Max Bazerman. "Goals Gone Wild: The Systematic Side Effects of Over-Prescribing Goal Setting." Working Paper, Harvard Business School, 2009.

Parker, James F. *Do the Right Thing: How Dedicated Employees Create Loyal Customers and Large Profits.* Upper Saddle River, NJ: Wharton School Publishing/Pearson Education, Inc., 2008.

Parnas, David L. "On the Criteria to Be Used in Decomposing Systems into Modules." *Communications of the ACM* 5, no. 12 (December 1972), pp. 1053–58.

———. "Software Aging." *International Conference on Software Engineering.* Sorrento, Italy: ACM, 1994.

———. "The Secret History of Information Hiding." In *Software Pioneers,* edited by Manfred Broy and Ernst Denert, pp. 399–409. New York: Springer, 2002.

Pfeffer, Jeffrey. *What Were They Thinking?* Boston: Harvard Business School Press, 2007.

Poppendieck, Mary and Tom. *Implementing Lean Software Development: From Concept to Cash*. Boston: Addison-Wesley, 2006.

———. *Lean Software Development: An Agile Toolkit*. Boston: Addison-Wesley, 2003.

Reinertsen, Donald G. *The Principles of Product Development Flow: Second Generation Lean Product Development*. Redondo Beach, CA: Celeritas Publishing, 2009.

Roseman, Neil. "Working Backwards & 2-Pizza Teams." NFAIS Annual Conference, Philadelphia, February 2006.

Royce, Winston W. "Managing the Development of Large Software Systems." *Proceedings, IEEE Wescon*, Los Angeles, August 25–28, 1970, pp. 1–9.

Savary, Louis, and Clare Crawford-Mason. *The Nun and the Bureaucrat: How They Found an Unlikely Cure for America's Sick Hospitals*. Washington, DC: CC-M Productions, Inc., 2006.

Scholtes, Peter. *The Leader's Handbook: A Guide to Inspiring Your People and Managing the Daily Workflow*. New York: McGraw-Hill, 1988.

Scotland, Karl. "Kanban, Flow, and Cadence." AvailAgility. 2009. http://availagility.wordpress.com/2008/10/28/kanban-flow-and-cadence.

Seddon, John. *Freedom from Command and Control: Rethinking Management for Lean Service*. Florence, KY: Productivity Press, 2005.

———. *Systems Thinking in the Public Sector*. Axminster, UK: Triarchy Press, 2008.

Shook, John. *Managing to Learn: Using the A3 Management Process to Solve Problems, Gain Agreement, Mentor, and Lead*. Cambridge, MA: The Lean Enterprise Institute, 2008.

———. "Purpose, Process, People." Lean.org, March 30, 2009. www.lean.org/shook/2009/03/purpose-process-people.html.

———. "Survive to Make Money or Make Money to Survive?" Lean.org, December 2008. www.lean.org/shook/2008/12/with-gms-demise-becoming-more-real.html.

Shreve, R. H. "The Economic Design of Office Buildings." *Architectural Record 67 (1930)*.

Smith, Adam. *An Inquiry into the Nature and Causes of the Wealth of Nations*. 1776.

Sobek, Durward, and Art Smalley. *Understanding A3 Thinking: A Critical Component of Toyota's PDCA Management System*. New York: CRC Press, 2008.

Spear, Steven. *Chasing the Rabbit.* New York: McGraw-Hill, 2009.

———. "Fixing Health Care from the Inside, Today." *Harvard Business Review,* September 2005, pp. 78–91.

———, interview by Sarah Jane Johnston. "How Toyota Turns Workers into Problem Solvers." Harvard Business School Working Knowledge, November 26, 2001.

Starrett, Paul. *Changing the Skyline: An Autobiography.* New York: McGraw-Hill, 1938.

Stewart, William. *The Living Internet.* n.d. http://livinginternet.com/i/ii_cerf.htm.

Surowiecki, James. *The Wisdom of Crowds.* New York: Anchor Books/Random House, 2004.

Swabey, Pete. "Agility Applied at Standard Life." *Information Age*, October 18, 2007.

Swartout, William, and Robert Balzer. "On the Inevitable Intertwining of Specification and Implementation." *Communications of ACM,* July 1982, pp. 438–40.

Tauranac, John. *Empire State Building: The Making of a Landmark.* New York: Macmillan, 1995.

Taylor, Suzanne, and Kathy Schroeder. *Inside Intuit.* Boston: Harvard Business School Press, 2003.

U.S. Department of the Army. *Mission Command: Command and Control of Army Forces,* field manual. 2003.

Vogels, Werner. "Availability & Consistency." InfoQ. London: Qcon Video, August 2007. www.infoq.com/presentations/availability-consistency.

———, interview by Jim Gray. "A Conversation with Werner Vogels." *ACM Queue* 4, no. 4 (May 2006), pp. 14–22.

———. Keynote. Structure08. San Francisco, September 2008. www.viddler.com/explore/michaelwilde/videos/11/.

———. "The Amazon.com Technology Platform: Building Blocks for Innovation." London: Qcon Video, 2007. www.infoq.com/presentations/vogels-amazon-platform.

Wallander, Jan. "Budgeting—An Unnecessary Evil." *Scandinavian Journal of Management* 15, no. 4 (1999), pp. 405–21.

Walton, Mary. *The Deming Management Method.* New York: Perigee, 1986.

Ward, Allen C. *Lean Product and Process Development*. Cambridge, MA: The Lean Enterprise Institute, 2007.

Watanabe, Katsuaki, interview by Thomas Stewart and Anand Raman. "Lessons from Toyota's Long Drive." *Harvard Business Review*, July–August 2007, pp. 74–83.

Weinberg, Gerald M. *Rethinking Systems Analysis and Design*. Boston: Little, Brown and Company, 1982.

Willis, Carol, and Donald Friedman. *Building the Empire State*. New York: The Skyscraper Museum, 1998.

Zeller, Andreas. "Predicting Bugs from History." In *Software Evolution*, edited by Tom Mens and Serge Demeyer, pp. 69–90. New York: Springer, 2008.

———. *Why Programs Fail*. San Francisco: Morgan Kaufmann, 2006.

Index

A

A3 problem-solving report, 176–180
Abe, Namiko, 187
Abstraction. *See* Information hiding.
Acceptance tests, 73–74
Adaptive control, 145
Adaptive control Frame 12, 143–147
  consumability, 145
  customer feedback, 143–144
  customer outcomes, 146–147
  escaped defects, 146
  frequent releases, 144–145
Adler, Nancy, 191
Agical AB, 25
Agile development
  cross-functional teams, 69
  future of, 61–63
  in large systems with tightly
    coupled architecture, 65
Agile Manifesto, 192
Agile@IBM
  changing the business process, 224
  continuous integration, 226
  creating a sense of urgency,
    229–230
  an early experiment, 223
  focus on customer outcomes, 228
  governance, 230
  key characteristics, 221
  key problems, 224–225
  lessons learned, 223–227
  stakeholder feedback, 226
  stakeholder involvement, 222
  support call reduction, 223,
    228–229

  technical debt, 226
  test automation, 227
  from theory to practice, 228–230
  training teams, 225–226
  transformation, 220–221
  understanding "done," 226
  WebSphere Service Registry and
    Repository team, 223
Airline industry. *See* Southwest
  Airlines.
Alcoa safety record, 156, 159–161
Alignment Frame, 236–241
Amazon.com
  experiencing the workplace, 172
  IT organization, statement of
    purpose, 9
  team size, 66–67
  waste, identifying, 172
Ambiguity, 157–158, 166, 190
Arbitrating with value, 134
Architectural vision, ideation, 41–42
ARPANET, history of software
  development, 57–60
The Art of Innovation, 39
Articles. *See* Publications.
Assembly language, history of
  software development, 52

B

B-17 bomber, case study, 154–155
Backus, John, 52
Bad news first, 38, 169–170
Balzer, Robert, 56
Barrier to rapid learning, 161

X

Y